BEGINNING WELL

CHRISTIAN CONVERSION &
AUTHENTIC TRANSFORMATION

GORDON T. SMITH

IVP Books

An imprint of InterVarsity Press
Downers Grove, Illinois

InterVarsity Press
P.O. Box 1400, Downers Grove, IL 60515-1426
World Wide Web: www.ivpress.com
E-mail: email@ivpress.com

InterVarsity Press® is the book-publishing division of InterVarsity Christian Fellowship/USA®, a student movement active on campus at hundreds of universities, colleges and schools of nursing in the United States of America, and a member movement of the International Fellowship of Evangelical Students. For information about local and regional activities, write Public Relations Dept., InterVarsity Christian Fellowship/USA, 6400 Schroeder Rd., P.O. Box 7895, Madison, WI 53707-7895, or visit the IVCF website at <www.intervarsity.org>.

Scripture quotations, unless otherwise noted, are from the New Revised Standard Version of the Bible, copyright 1989 by the Division of Christian Education of the National Council of the Churches of Christ in the USA. Used by permission. All rights reserved.

Cover photograph: Roy Morsch/The Stock Market

ISBN 978-0-8308-2297-3

Printed in the United States of America ∞

Library of Congress Cataloging-in-Publication Data

Smith, Gordon T., 1953-
 Beginning well: Christian conversion & authentic transformation/Gordon T. Smith.
  p. cm.
 Includes bibliographical references.
 ISBN 0-8308-2297-6 (pbk.: alk. paper)
  1. Conversion—Christianity. 2. Evangelicalism. I. Title.

 BV4916.3 .S55 2001
 248.2'4—dc21

                                                                2001024040

| P | 19 | 18 | 17 | 16 | 15 | 14 | 13 | 12 | 11 | 10 | 9 | 8 | 7 | 6 | 5 | 4 |
| Y | 22 | 21 | 20 | 19 | 18 | 17 | 16 | 15 | 14 | 13 | 12 | 11 | 10 | 09 | | | |

to joella

Contents

Preface

Conversion merits the focused, critical attention of all Christians. But to those of the evangelical Christian tradition[1] a theology of conversion is particularly important. In *Evangelicalism in Modern Britain* D. W. Bebbington provides what has increasingly become a standard definition for evangelicalism. He contends that the four defining features of the movement are *"conversionism,* the belief that lives need to be changed; *activism,* the expression of the gospel in effort; *biblicism,* a particular regard for the Bible; and what may be called *crucicentrism,* a stress on the sacrifice of Christ on the cross."[2]

Bebbington calls conversion the content of the gospel for evangelicals.[3] It could be said that nothing has quite so defined this movement as the element of religious experience. Stanley J. Grenz echoes Bebbington, suggesting that "the genius of classical evangelicalism is its concern for or emphasis on a conscious experience of the grace of God in conversion. It is characterized by what [Donald] Dayton calls 'convertive piety.' "[4] Thus there is a pressing need to think theologically and critically about conversion as a standard mark or defining element of the movement. Only with a proper understanding of conversion can we truly appreciate the charac-

---

[1]I am using *evangelical* to specify a particular theological and spiritual tradition whose roots are in both the Puritans and Pietists of the seventeenth and eighteenth centuries; this will be covered more fully in chapter two.

[2]D. W. Bebbington, *Evangelicalism in Modern Britain: A History from the 1730s to the 1980s* (London: Unwin Hyman, 1989), p. 3.

[3]Ibid., p. 5.

[4]Stanley J. Grenz, *Revisioning Evangelical Theology: A Fresh Agenda for the Twenty-first Century* (Downers Grove, Ill.: InterVarsity Press, 1993), p. 24.

ter of our religious heritage and what it means to be evangelical.

In spite of the importance of conversion to evangelicals, as late as the mid-1980s the Reverend George Carey noted that "literature on conversion is disappointingly meagre."[5] While there has been some attempt to redress that imbalance, within the evangelical tradition we have few major studies of religious conversion in general and Christian conversion in particular. This book is meant to contribute to what I hope will be a renewed and vital theological interest in this subject.

How *Beginning Well* Can Help

A careful study of conversion has relevance for personal self-understanding, for the church's ministry and for the task of theology.

Personal self-understanding. A sound theology of conversion has remarkable potential to facilitate personal self-understanding. A critical element in self-knowledge is an appreciation of one's religious or spiritual pilgrimage. Some are alienated from their own experience because it does not fit a preconceived pattern of what a conversion should be. They feel as though their own experience is not legitimate. Others simply have never been given the theological tools to understand their experience.

Our whole life is in one sense the working out of the full meaning of our conversion. To live in truth is to act in a manner consistent with our conversion. Nowhere is this more dramatically portrayed than in the life of St. Paul, whose conversion is the fountain from which he lived and in which the early missionary movement found its impetus. So it makes sense for us to reflect intentionally and theologically about our coming to faith. And we need an outline of the nature and character of conversion that is internally consistent and congruent with our own experience—so that we can understand and interpret our own experience, strengthen and deepen it and know that it leads to transformation.

Church ministry. Critical theological reflection on conversion will also facilitate the conversion of others. Both as individuals and as communities of faith we have the privilege of encouraging and enabling others to come to faith in Christ Jesus. But we need to learn how to do this well. The practice of evangelism is undermined by an inconsistent and flawed notion of conversion.

Evangelism is a vital part of our common life as Christians. We will be

---

[5]George Carey, "A Biblical Perspective," in *Entering the Kingdom*, ed. Monica Hill (British Church Growth Association/MARC Europe, 1986), p. 21n.

more effective evangelists when we develop a clear understanding of the meaning and character of conversion. A theological appreciation of conversion is an essential tool for evangelists, pastors and all who have opportunity to enable the conversion of others—children, friends, office coworkers or neighbors.

Evangelism is not the task of a few individuals with special gifts. It is the responsibility of the whole church, which fosters the context in which men and women come to a full experience of Christ. As a church we will be able to do this well only when we appreciate the complex character of conversion. This study should prompt rich conversations about the nature of conversion so that together we can more effectively bring others to Christ.

The theological task. Third, critical reflection on conversion is vital to the task of theology. Bernard Lonergan probably has done more than any other contemporary theologian to stress the urgent need for intentional theological reflection on conversion. He suggests that the renewal of theology could come as a result of this analysis; that is, conversion itself could be the starting point for the theological task. Lonergan argues that conversion is one of the fundamental elements of religious life and experience. "It follows that reflection on conversion can supply theology with its foundation and, indeed, with a foundation that is concrete, dynamic, personal, communal and historical."[6]

Because of evangelicals' deep indebtedness to John Wesley and Jonathan Edwards, Lonergan's analysis rings true. For Edwards and Wesley, divine grace, particularly the grace experienced at conversion, is the crucial energy sustaining all theological reflection. The experience of conversion—rather than abstract theological propositions—defined both the agenda and the application of their work to the life of the church. I am not suggesting by this that theological propositions are not essential to the task of theology or the life of the Christian community. Rather, properly speaking, conversion and intentional reflection on it have the capacity to bring renewal and focus to our theological work.

Each person's experience of God's mercy and grace is a necessary window through which we see and appreciate the mercy of God toward the whole of creation. We are not being narcissistic when we are very conscious of our own experience. Instead we are allowing God's work of

---

[6]Bernard Lonergan, "Theology in Its New Context," in *Conversion: Perspectives on Personal and Social Transformation*, ed. Walter Conn (New York: Alba House, 1978), p. 14.

grace in our lives to be the means by which we see the big picture, the unfolding of God's work of redemption and transformation in the lives of others and in the whole of the cosmos.

The Approach Taken in This Study

Perhaps more than anything else, what follows demonstrates that conversion is a complex experience. Humans are terribly complex creatures, and we will appreciate what it means to begin the Christian journey well only when we find a model or approach to conversion that incorporates and takes full account of this complexity.

It would be helpful to divide the ten chapters of this book into three parts. Chapters one through four are largely foundational, establishing the conversation about conversion and primal religious experience. They set the stage for the rest of the book. Chapters five through eight are the heart of the presentation, including both the study of New Testament texts on conversion and a comprehensive outline of the elements of a Christian conversion. Some readers might be inclined to jump straight to this material, but ideally these chapters should be read in the light of what has been said in the first four chapters. Chapters nine and ten address religious autobiography and evangelism, including a discussion of conversion for second-generation Christians.

1

Thinking About Conversion

Ninoy Aquino is well known as the exiled leader of the Philippines' political opposition in the 1970s and 1980s. He returned to the Philippines only to be assassinated on the tarmac of what was then the Manila International Airport (now called the Ninoy Aquino International Airport).

What is not as well known is his conversion to faith in Christ. Dictator Ferdinand Marcos considered Aquino a political enemy, and in 1972 Aquino was captured as part of a massive military round-up of opposition leaders. Security forces arrested him along with many others (at one point as many as sixty thousand were incarcerated for their opposition to Marcos over the course of eight years of martial law). Tragically, the American Chamber of Commerce actually praised and supported Marcos for bringing economic stability to the country and seemingly turned a blind eye to the travesty of justice. Of those initially arrested—about eight hundred that first night of martial law—all were released within three months, with the exception of Aquino and Senator Jose ("Pepe") Diokno.

Aquino was first held in a cubicle in a bungalow at Fort Bonifacio, a military camp outside Manila; from there he was transferred to Fort Magsaysay north of Manila (in Laur), where he was kept in a tiny cell with only a narrow opening. For a whole month he was in solitary confinement, allowed to wear only his underclothes and to eat very limited rations.

After his return to Fort Bonifacio, many noted a dramatic transformation in Aquino. At Magsaysay he had undergone a significant religious experience. As Aquino himself described it, he started out angry and irritated with his circumstances, since he was innocent and undeserving of such harsh treatment. In the midst of his frustration he heard a voice: "Why do you cry? I have gifted you with consolations, honors and glory which have been denied to millions of your countrymen. Now that I visit you with a slight desolation, you cry and whimper like a spoiled brat."

Aquino later wrote that he fell to his knees, asked for forgiveness and chose to give his life to the service of God, then "picked up my cross and followed Him." In the long hours of meditation that followed, he found inner peace. He recognized that pride had blinded him to the presence of God in his life—the same pride that had fostered a love of temporal power, honors and joys. In the end he saw something providential even in the persecution of a dictator: "If only for my conversion, I should owe the tyrant my eternal gratitude."

I have a vivid memory of the first Sunday that Bob Brewster showed up for worship at the church in central Ontario where I was the pastor. I learned later that morning that his wife had left him the previous week. He had decided that he could not cope alone; since he had some friends at this church, he showed up with his two young daughters, wondering how to piece his life back together.

At first Bob stayed in the back pew during Sunday worship. But after two or three months he was sitting farther forward. And after a time he was involved in a variety of ways, one of which was as an assistant Sunday school teacher.

For a number of months I chose to say nothing to Bob about Christian faith or ask him about his religious commitments. I'm not sure why I was reticent; it just seemed best to let him be on his own. But after about a year he came to me and, without any prior warning, asked to be baptized.

I asked then about his journey. As he described his coming to faith, a process that had taken at least a year, I realized that Bob would have never accepted God's love or given himself to God until he felt loved and accepted by the Christian community. I thanked God that our community had been a means by which he had come to see and embrace the love of God. No one person had been an evangelist to Bob; rather the whole community had been the vehicle through which he came to understand the gospel and gained confidence to choose to follow Jesus.

Ninoy Aquino's conversion story may seem more compelling and dramatic, and many Christians wish they had such a story to tell. But most Christians' story is much more like that of Bob Brewster.

And Bob's experience of coming to faith suggests something else. We have tended to think of church involvement as following conversion: one becomes a Christian and then joins the church. The church, in other words, was viewed as the consequence of conversions. But Bob's experience during my first pastorate made me wonder if it might not be the opposite—that conversion follows from the church. That is, someone first joins the Christian community, and as a member one learns about the Christian faith and is enabled by the community to become a follower, a disciple, of Jesus.

But there is another question that underlies all of this and is a pressing question whenever we think about conversion. What is the relationship between conversion and transformation? What will make it possible and likely that Bob will become a mature Christian believer, an individual who lives fully and thoroughly in the light of the kingdom reign of Jesus Christ, at home with his daughters, in his place of work, in relationships with fellow believers in the church? What difference will his conversion make—in the next life, of course, but particularly in this life? Will he truly become a transformed person? And if so, what will make that possible?

We are only going to respond well to these questions if we think well about conversion—which means that we must take both conversion and transformation seriously.

Taking Conversion Seriously

Scripture, from beginning to end, stresses the vital need for conversion, for it is the means of knowing life, eternal life. The need for conversion is universal, and it is essential because of sin. All have sinned and fallen short of glory. We need conversion because of guilt, the consequence of rebellion; because of bondage and alienation, the consequences of sin. The only hope for transformation, for life with God as a child of God, is a complete and radical conversion.

Further, the Bible assumes that such a conversion is possible. The Scriptures are an extraordinary declaration of hope, stressing that change and transformation are possible in the mercy and goodness of God—justice and peace can and will embrace; the reign of God will come. Lives need to be changed; lives can be changed; lives will be changed.

When we speak of the importance of conversion, it is imperative to do so in light of the Lord Jesus Christ. Only then can we speak of a Christian conversion. The notion of conversion in the New Testament is expressly trinitarian and christocentric. A conversion comes in response to the election, call and initiative of the Father and is enabled by the Spirit; there is no conversion without this call and enabling. But the very heart of conversion is encounter with Christ, and without this conscious encounter a conversion is not, properly speaking, Christian conversion.

Thus conversion comes in response to an encounter with God—God's holiness, truth and love—and it can generally be viewed as an act in response to the call of God, though that call may be presented and understood in a wide variety of ways.

The work of Christ makes conversion possible; even more, the actual focus and dynamic of conversion is that an individual comes to faith in Christ Jesus. Conversion is the act of believing in Jesus, choosing to follow Jesus and being united with Jesus as Lord and Savior. To be converted is to become a Christ-ian. And the purpose of conversion is that we may ultimately be transformed into the image of Christ Jesus. Although all three members of the Trinity are actively involved in the conversion experience, the focus is on Christ. In fact, conversion is the fruit of an encounter with the risen Christ himself, as witnessed to and experienced within a Christian community. Conversion is not the result of an encounter with truth or principles or spiritual laws; rather, it comes from meeting Jesus.

We cannot think well about conversion unless we take the experience itself seriously. By this I mean not merely that conversion is necessary but also that it merits focused, critical attention.

However, here we need to consider a crucial distinction that is inherent in this call to take conversion seriously: conversion is human activity. *Conversion* and *salvation* are not synonymous.

Conversion is the human response to the saving work of God through Christ. Conversion is the initial encounter with God's saving grace—the steps or the means by which we enter into a redemptive relationship with God.

Salvation is God's work and God's work alone, unequivocally. God saves. There is no such thing as self-salvation. The salvation and transformation that we seek come wholly from the hands of God.

Subsequently, conversion is the means by which we appropriate and experience God's saving grace. Therefore conversion has an obvioius human element. It is those things that are done following such questions as "What then must I do in order to be saved?" and "How can I appropriate eternal life?"

Conversion, theologically speaking, is the parallel to God's work of making all things new. Thus we are making a theological examination of human activity, with particular reference to that activity that enables us to appropriate as fully as possible the grace of God.

In the pages that follow, God's saving initiative and grace will be sometimes celebrated, sometimes discussed and sometimes assumed. But the primary focus of this study is conversion, the human response to God's offer of salvation. It is critical that this distinction be maintained.

When we consider conversion as a matter of theological reflection, we focus our attention on religious experience. Religious experience has been studied by social scientists, and a study of conversion must of necessity draw on their insights. Psychological, sociological and cultural issues will be addressed insofar as they enable us to locate a theologically sound understanding of conversion and religious experience in the actual circumstances of our lives. But for our purposes the primary question will be theological: what, from a theological perspective, is the meaning of conversion, and what implications follow for us as individuals and for the life and ministry of the church?

In the formulation of a theology of conversion the Scriptures must remain primary—not in the sense of first or foremost but as a basic and authoritative source for our theology. The experience of the church is a secondary source—not in the sense of minor but as interpreter of the primary source, enabling us to appreciate its meaning and understand its implications. Our theology of conversion must be informed by an analysis of the work of the Holy Spirit in the lives of persons. Our understanding of the meaning of conversion, while informed by Scripture, will be shaped by the actual experience of the church—by the religious experience (especially conversion experiences) of Christians.

Taking experience seriously means we take ourselves seriously. Of course, an authentic study of conversion above all emphasizes the priority of God's initiative and the unilateral character of God's salvation. However, we cannot examine religious experience adequately without acknowledging the uniqueness of each person and the distinctive character of each person's experience. I trust this is evident in the pages that follow. But it is most evident in the legitimacy we give to the individual conversion narrative—the fact that each person is a story of God's grace. While there are parallels between us and we can compare our stories and celebrate the common elements, each person's conversion narrative is unique. No two are identical.

When we take experience seriously, we highlight what actually does happen rather than insist on what *should* happen. This does not for a moment mean that all experiences are equally valid or equally Christian. We seek to understand the character of an authentically *Christian* conversion. However, the expression or experience of each Christian conversion is unique. And the genius of a good conversion narrative is the capacity to describe what has actually happened in the life of an individual. I hope that after reading this book you will have a greater capacity to interpret your own experience, make sense of its distinctive character, probe into its unique meaning in your life, and consider its implications within your whole journey of faith.

Finally, we take experience seriously when we recognize its complexity. Conversion is a complex experience. We are complex beings, women and men of heart, mind, will and strength. While the language used by many Christian communities implies that conversion is simple, punctiliar and definitive, in actual fact conversion is usually drawn out over many years. This means that when we speak of Christian conversion, we are serious about it only when we allow for the complexity of the *actual* experience.

One more thing: if we take conversion and religious experience seriously, then religious experience can be properly interpreted only by the person who has the experience.[1] This implies that religious experience, by its very nature, cannot be analyzed by someone who has not had a comparable experience. Experience of any kind can be understood and appreciated only from within, for in the words of Louis Dupré, "the philosopher deprived of empathy with religion is incapable of successfully analyzing its acts, meanings, and symbols."[2] We must accept religious acts on their own terms and merits; we cannot prove something to be true by appealing to a "truth" that stands outside of it.[3]

For the Christian this finds expression in the conviction that the Word of God testifies to itself, and further, that the Spirit testifies to the Word in the heart and mind of the believer. When it comes to religious experience,

---

[1] I find particularly helpful the perspective of Louis Dupré in his collection of essays *Religious Mystery and Rational Reflection: Excursions in the Phenomenology and Philosophy of Religion* (Grand Rapids, Mich.: Eerdmans, 1998). Dupré demonstrates that philosophers are increasingly recognizing the importance of religious experience, insisting that "the analysis of religious concepts needs to be complemented by a reflection on religious experience" (p. vii).
[2] Ibid., pp. vii, 8.
[3] Ibid., p. 28.

as Dupré contends, "experience defines its own meaning: those who experience learn in the process itself what they are experiencing"; also, "precisely in following the very course of consciousness in time, experience acquires its unique purchase on truth—namely, . . . it is and becomes increasingly my own experience."[4]

This does not mean, Dupré insists, that the experience is then purely subjective, for "the reality we experience . . . defines the nature of the experience and endows it with its own authority."[5] I would add that an experience is always mediated by a community governed and sustained by the Scriptures. Yet in the end the experience is nevertheless interpreted from within.

What Christians need is not so much to be informed of what they should experience or have experienced as to be given means to conduct their own self-examination, theological tools that enable them to reflect on and interpret their own experience.

The most critical of these tools is a fresh reading of Scripture. An emphasis on experience does not for a moment imply that we neglect the Bible. To the contrary, we will think clearly about conversion only when we allow the Scriptures to speak. In what follows I hope to enable us to hear the New Testament afresh. However, we cannot hear the Bible unless we acknowledge a certain inevitability: we hear the text of Scripture through the filter of both our religious experience and the particular theological traditions within which we have come to faith. We read the Bible not from a detached, objective stance but as individuals shaped and informed by the particularity of our own experience in certain theological and spiritual traditions. If we are to allow the Bible to have a fresh voice on the matter of conversion, we must acknowledge our own experience and appreciate the character of our theological tradition.

Consequently, in what follows it should be clear that the text of the New Testament is the primary source for a Christian understanding of conversion. However, we will consider the text only after we place both experience and an overview of the evangelical Christian tradition on the table.

Taking Transformation Seriously
We cannot think effectively and biblically about conversion until we take seriously both the possibility of and the call to transformation. This is,

---

[4]Ibid., p. 39.
[5]Ibid.

properly speaking, the goal of all of the church's life and thus of theological reflection. Conversion therefore is not an end but a beginning; we give it particular attention to encourage the spiritual transformation that it is meant to begin.

Transformation must be the goal of our study of conversion. To appreciate this, we need to place our discussion about conversion in its broader theological context. Conversion and religious experience must fit within the whole spectrum of the biblical doctrine of salvation.

Conversion, as stressed above, is fundamentally a human activity. However, human activity within conversion must be understood in the context of God's saving work. To develop a theologically consistent understanding of human response to God's saving initiative, we need a sense of how God is acting. In other words, to appropriate God's saving work through conversion, we must know the nature of this saving work. What follows, then, is a survey of the big picture—the doctrine of salvation—within which we must locate the human activity of conversion.

Human Predicament and Divine Solution

The doctrine of salvation assumes two things: the depth and complexity of the human predicament and the provision of a resolution in and through Jesus Christ. The seriousness of our predicament is captured in the Christian doctrine of sin. Through rebellion, humanity has experienced a horrific Fall: this sinful predicament has three elements, each of which is a form of death.

First, humanity is guilty of rebellion against God, having violated God's holy law and rejected God's perfect love. Second, humanity is not merely guilty but in bondage to sin. Sin is not only a failure to observe God's laws and ways; sin is bondage. When a person is guilty of sin, that guilt results in bondage to the very sin of which he or she is guilty. Having rebelled against God, humanity found itself in bondage to the sin it had committed. Third, the human predicament involves alienation. Because of sin, we are alienated from God, from ourselves, from others and from the whole created order.

This sinful state is so pervasive and invasive that humanity is incapable of self-salvation. Further, sin is universal—all of humanity is caught in the same deathly situation. It follows then that the only hope is divine intervention. And the gospel captures this reality in the glorious news that through Jesus Christ God has chosen to act, to intervene and break into human affairs.

The human predicament is guilt. But in Christ we have propitiation; Christ provides a vicarious sacrifice that enables human beings to experience forgiveness and cleansing.

The human predicament is bondage. But in Christ we have redemption: we can speak of One who has acted powerfully on our behalf to break the power of sin and release us from bondage.

The human predicament is alienation. But in Christ we have reconciliation. Through Jesus we have experienced the transforming love of God, a love that overcomes alienation and brings peace.

Propitiation, redemption and reconciliation assume God's initiative. We know the life of God through the grace of God; it is effected in us by the Spirit. God invites, God enables, God transforms. Conversion, biblically understood, is always a response to the invitation, love and work of God in Christ. But precisely at this point we need to stress that the purpose of conversion is personal transformation. Conversion is not an end, it is the bridge to the goal of our salvation, which is nothing less than transformation into the image of the Lord Jesus Christ (Rom 8:28-29).

The Unity of God's Salvation

The goal of conversion is *not* merely to expedite a release from the consequences of sin—hell or damnation or punishment. There is no doubt that conversion does bring about a release from guilt, bondage and alienation; however, the purpose of conversion is not only to get us out of a sinful predicament but that we might be a transformed people.

This basic working principle arises from a theological conviction: the fundamental unity of God's salvation. One way to appreciate this is through the classic theological concepts of justification and sanctification and the relationship between them.

Justification refers to the initial or foundational work of God in the life of the Christian. While various Christian traditions differ on what it means to be justified, most would agree with the following: to be justified is to be accepted, forgiven and adopted by God through Christ. We define *justification* too narrowly when we speak of it in purely forensic terms—that we gain a good or right standing before God, with no actual or substantial change in our being. There *is* change; we experience the transforming grace of God. However, it is true that justification sets the stage for what follows in our Christian experience. When we are justified, we are given a new standing in relationship with God. This right standing turns us around, sets us on the right course and establishes a right relationship with God. As such, justification is not only the good beginning of the Christian life; it is the only possible beginning.

Returning to what we began with—the human predicament of guilt, bondage and alienation: a justified person is not a transformed person, with all guilt, bondage and alienation removed or resolved. Rather, the justified person is accepted by God, forgiven by God and set in the right direction and relationship with God with the hope and goal that full salvation will actually be experienced.

The goal we seek is sanctification. *Sanctification* speaks of our transformation into the image of Christ, a transformation that comes purely and solely by God's gracious work in our lives. We do not bring it about; it comes as we trust, by faith, in what God and only God can do.

Justification speaks of a good beginning—accepted, forgiven and set right in Christ. *Sanctification* speaks of the goal of our human life and identity in Christ—that we be mature, whole and complete in Christ. Thus both justification and sanctification are integral and essential to biblical salvation.

To put it differently, justification and sanctification are distinct but inseparable. Sanctification is not possible without justification; we cannot hope for personal transformation until we are accepted, forgiven and set right in Christ. But sanctification must follow justification. Sanctification is the very purpose of justification. We are justified so that through the work of the Spirit we might be transformed into the image of Christ, sanctified in him and enabled to live in maturity in Christ. Something is profoundly flawed when justification does not lead to sanctification, for this is the very purpose for which we are justified.

Within this scenario, conversion is the human activity that enables us to appropriate the justifying grace of God. It follows, therefore, that we have an authentic conversion, a theologically sound and biblically consistent conversion, only when this initial experience enables us to complement justification with sanctification. It is a true conversion only when it leads to transformation, for the simple reason that conversion is not an end in itself. It is a beginning, ideally a good beginning, that enables us to eventually experience transformation in Christ.

Justification is the glorious gift through which the children of God experience God's love and acceptance and are enabled to live in relationship with God. But a justified person is not necessarily transformed. When justified, we are not changed, we are merely set in a right direction. Better yet, we are set in a right *relationship,* a relationship that has the capacity to eventually lead to personal transformation.

I once heard it said that there is really only one tragedy in human life—the failure to become a saint. The purpose of human existence is to be holy as God is holy (1 Pet 1:16), to grow up into him who is our head, Jesus Christ (Eph 4:15), so that we become mature or perfect in Christ (Eph 4:13). Tragically, many evangelical Christians resist this. They believe that conversion is an end—all that really matters in our lives—and the only tragedy is when we fail to enable others to come to Christ. While there is merit to the second part of this equation, the first part subtly turns a blind eye to the very purpose for which God sent his Son and the Spirit.

Here is a simplified but helpful way to view the two sides of God's saving work in our lives. Some have noted that the Roman Catholic tradition effectively sustained the second part of the equation, the call to perfection or sanctification in Christ. But unfortunately it did not maintain a good foundation, for the only legitimate foundation or beginning is justification, acceptance and forgiveness in Jesus Christ. Without justification as the foundation, sanctification becomes nothing more than human effort and easily descends to legalism or works righteousness.[6]

The evangelical tradition has made the opposite mistake: it has affirmed justification but, ironically, as an end rather than as a good beginning. Evangelicals have denied—explicitly or implicitly—the need for genuine transformation. In contrast to both traditions, salvation is both justification and sanctification. Christian believers in all traditions have recognized that we cannot be transformed unless we know we are loved and accepted in Christ; but just as surely, they have also known and affirmed that this initial saving work of Christ is merely that—a good beginning that can and must eventually lead to maturity in Christ.

Underlying Problems
The language of conversion has often failed those of us within the evangelical tradition. The most common language for conversion within evangelicalism has revolved around "salvation." To be converted is to be "saved." To be born again is to be "saved." The problem with this lan-

---

[6]Yet while many Roman Catholics do not use the language of "justification," they affirm the principle that the only possible point of departure in the Christian life is that we live with an assurance that we are loved and accepted by God. This perspective is remarkably congruent with the Protestant notion of justification, in experience and practice if not in formal doctrine.

guage is twofold. First, salvation is more than what we experience at conversion; thus our language is only partially correct. But second, and just as problematic, our usage does not accurately reflect the language of the New Testament. The biblical word *save* is used in the past tense, such as in Titus 3:5, where we read that God "saved us," not because of our works of righteousness "but according to his mercy." But the language of salvation is also found in the present tense, as in "work out your own salvation" (Phil 2:12). And just as commonly if not even more, the verb *save* in Paul's vocabulary is future—he looks forward to the day of his salvation. Even when used in the past (aorist) tense, it often has a future reference. Romans 8:24, for example, speaks of being saved "in hope"; that is, the consummation of our salvation is, inevitably, future.

The exclusive use of the past tense of *save* to refer to conversion, then, subtly undercuts the biblical notion of salvation and fails to properly embrace all that conversion means. It is but one example of how our language of conversion urgently needs rethinking.

One of the great longings of our day is for dramatic and radical renewal in the life of the church. The word *revival* is used as a catch phrase for the deepest aspirations we have for our communities of faith, churches, denominations and nations. I am convinced the renewal of the church will not come through efforts to foster revival but through a renewed appreciation and formulation of the nature of conversion. Renewal will come as we embrace three things:

☐ a clear goal—a well-articulated, thoroughly biblical and relevant notion of sanctification as transformation in Christ, capturing the longings of our hearts to be a people who grow in holiness and become saints as we grow older

☐ a good beginning—a thorough and radical conversion, for there is no sanctification without justification, no transformation without a complete conversion

☐ an intentional program of spiritual formation that has the clear goal of personal transformation and builds on a good beginning—a complete conversion

What follows addresses the second of these: the nature and character of a good conversion. But the stress will be on conversion as a good *beginning*.

Many Christians have anemic spiritual lives with little freedom, little growth in grace and little commitment to obedience and service. I propose that an appropriate response to this predicament includes facing up to the fact that the church has a weak notion of conversion. True conversion leads to growth, commitment and service.

Evangelicals wrestle with the lack of spiritual maturity in our congregations. Pastors and laypersons bemoan a lack of even minimally qualified elders to give effective leadership. We can be encouraged by the many creative programs of spiritual formation and discipleship developed in the last fifty years. These are indications of a profound spiritual hunger. However, are we trying to fix a problem that is really rooted in an incomplete experience of conversion? Are our efforts at spiritual formation building on a faulty foundation? Effective spiritual formation is essential, but won't we continue to be frustrated until we rework our understanding of conversion? Shouldn't we reevaluate the way we think about beginning the Christian life?

The dilemma is caused in part by the activism of evangelicalism. The purpose of the church is generally defined in terms of evangelism (or evangelism and church planting). And evangelism and church planting are not always seen as means to an end—maturity in Christ. Depth of commitment to Christ is defined by level of participation in church activities rather than by more holistic criteria such as service, depth of joy, moral transformation, capacity to love others and work with others, and ultimately love for Jesus.

More than a generation ago A. W. Tozer, a well-known spiritual author in my own tradition, gravely spoke of notions of conversion, making particular reference to the language we use:

> Today all is made to depend upon an initial act of believing. At a given moment a "decision" is made for Christ, and after that everything is automatic. . . . In our eagerness to make converts we allow our hearers to absorb the idea that they can deal with their entire responsibility once and for all by an act of believing. This is in some vague way supposed to honor grace and glorify God, whereas actually it is to make Christ the author of a grotesque, unworkable system that has no counterpart in the Scriptures of truth.[7]

He goes on to decry the use of *accept* to encompass what it means to become a Christian, as though this could approximate what the early church understood to be the cost of choosing to follow Christ.

Almost half a century later the situation has hardly changed in many

---

[7]A. W. Tozer, "Faith Is a Journey, Not a Destination," *The Alliance Weekly* 92, no. 45 (1957): 2.

evangelical communities. Yet we are beginning to realize that to grow into communities of faith that genuinely experience spiritual maturity, individually and corporately, we need to rethink what it means to become a Christian believer. We need to think theologically and critically about the meaning and character of conversion.

The Transformation We Seek

I need to specify just what I mean by *transformation,* the goal of our Christian experience. Christians within different cultural and social settings read Scripture through different experiential lenses, and Christians of different temperaments and personalities no doubt stress different aspects of what it means to be a mature or transformed Christian believer. So this is not offered as an exhaustive outline but as one attempt to capture the longing of our hearts: to be mature in Christ, to know the fullness of his grace and the full experience of walking in the Spirit.

The goal of our conversion is a transformed humanity. We seek to be what we were created to be—fully human, transformed into the image of Jesus Christ. Through conversion, the Spirit of Christ enables us to be like himself that we might be fully ourselves. Christ is the head of a new humanity, true humanity infused with divine grace; and it is this humanity, with Christ as its head, for which we long. When we identify with Christ and live in gracious union with him, we become all we were created to be. The righteousness and transformation for which we strive can be summarized as follows.

First, we seek dynamic communion with God our Maker. This is experienced through an intentional union with Jesus Christ made possible when we live in fellowship with the Holy Spirit. Regardless of whether the reference is to Christ Jesus or the Spirit, the clear witness of Scripture is that a transformed humanity finds joy, strength and life through a profound fellowship, or communion, with God. Very simply, to be transformed is to know the love of God and to love God in response.

Second, the transformation we seek has a social dimension. To be fully human, transformed into the image of Christ Jesus, is to experience the love of others, to have the mature capacity to live in mutual love and submission with others. Transformation has a corporate expression, which means that we mature in our capacity to live in community. A person who is transformed into the image of Christ necessarily knows how to be loved by others and to love others. This means, at the very least, demonstration of genuine hospitality and generosity toward others, perhaps most evident in the capacity to forgive and serve. A person of spiritual maturity has learned how to forgive when wronged, how to bear with others' weaknesses and how to serve others sacrificially.

Third, spiritual transformation is manifested in personal integrity, seen particularly in the quality of our speech, finances and sexuality, each a key moral indicator. It also means that we have come to terms with our own identity; we know who we are and what we are called to be. We are at peace with our personal identity. Humility plays a vital role. We might say humility is nothing more than living in truth. Personal integrity also involves emotional maturity: peace with God and ourselves allows us to live with joy, even in a broken world. Emotional maturity—the capacity to live honestly from the heart, with emotional depth, expressing the appropriate emotion in the appropriate context—is a critical indicator of spiritual transformation.

Fourth, all these signs of transformation are summed up in the principle of wisdom, which represents humanity at its fullest potential. In Proverbs 4 we find an extraordinary expression of both call and longing as we are urged to seek wisdom no matter the cost. Wisdom is described as supreme, the highest aspiration for the human soul, that which will protect and bring honor and even exaltation to a person. Wisdom is embodied in Christ Jesus, and wisdom represents all that it means to be a mature person in Christ.

The bottom line is that we are enabled through conversion to experience the grace of a good beginning, a beginning so good that it serves as the foundation for a life growing and maturing in grace, wisdom, strength and joy. The goal of conversion is that we are enabled to live under the kingdom reign of the Lord Jesus Christ, the reign that ultimately frees us from the power of sin and transforms us into the image of Jesus.

Transformation never just happens. While it is the work of the Spirit, it is also, as mentioned above, the fruit of three distinct factors. First, transformation is the fruit of a full and complete conversion. Second, it is also the fruit of clarity in our spiritual aspirations. That is, we need to clearly identify what it means to be transformed—mature in Christ. Third, transformation is the fruit of an intentional program of spiritual formation. It follows that this program is congruent with the nature of a Christian conversion and aligned toward the goal of the Christian life, as described above.

Transformation: Continuity and Discontinuity
The Scriptures use dramatic language to describe what it means to come

to Christ in response to the call of God and the enabling of the Spirit. It is the act of being made new. This renewal is radical; a believer is made whole and complete. The Christian moves from darkness to light, from being a slave of sin to being a slave of righteousness. Once dead, the convert is now alive. Having had no mercy and living in hopelessness, the convert finds purpose and meaning. In becoming Christians we find faith, hope and love. Jesus intends to capture the radical character of conversion when he speaks of this as a "new birth" (Jn 3).

However, affirmation of the radical, transforming character of Christian conversion requires that we recognize some critical qualifiers. First, this transformation must be viewed eschatologically. Within Scripture the transforming vision of conversion always has a future component. Transformation is ultimately eschatological—it will come and will be complete in the kingdom that is yet to come. The experience of conversion enables us to know the transforming grace of God in this life, but it is given to us only as a "down payment" of the final and ultimate experience of God's grace, which will be experienced at the consummation of the kingdom. Therefore it is theologically imperative not to overstate the effects the possibilities of grace have in this life. We are new creatures, but the full experience of what it means to be a new creature is not yet known or experienced.

Second, given that this vision is eschatological, we must nevertheless understand that conversion is not solely intended to take care of matters of the afterlife. Scripture clearly assumes that when we come to Christ we begin a new "walk" with a new ethic. Conversion is both the beginning of the process of personal transformation and the act that makes transformation possible. Through God's initiative we are led to and through a conversion experience for a particular end: that we might be transformed into the image of Christ. Again, conversion is not an end: it is a means to an end—our transformation.

Third, transformation involves the whole person. Within the New Testament, conversion is conceived holistically: its outcome is the transformation of the whole person. The goal is that we might be sanctified entirely (1 Thess 5:23-24). We are not merely seeking the salvation of souls or disembodied spirits but a transformation that enables us to be whole persons. This means that in our consideration of the nature and character of conversion, we must be attentive to all that it means to be human: our intellect (a reorientation of our worldview), our emotions (matters of affect), our relationships, our bodies, our volition and our vocation.

Fourth, in speaking of transformation, we must affirm that this experience points to both continuity and discontinuity. Within our understanding of the transforming character of conversion—however dramatic or radical the conversion—there is always in biblical thought both a discontinuity (from death to life, from darkness to light, from no mercy to mercy) and a continuity.

God saves what God has created. At conversion grace is bestowed on a life that is already there, already created, a life in which the principle and possibility of grace were already present. We must not speak of conversion as so radical a change that we either neglect or, worse, deny the previous existence of a person. There is continuity with our preconversion selves— for in conversion our lives experience transformation and renewal, a renewal of what God has created. Transformation is always the transformation *of something;* in conversion, it is the transformation of our lives. And no life is so wasted that there is no possibility of change or transformation.

Austrian theologian Karl Rahner can help us see that there is "no wasted time," given the necessary continuities that exist in a converted life. Rahner stresses that conversion is never so radical a break from the past that the past is either erased or merged with the present:

> Your whole life remains always preserved for you; everything you have done and suffered is gathered together in your being, you may have forgotten it, yet it is still there. It may appear to you as a pale dream even when you remember what you once were, did and thought. All this you still are. All this has perhaps been transformed . . . incorporated into a better, more comprehensive framework, has been integrated more into a great love . . . and silent loyalty towards God which was, remained and grew throughout everything life did with you; but everything has remained in this way, nothing has simply ceased, everything which happened—as long as we are pilgrims maturing in freedom—can still be retrieved and transformed into the one action of the heart in what you do today. . . . Life gathers more and more.[8]

Conversion, then, is not creating something new out of nothing; it is rather enabling a life that is misdirected and confused to find purpose, direction and meaning. Conversion is the renewal and transformation of what had been lost and severely damaged.

---

[8]Karl Rahner, *Theological Investigations III: The Theology of the Spiritual Life,* ed. and trans. Karl H. Kruger and Boniface Kruger (London: Darton, Longman & Todd, 1967), pp. 141-57.

Primal Religious Experience

This book is essentially a critical reflection on primal religious experience. By "religious experience" I mean experience that cannot in the end be attributed solely to the natural; it can be explained only by appealing to a supernatural reality. For the Christian, this other reality is the risen Christ and the presence of the Holy Spirit in the world. By "*primal* religious experience" I mean the genesis of this experience of Christ and the Spirit; it is our beginning, the early stages of our life as Christian believers.

We are speaking, then, of the work of God in our lives. And this work is miraculous and wonderful; we experience grace and life and renewal that we cannot attribute to natural or sensible phenomena in our world. Yet part of the wonder of our conversion is that God drew us to himself and enabled us to appropriate his grace through means that seem remarkably ordinary. In other words, every conversion can be explained. Even though every conversion is a testimony to the grace of God, each conversion is also the product of natural, human and ordinary factors that shape our lives and enable us to know the God who calls us.

This does not for a moment make the experience less miraculous. Quite the opposite: the human and ordinary factors help us to appreciate the wonder of God's grace in our lives. All religious experience happens within the context of God's created order. God always works in concert with the natural and the ordinary, real people who are the means by which we hear the gospel, real events that cause us to appreciate our need for God. The human and the ordinary are never the total explanation for religious experience, but they must be considered in a thoughtful study of conversion and religious change.

Therefore we can draw without apology on the insights of students of psychology, anthropology and sociology. A sociological explanation of conversion is not antithetical to a Christian or theological explanation. Rather, it is a necessary complement to a theological study of conversion. Even more, a theological interpretation is incomplete without the insights into the nature of human experience that may come to us through social scientists. Though this book is primarily a theological study of conversion, I recognize a partnership with and dependence on those whose expertise is the nature of human experience, including the social-scientific analysis of religious experience.

Further, in speaking of primal religious experience, we are speaking of the beginning of the life of a Christian believer. This may seem to imply that conversion is decisive and dramatic, a definitive moment that is the turning point in a person's life. The language of revivalism has left many assuming that the word *conversion* necessarily refers to one event, one moment.

In reaction to revivalism some have concluded that conversion is really a lifelong process of incremental and gradual change. If they use the language of conversion, they do so to stress that the whole of life is a continual turning, a movement away from death to life, an ongoing conversion that enables us to increasingly live authentically in response to the call of God.

However, the witness of Scripture and the church suggests that perhaps a third alternative is a more accurate rendering of how people normally come to faith in Jesus Christ. The weight of the evidence suggests that most if not all people come to faith in Christ through a protracted series of events. These events in concert constitute a Christian conversion and thus a good beginning. Conversion is complex, protracted and unhurried. Appreciation of this can enable us to understand our own experience better. But more, it can help us discover implications for the life of the church. If conversion is an extended process, then evangelism can be hopeful, loving, compassionate and patient, allowing women and men to come to faith in Christ at their own pace.

For most if not for all, conversion is a protracted experience, a series of events over many months or even years. Yet there is distinctive value in thinking about the beginning of the Christian life (primal religious experience). On the one hand, the New Testament clearly highlights what it means to come to faith in Christ and shows us how to respond to the question "What must I do to become a Christian?" This presupposes that it is possible to speak of not being a Christian and being a Christian, and thus that it is possible if not actually necessary that we speak of a beginning.

Further, many Christians legitimately long for clarity, what older evangelicalism called "assurance," a deep, heartfelt confidence that one is indeed a child of God. People have a reasonable desire to know if they are part of the family of God.

Finally, as will be noted, New Testament authors, particularly the apostle Paul, repeatedly appeal to the conversion experience of their readers as part of the call to greater faithfulness in their spiritual experience. They thus demonstrate the value of a benchmark, a point of departure, a good beginning. This good beginning becomes, then, the foundation from which the whole Christian life is lived. So there is value in thinking about primal religious experience, the beginning of the Christian life. But we speak of a good beginning so that we can ultimately speak of authentic transformation.

2

The Community of Faith & the Language of Conversion

It is helpful to think of a Christian conversion as the experience of three kinds of persons:

☐ those with no Christian orientation who become Christians and choose to follow Christ

☐ those who have been nominally Christian who come to new or actual faith in Christ and through this experience embrace a new life orientation (that is, although no change of religion is involved per se, they come to see themselves as "true Christians" in a way that they were not before)[1]

☐ those who grow up in a Christian community with sincere faith and who eventually make an adult decision to be Christian

Although there are common elements among these Christian conversions, the actual experiences may be very different. The common elements will be considered in the chapters that follow. First, though, we need to consider something else that is basic to a Christian conversion: the role of the community of faith as the mediator of the conversion. For

---

[1]See the helpful distinctions outlined in R. T. France, "Conversion and the Bible," *The Evangelical Quarterly* 65, no. 4 (1993): 292.

conversion is both an individual and a communal event or process. Conversion is individual in being personal: we each must take responsibility for our own response to divine grace. Christ calls us each by name and chooses us as his own. Few things are so powerful in a person's life as the extraordinary recognition that God loves *each of us,* knows us by name, and calls us into his company and into his service.

But a Christian conversion is also communal. As Bernard Lonergan has aptly put it, conversion is never so private that it is solitary.[2] And one of the most critical (and neglected) tasks in theological reflection on conversion is appreciating the communal character of religious experience.

In a genuine Christian conversion, through an encounter with Christ we become part of the community of those who are called *(ekklēsia)* and who, in response to that call, become one in Christ. There is no such thing as an isolated Christian; a conversion to be properly Christian includes incorporation into a community of faith. More will be said on this in the chapters that follow.

When it comes to conversion, many assume that the religious community is derivative of individual religious experience: first come conversions, and then the people who have been converted join the religious community. Until one is converted one would have no reason to be part of the community, and one would not, properly speaking, be a legitimate member of that community. Many fail to appreciate the communal character of conversion because of the radical individualism of Western thought and piety. In the West conversion is easily thought of as an individual matter occurring in the interior (and solitary) life of the individual. Yet in a profound and mysterious way it may well be that the opposite is true: that conversion is derivative of the community. If this is so, it is because the community is the mediator of conversion.

The Community as the Mediator of Conversion

Central to Paul's teaching in Romans 9—11 is the principle that no one can claim special or direction revelation; we all know the grace of Christ through the witness of another. Faith is passed on from one generation to another; and the faith is proclaimed and shared across cultures and ethnic boundaries. The gospel is communicated to us, in word and deed, by others.

---

[2]Bernard Lonergan, "Theology in Its New Context," in *Conversion: Perspectives on Personal and Social Transformation,* ed. Walter Conn (New York: Alba House, 1978), p. 13.

The human person is fundamentally communal, and we are formed by the communities of which we are a part. It only follows, then, that we will not be formed in the Christian faith apart from the religious communities that enable us to know, love and serve Christ. As William J. Abraham has put it: "It is inadequate to think that the new convert can undergo the kind of change envisaged in the coming of the rule of God in isolation, situated alone, so to speak, in a religious cell that is only marginally and accidentally related to the church."[3] As Abraham stresses, building on the thought of José Míguez Bonino, "The higher the initial demands, the greater the need for communal support."[4]

Small groups and communities of faith have always played a critical role in enabling women and men to come to faith. Whether in the class meetings of John Wesley, so integral to his ministry of evangelism, or the contemporary base communities *(comunidades eclesiales de base)* that are playing a pivotal role in the reevangelization of Latin America, Christian faith is sustained by community. This applies to the nurture of Christian belief; but it is equally true to how individuals begin their Christian pilgrimage.

The Holy Spirit effects Christian conversion. It is the Holy Spirit who illuminates the mind, convicts the heart of sin and enables the will to act in response to truth. But the context in which this takes place is the community of faith. The outpouring of the Spirit as described in Acts 2 coincides with the formation of the church; we cannot divorce the work of the Spirit from the formative role of the Christian community. The church, the community of faith, is necessarily the mediator of religious experience. Only the Spirit of God can bring about the spiritual renewal and regeneration that is sought by those coming to faith. But the church is a kind of midwife, a necessary and critical means by which this new birth is experienced.

This applies equally to the experience of conversion and to the formation of Christian virtues and character: spiritual maturity is the fruit of the common life of the people of God. It is through our communal practices of worship, learning and service that we are formed, not just communally but also as individuals. By this I do not mean that there is no religious experience outside of the church, but that the Christian community inter-

---

[3]William J. Abraham, *The Logic of Evangelism* (Grand Rapids, Mich.: Eerdmans, 1989), p. 129.
[4]Ibid.

prets and gives meaning to such experiences and eventually enables them
to be the basis for ongoing transformation.

Some may suggest that this affirmation of the community seems to
undermine the central place of Christ Jesus in the life of the Christian
and the process of conversion. We must certainly make a distinction
between Christ and the church. Jesus Christ is the object of faith, not the
church and its teaching. John Calvin made this critical distinction a central tenet of Reformed faith.[5]

But to affirm that Jesus and Jesus alone is the object of faith is not to
negate the vital place of tradition and the community of faith. Calvin himself, while insisting that Christ is the object of faith, points out that the witness of the Samaritan woman eventually led others in the village to
believe[6] and that in a similar way tradition mediates faith in Christ. We
"trust" and depend on the witness of another—representing a specific
religious tradition—and that trust enables us to place our confidence ultimately in Christ himself. The tradition and the community are not the
objects of faith; however, the community does play a critical role in mediating faith.

Even though we are each called to have faith in Christ, the community
fosters and encourages this faith in us, including the individual who is
coming to faith in Christ. The community, then, is not acting apart from
God's grace; it is the very means by which this grace is known and experienced. The church does not have authority over that grace (as a kind of
dispenser of grace) but is the means, wittingly and unwittingly, by which
God brings grace to those God is calling.

Bounded sets and centered sets. The church has always recognized that it
has a definitive and formative role in the way individuals come to Christian faith. But the mainstream of thought, historically, has viewed the
responsibility of the church as twofold. First, Christian communities have
viewed themselves as arbiters of the boundaries—those who define who is
in and who is not when it comes to identity in the kingdom of God. And
second, the church has traditionally viewed evangelism as that which
enables individuals to cross the line—the boundary between nonsalvation
and salvation.

Some theologians today say it is imperative that the church reconsider
this interpretation of its role. Paul Hiebert has approached the question

---

[5]John Calvin *Institutes of the Christian Religion* 3.2.3.
[6]Ibid., 3.2.5.

through set theory.[7] He speaks first of bounded sets, where categories are defined by clear boundaries: for example, an item is either an apple or not an apple. And all apples are 100 percent apples. "One is not more apple than another. Either a fruit is an apple or it is not." Bounded sets are essentially static sets; you are in or you are out.

Hiebert asks whether the same form of classification can be used to describe Christians. Are there really such clear distinctions between Christians and non-Christians as between apples and nonapples? Is it not more appropriate to recognize that some people—*many* people—are in process of becoming Christians? If so, Hiebert suggests, we would be better advised to think about conversion in terms of "centered sets."

In a centered set, things are classified not by whether they are "in" or "out" but by how they relate to one another. Here things are defined and understood in terms of relationship to a particular entity. What this means is that things are classified not by absolute, in-or-out categories but by their relationship to the center of the set of classification. The focus is not on the boundary but on the center. A boundary of some sort is still essential. But in a centered-set approach, while there is a boundary, the focus of attention is on the center.

When the boundary remains our primary point of reference, we encounter inherent difficulties and obstacles in thinking about what it means to become a Christian. For example, the bounded-set model implies that God's saving work is limited to the church and the confines of the church. But the Christian community cannot take this position. God is always at work everywhere within the world and among all peoples. Clearly, for example, the Spirit of God was at work in the heart and mind of Cornelius long before Peter arrived on the scene (Acts 10).

Second, the bounded-set way of thinking implies that the church or the Christian community is in a position of judgment, called on to decide who is in and who is not in the kingdom. But the New Testament Scriptures regularly warn against such a posture; Jesus tells us that in the coming kingdom we will be surprised by all those to whom God has chosen to show mercy. Further, the bounded-set assumption places the Christian community in an impossible position of defining the boundary as well as determining who is on the right side of the boundary.

Third, the bounded-set model is faulty because conversion is more com-

---

[7]Paul G. Hiebert, "The Category 'Christian' in the Mission Task," *International Review of Mission* 72 (July 1983): 421-27.

plex than "crossing a boundary." Conversion, as I hope to show in the chapters that follow, is rarely if ever a single, defining moment at which we can state definitively that a person has fully converted and is truly "in" (or out).

This does not mean that the boundary between faith and lack of faith either is not important or does not exist. It most certainly is and does. Indeed the church is mandated to proclaim the extraordinary claims of Christ upon each person—to declare that Jesus is Lord and to call people to affirm the unequivocal supremacy of Christ and his kingdom. Challenging the boundary approach to evangelism and mission simply means questioning the assumption that the church knows precisely where the boundary is between faith and nonfaith, that the church is the manager of this boundary, and that evangelism, mission and childrearing should be defined in terms of this boundary. And it means calling the church to place the focus in evangelism and witness where it belongs: on Christ Jesus.

The appropriateness of a centered-set model. There are several reasons a centered-set model is more helpful and appropriate when it comes to thinking about the relationship between church and conversion. First, the centered-set perspective gives allowance for variation and movement; it is dynamic rather than static, so that things are defined as they are moving toward (or away from) the center. Christians, then, would be defined in terms of their relationship with Christ Jesus—by their allegiance and worship, by the fundamental orientation of their lives as followers of Jesus— and not by whether they fit preconceived notions of what makes a person religious, nor by whether they are part of a religious community. In other words, those who are religious but whose orientation is not toward Christ (e.g., the Pharisees) would not be seen as Christian regardless of how religious they are.

Further, while there is a boundary in this perspective, it is possible with a centered set to be intentionally ambiguous or imprecise about the boundary. We do not need to insist on defining the clear and undebatable boundary one would presumably cross and thus be defined as a Christian. Hiebert uses the example of traveling from the mountains to the prairies. The transition is definitive and distinct; yet it is so subtle that the traveler never knows exactly when she has left the mountains and entered the plain. In the same way, Hiebert notes, "conversion to Christianity . . . might not be a decisive event. It could also be a gradual movement from outside to in, based on a series of small decisions."[8]

---

[8]Ibid.

With this perspective, then, the Christian community views itself as responsible to witness to Christ (rather than to the boundaries) and to what it means to follow Christ (regardless of how religious or pagan one might be, or how active in the local church). The issue at hand is one's relationship with Christ Jesus, not the level of one's religious aspirations and practices.

Under this model, the Christian community is not so much a manager of the boundary as a witness to the center. It is freed from the burden of manipulating conversions and instead focuses its attention on its true responsibility, serving as a witness to the reign of Christ. This frees us from any temptation to think of the church and the kingdom as synonymous, and from the trap of thinking of the church as the owner or manager of the kingdom. A centered-set perspective frees the church to think of itself as a sign of the kingdom and as bearing responsibility to witness to that kingdom through word and deed.

Vital in all of this and pivotal to our understanding of the relationship between the church and conversion is the conviction that the church is the midwife, not the manager, of the process by which women and men come to Christ. As George Hunsberger aptly puts it, building on the thought of Lesslie Newbigin, the church "is neither the author nor agent of conversion, which remains a miracle of the Holy Spirit. The body owes its life to the Spirit, but the Spirit is not 'domesticated' within it."[9]

The final chapter of this study will explore more fully some of the implications of thinking this way about the connection between the church and conversion. For now, we turn to another dimension of this relationship: the language of conversion.

The Language of Conversion

Paul Helm makes a sobering observation: "Such is the close relationship between language, thought and experience that vague and indefinite language is invariably accompanied by vague and indefinite experience."[10] If this is so, the language used within religious communities, especially by religious leaders, and especially the language of religious experience and of conversion, requires careful attention. The reason for such urgency is

---

[9]George R. Hunsberger, *Bearing the Witness of the Spirit: Lesslie Newbigin's Theology of Cultural Plurality* (Grand Rapids, Mich.: Eerdmans, 1998), p. 168.

[10]Paul Helm, *The Beginnings: Word and Spirit in Conversion* (Edinburgh: Banner of Truth, 1986), pp. 9-10.

that language, especially religious language, is formative. The community of faith is both the setting and the means by which a person becomes a Christian. And what enables the community to have this formative influence is the story its members sustain together, particularly the story of Jesus.

Language and religious experience. There is no religious experience that is not rooted in language—language that both enables and interprets the experience, and apart from which it is meaningless. Religious experience does not occur in a linguistic vacuum. Language gives conceptual and structural context to our experience.

For many, Ludwig Wittgenstein has served as a catalyst for the conversation about the ways language shapes both understanding and experience—such that the means by which a person becomes a Christian is a process of enculturation rather than indoctrination.[11] Wittgenstein suggested that we become religious by learning a language of faith, learned in much the same way that a child learns a language. In echo of this, George Lindbeck in *The Nature of Doctrine* contends that religious experience is formed by linguistic and cultural forms through religious symbol systems. Religious conversion, then, cannot be conceived of as merely the adoption of and following of certain propositions. "Rather," he writes, "to become religious—no less than to become culturally or linguistically competent—is to interiorize a set of skills by practice and training. One learns how to feel, act and think in conformity with a religious tradition that is, in its inner structure, far richer and more subtle than can be explicitly articulated."[12]

There is so such thing as a "private" language. Religious experience is impossible without a language scheme, and all language is inherently communal. We cannot know and speak and live a language, any language, apart from the community that defines and sustains that language. The Christian proclamation of the gospel has significance and power only as it is embodied in the common life of a community of believers.

Dean Martin notes that the language of faith is not learned through

---

[11]Ludwig Wittgenstein's works addressing the matter of religious experience and language include *Lectures and Conversations on Aesthetics, Psychology and Religious Belief* and *Culture and Value.* For much of what follows I am indebted to the insights of Dean M. Martin, "Learning to Become a Christian," *Religious Education* 82, no. 1 (winter 1987): 94-114. See also Paul Holmer, *The Grammar of Faith* (San Francisco: Harper & Row, 1978).

[12]George Lindbeck, *The Nature of Doctrine* (Philadelphia: Westminster Press, 1984), p. 35.

discourse so much as through the ordinary life of a congregation, particularly the common act of worship. Describing how a person learns religious faith while growing up within a religious community, he says, "The language of religion (like any other language) is mainly learned by long exposure to the spontaneous and unrehearsed fashion in which adult believers—often, though not only, one's parents—speak to one another and with those outside the faith."[13] It follows, then, that "the learning of the language of faith is gradual and piecemeal—as it is with the rest of our concepts. There is no short route to an understanding of that language, no immediate and intuitive grasp."[14]

The learning of a language is not merely a cerebral or cognitive process. What a learner appropriates is both intellectual and affective, including the meaning and character of both sorrow and joy, and what it means to live with faith, hope and love. Yet what is learned determines foundational beliefs that shape the life, worship and character of a religious community. Martin speaks of these as the *governing beliefs* of the faith community.[15]

Thus the way a person learns the faith is not through rational presentation so much as through conversation around life lived. There is a close interconnection between belief and behavior, between confession and life, for one's faith convictions are learned within a community that lives the faith it professes. One learns of the person and work of Christ in the context of the worship of Christ and a community that is seeking to live in the service of Christ.

Language is communal. In the community of faith we learn the language of faith and conversion through sermons, hymns, prayers and readings of Scripture. But we also learn this faith language through ongoing conversations day in and day out in the context of both play and work. This communal language enables us to make sense of and give definition to our human predicament, the longings and aspirations of our hearts, the reality of God and the work of the Spirit in our lives. And this language outlines an authentic and life-transforming response to God.

So the community's language of faith increasingly becomes our own language, enabling us to make sense of our experience and fostering depth and breadth to that experience. Conversion requires that we

---

[13]Dean Martin, "Learning to Become a Christian," p. 99.
[14]Ibid., p. 100.
[15]Ibid., p. 110.

embrace this language. It involves not only trusting in Jesus but also trusting in the community that mediates Jesus to us through the language of faith. Conversion is largely an experience of learning and appropriating a faith language, a language that is sustained by a particular religious community.

The irony is that we cannot learn the language of faith unless we are part of a community. We cannot become converted unless we first become part of a community, a community of faith, so that we can learn the language that will enable and interpret our conversion. In other words, the community of faith mediates a conversion, and it does so largely through enabling others to learn the language of faith.

Further, a convert may develop a personal conversion narrative, a story of his or her experience of divine grace. The language for this narrative is provided by the community; the common language of the community provides the interpretive framework for personal narratives.

Among evangelicals the language of conversion has traditionally and consistently found its place within conversion narratives. Although as a popular genre the conversion narrative is at least a hundred years older than the evangelical renewal movements of the eighteenth century, conversion narratives multiplied and became a standard form of spiritual autobiography with the advent of the Evangelical Revival.[16] But though it has not been as dominant in the nineteenth and twentieth centuries, what many have called the "testimony" continued to be an inescapable element of evangelical religious life well past the middle of the twentieth century.

Many see the common testimony as a bit archaic and of little value since often these narratives have little theological content and do not truly capture the angst and ambiguity of spiritual experience. The traditional "testimony" was simply too black and white, too dramatic; those whose experience was quieter and more gradual tended to assume that their narrative had little if any value or significance.

But if we intend to seek an authentic language of conversion, it seems appropriate that we seek to recover the conversion narrative. According to D. Bruce Hindmarsh, the seventeenth and eighteenth centuries were particularly fertile ground for this genre of spiritual autobiography, in com-

---

[16]For an illuminating and insightful study of conversion narratives see, D. Bruce Hindmarsh, "Early Evangelical Conversion in the Light of Early Evangelical Mission History," *The North Atlantic Missiology Project,* Position Paper 25 (Cambridge, U.K.: Westminister College, 1997), p. 2.

parison with other periods of evangelical witness and conversion. He contends that the features of this period that bred conversion narratives were a heightened sense of introspection and a distinctive self-consciousness (or a distinctive sense of the self), something that arises in societies where "self-determination is given significant scope."[17] The evangelical conversion narrative, he says, "flourished . . . when Christendom, or Christian civil society, had eroded far enough to allow for toleration, dissent, experimentation, and the manifestation of nominal and sincere forms of adherence to faith, but not so far as to elude a traditional sense of Christian moral norms and basic cosmological assumptions."[18]

While the circumstances of the early twenty-first century are certainly very different, perhaps the climate is right for us to recover the art of the conversion narrative. The postmodern context is particularly alive to the possibilities of narrative and story, recognizing their significance. One of the outcomes of a thoughtful study of conversion might be to encourage spiritual autobiography—a sense of one's own journey of faith and how an appreciation of one's past can provide impetus, a sense of purpose and hope for the future. If we are to encourage and nurture spiritual autobiography, the purpose is not only to appreciate the power and significance of experience but also to develop a language that is both informed by the Scriptures and consistent with our experience—a language that enables us to tell the story well.

In my experience of teaching on conversion in both academic settings and within congregational life, one of the most fruitful exercises has been for participants to formulate a conversion narrative that is consistent with their experience, that authenticates it (gives it significance and value) and that then enables that experience to foster a positive focus toward the future and to enable continuing transformation.

Early evangelicals, according to Hindmarsh, viewed the conversion narrative as an opportunity to point to something larger and beyond the self.[19] In other words, while the conversion narrative might be viewed as self-centered, in practice it enabled persons to see and appreciate how their own story was but a small part of the story of God and God's saving activity. A contemporary quest to recover the conversion narrative as a means of self-expression should have this very end in mind: to see and

---

[17]Ibid., pp. 16-17.
[18]Ibid., p. 19.
[19]Ibid.

embrace the work of God in our lives and our communities. But to do this well, we must find a meaningful and authentic language of conversion.

Language that fosters and enables conversion. We need to ask ourselves, then, how do we settle on language that will enable and foster conversion? It should be clear that religious leaders bear particular responsibility in the language of faith and conversion. Pastors and teachers within the church necessarily play a key role in the formation of a shared language of faith.

We must be both careful and intentional. Language shapes thought and behavior. When language is weak and meaningless, we fail to effectively communicate truth and grace. When language is dynamic and consistent with truth, it has the capacity to profoundly shape understanding and behavior. It makes a difference.

In the late 1950s A. W. Tozer suggested that the words *accept* and *receive* had long since lost their usefulness in reference to conversion. He argued that these words no longer effectively communicated the meaning of conversion as taught in Scripture. Yet familiar and favorite expressions have remarkable power of persistence in the popular language of the Christian community. If as Tozer suggests, these words have lost their power, then we indeed have a crisis of failure on two accounts: the New Testament doctrine is not faithfully represented, and we do not have a dynamic way of articulating and describing this vital dimension of Christian experience.

Tozer's observations are a reminder that the language of conversion within evangelical communities is in a state of flux. We have one foot in the postwar language of the 1950s and the other foot stretching to find a new language to make sense of our religious experience.

Virginia Lieson Brereton makes some astute observations in a study of women's conversion narratives of the nineteenth and twentieth centuries.[20] For example, she notes that in the twentieth century the "most persistent one-sentence signification of conversion has been for a narrator to say that she had 'accepted Christ as her personal Lord and Savior' (or, less frequently, as 'Lord of her life')"; the second most common involved references to yielding one's life or surrendering one's life. There was also fairly common language of "finding Christ" or "being

---

[20]Virginia Lieson Brereton, *From Sin to Salvation: Stories of Women's Conversions, 1800 to the Present* (Indianapolis: Indiana University Press. 1991), pp. 54-55.

saved" or "being born again." And Brereton highlights corresponding language of evangelism as "leading" or "winning" or "bringing someone to Christ."[21]

Twentieth-century narratives, she points out, make primary reference to receiving Christ into one's heart.[22] But significantly, in the twentieth-century narrative the emphasis is on accepting Christ rather than being accepted by Christ. The experience of divine grace is described as the fruit of a decision—something that happens on a fundamentally human level. In the previous century there was much more emphasis on the convicting and persuading work of the Spirit who draws people to God. Further, Brereton notes, in the twentieth century there was much more emphasis on a "personal relationship with Jesus" or reference to Christ as one's personal Savior.[23] The language of conversion has had a strong emphasis on Christ to the neglect of Father and Spirit.

Brereton's observations serve to highlight and reinforce the need to be attentive to the meaning and formative influence of language, particularly when it comes to a consideration of conversion and the nature of religious experience.

In *The Transformation of Man: A Study of Conversion and Community* Rosemary Haughton effectively stresses that an authentic language of conversion clarifies and fosters an integral relationship between conversion and transformation. Haughton calls for a "total language" that encompasses the full range of experience, feeling, hope and desires of a particular community in symbol: word, rite and gesture.[24] An authentic language of conversion has the capacity to foster substantial change, even if ultimate change and transformation is "beyond death."

> The language of conversion is of crucial importance, because it determines the way in which conversion is worked out, and the area of living which it affects. Conversion affects the whole person, but a human being is a person only in the degree of this self-awareness, developed in the saving (or damning) encounter. And the effect of conversion is to convert the language of self-understanding, so that a whole area of ordinary living has a new type of awareness.[25]

---

[21]Ibid., p. 55.
[22]Ibid., p. 56.
[23]Ibid., p. 57.
[24]Rosemary Haughton, *The Transformation of Man: A Study of Conversion and Community* (London: Geoffrey Chapman, 1968), p. 225.
[25]Ibid., p. 245.

"The language of conversion . . . determines the way in which a conversion is worked out." If we are negligent or careless in our language of conversion, we are undermining the possibility that a conversion experience will lead to genuine transformation.

We must find language that enables us to speak of both the simple fact that we have become Christians and the reality that this experience is complex and often filled with ambiguities. We need a language that affirms that religious experience involves the whole person. While evangelicals have moved beyond the language of "saving souls," we must still work to find language of the conversion of the whole person: intellect, emotion, will, the whole person in response to God and in connection with others. Finally, we need a language of religious experience that aptly captures the reality of divine initiative and the call for human responsibility in response. Christian humility will be key to the formation of an authentic language of conversion.

Sources for language of faith and conversion. If we are to be intentional in our use of language, we begin by attending to its sources. First and perhaps most obviously, an authentic language of faith and conversion will draw on the Scriptures as its primary source. This does not mean that we do not use language in translation; neither does it mean that we do not use language and concepts that are rooted in our own cultural and societal context. Our contemporary context and speech can integrate and provide a synthesis of biblical concepts and "words." But the ancient text of Scripture takes primacy for the simple reason that it is the abiding record of God's self-revelation. In reading the text of Holy Scripture with humility and receptivity, we allow it to be a new word to us and thus to continually form and reform our language of faith and conversion.

Second, our own spiritual heritage and tradition will be a source for the language of conversion. On one hand this is necessarily the case; we cannot deny or ignore the formative influence of our religious upbringing. Indeed all theological reflection is necessarily linked to a particular theological and spiritual tradition. Theological reflection is meaningful only when we recognize that it is embodied within particular faith communities and kept alive by those communities. The place of tradition is inherent in theological study. However, we must also acknowledge the danger that a particular community's language can take on an insular quality and become a language unto itself. Many people leave one church and find faith in another community for the very simple reason that the second offers a language of faith that is more congruent with their experience;

their own heritage has a language that makes little sense to them or may actually be an obstacle to genuine Christian faith. Further, it is very possible for a tradition to lose its capacity to point us to a humble, receptive approach to Holy Scripture that would allow it to speak afresh.

Wisdom therefore requires that we recognize both the strengths and the limitations of our own religious heritage. With critical appreciation we can celebrate the strengths of our tradition while acknowledging the limitations it represents. It is possible for a community to allow its language of faith to be challenged anew, again and again, by the text of Scripture. And the language of a tradition is a vital and necessary resource. None of us come to faith in a linguistic vacuum; inevitably our faith is nurtured within the context of a particular tradition.

The genius of vitality within our faith traditions and communities is that we allow Scripture to be read freshly. But we sustain a lively language of faith when we allow other Christian traditions to shape, inform and challenge how we speak of conversion and transformation. Faith communities that have lost the capacity to sustain a dynamic language of conversion have usually not only failed to allow Scripture to be alive to them but also become insular and failed to appreciate the value of learning from other traditions.

In this study of conversion I draw on a whole range of Christian traditions. This is intentional. Though I speak out of my own evangelical tradition, I lean heavily on the insights and perspectives of those from other traditions, and I hope that this study will enable those in other traditions to appreciate more fully, within their context, the meaning of conversion.

Third, the language of faith and conversion finds a necessary source in its societal and cultural context. Conversion never happens in a historical vacuum but always in the lives of people shaped by psychological, social and cultural factors and influences. Inevitably conversion has a very particular context. There is the macro context of cultural and linguistic milieu, the micro context of family, religious community, work and neighborhood, and the personal context of one's own personality, temperament and experience.[26]

Conversion arises out of a personal longing for change or transformation. As often as not, conversion is occasioned by some stress or turmoil,

---

[26]For this distinction I am indebted to Lewis R. Rambo, "The Psychology of Conversion," in *Handbook of Religious Conversion*, ed. H. Newton Malony and Samuel Southhard (Birmingham, Ala.: Religious Education Press, 1992), pp. 163-65.

some inner conflict that seeks resolution. This psychological crisis represents a possibility for a resolution of the conflict or, beyond this, to some form of self-realization.

A conversion experience might be the means by which a persistent sense of guilt is resolved or an individual finds peace in life circumstances that have been filled with fear and anxiety. But ultimately a conversion experience taps into the human longing for significance, meaning, integration and purpose.

For some, conversion is a means to find cognitive coherence, intellectual resolution or meaning. For others the resolution is part of a quest for meaning and life purpose (creative meaning), and thus conversion is a means to mature emotionally, morally and intellectually. This would be the posture of most theorists of adult development. For others, religious change and conversion arises from the need to love and be loved.

It should be stressed that while it is possible that the inner conflict or crisis is pathological—a person may be in deep depression or overcome by guilt and fear—this is not necessarily the case. Instead the tension may be a sign of emotional and psychological health, a longing to grasp the nature and meaning of human life in general and of one's own life.

While some psychological studies of conversion seek to establish one overriding theme or motivation, likely in almost everyone there are multiple factors that shape the experience and the process. But the end is the same: conversion brings psychological equilibrium, personal integration, meaning and purpose.

The deep longings and aspirations that may lead to and find resolution in Christian conversion, however, are never merely individual matters. Everyone is enculturated and socialized. We are social beings. We are members of social entities, and our identities are deeply formed by social realities.

Christopher Lasch, in *The Culture of Narcissism*,[27] describes a "narcissistic personality" of our time. Given his devastating critique, should we give no serious attention to the longings evident within Western culture? Wade Clark Roof challenges such a conclusion. In *A Generation of Seekers* Roof speaks of Americans as a people searching for direction, purpose and meaning. And increasingly the search is guided by spiritual aspirations or longings and seeks expression in a commitment to self and to others.[28]

---

[27]Christopher Lasch, *The Culture of Narcissism* (New York: W. W. Norton, 1978).
[28]Wade Clark Roof, *A Generation of Seekers* (San Francisco: Harper, 1993), p. 133.

Roof actually sees this quest as a potential antidote to the radical individualism of Western societies. He believes the self-centeredness theme has been overplayed and many—particularly many baby boomers—are ready to commit themselves to something that they believe in.[29]

If Roof is right, the church does not need to pander to anyone; the community of faith can without apology outline the claims of the gospel and the call to live in service of the truth. That is, the church can take seriously the longings within its social and cultural context without compromising its commitment to the authority of Scripture and its fundamental religious practices. The culture's deep longings will actually be met through God's self-revelation in Scripture and lived out within a community that through its religious practices sustains its capacity to know and live this Word.

In Western society there are deep longings for genuine community, self-actualization, spiritual transcendence and wisdom. In fact, everyone enculturated or socialized within the West will demonstrate these longings in some form or another—aspirations that in themselves are legitimate.

The bottom line is that our language of conversion needs to resonate with the deepest longings of the people among whom we live and work. For an evangelistic mission to set up a billboard in India that reads "Ye must be born again" makes little sense in a culture where the majority assume reincarnation and long to be freed from it. In other words, the language of conversion must not only be faithful to the text of Holy Scripture and our religious traditions; it must tap into the longings of its cultural context. This assumes, of course, that these longings are not inherently evil, though they may be expressed in ways that are destructive. The gospel promises the fulfillment of our deepest longings in Christ Jesus.

Conclusion

This study, then, is a call to rethink the language of conversion within our faith communities that informs our experience of Christian conversion. We need a language that enables us to both make sense of our own experience and foster a genuine experience of God's saving grace in others, so that we all might more deeply know the transforming grace of God.

---

[29]Ibid., p. 184.

3

Autobiography

The Church's Experience of Conversion

The hymn "Blessed Assurance" has as its chorus:

This is my story, this is my song,
praising my Savior all the day long;
this is my story, this is my song,
praising my Savior all the day long.

Not great poetry perhaps, but great sentiment. This gospel song was for many years a kind of theme song for evangelicals. While the hymn is sung less frequently today, it captures the reality that story, particularly the narrative of one's own religious experience, is an important if not essential element in the evangelical understanding of conversion.

It is through narrative that the language of conversion has shaped experience in the evangelical tradition. The affirmation of story or narrative is an implicit recognition of the significance of experience in Christian theology. The same kind of sentiment is expressed in another gospel song, "He Lives":

You ask me how I know he lives?
He lives within my heart.

As one raised on the rational apologetic that stressed the need for evidence—concrete, tangible, hard facts that were, in our minds, irrefutable—I responded with great skepticism to the suggestion that we would be able to attest to the resurrection by the sentiment of our hearts! Only later in my Christian journey did I came to appreciate the power of experience, and the role of narrative in particular, to inform our reading of Holy Scripture.

Indeed, a comprehensive theology of conversion needs to include an examination of conversion narratives—autobiographical accounts that give us glimpses into the actual experience of conversion in the history of the church. Such narratives do not merely illustrate the text of Scripture; nor is a conversion narrative merely a source by which we supplement or highlight Scripture. Rather, the experience of the church is a critical lens through which we read Scripture. Encounter with these narratives in fact led me to reconsider my own prior understanding of the theology of the New Testament. Further, these narratives are testimony to the work of the Spirit in the lives of God's people, and as such they have significant instructional potential for the contemporary Christian. They are critical means by which we can interpret Scripture, but they also serve as windows through which we can view our own experience.

Experience and Context

Narrative is a reminder that all theology is contextual. It shows us that understanding conversion is not merely a matter of knowing what is right or wrong on the basis of certain biblical texts or doctrines. Rather, all theology is lived theology, lived out by particular individuals in actual communities. Narratives of individuals and communities constitute, then, embodiments of the theology (the summary of the biblical texts and doctrines) by which we live.

I have been forced to reread scriptural texts because my own religious experience did not fit the language of conversion of my religious community. My experience gave me new eyes through which to read the text, which in turn informed my experience. There is no reading of Scripture that is not in some way or another informed by experience; and the ideal of course is that as we continue to experience the grace of God we will continue to allow the text to inform and reform our experience.

Experience and Self-Knowledge

Narrative, particularly conversion narrative, is a central means by which we understand human life in general and our own lives in particular. We really know ourselves only when we know how God has worked in particular ways in our lives. A narrative of our religious experience is, then, a narrative of God's gracious work in our particular circumstances. Such a narrative helps us know who we are, where we have come from and where we are going.

As noted by L. Gregory Jones, some resist references to autobiography in Christian theology because they think theology should focus our attention on God rather than human beings. That is, we should be telling God's story, not our story. But to do so, as Jones demonstrates, fails to appreciate that "autobiography can be important as a means of locating our lives in the story of God."[1] This, Jones says, is precisely what Augustine was doing in his magisterial *Confessions:* giving an account of how his life demonstrated the work of God, the story of God, and how God's grace in his life led him to confess faith in God. His narrative certainly turns inward at points to give account of the grace of God; but "his autobiographical turn inward is at the same time a turn outward to the God in whom he lives and moves and has his being."[2]

So while some may protest that an examination of personal experience is self-centered and narcissistic, telling our conversion stories does just the opposite, for our own experience enables us to see and enter into the grand picture of God's work. Paul's repeated narration of his own experience did not reflect self-fascination; it was rather a lens through which he was able to see all of God's merciful work.

My own self-understanding has been deeply affected by John Wesley's experience. An appreciation of the way God was attentive to Wesley has enabled me to make sense of my own narrative and gain awareness of the ways God has been present in my life. Self-knowledge and knowledge of God are integrally linked.

Experience and Imitation

A study of conversions within the history of the church will of necessity give particular attention to those that are dramatic, decisive and determi-

---

[1] L. Gregory Jones, "For All the Saints: Autobiography in Christian Theology," *The Asbury Theological Journal* 47, no. 1 (spring 1992): 35.
[2] Ibid., p. 34.

native. But these cannot be viewed as prescriptive, as examples of ideal conversions. It is more helpful to think of them as laboratory material, so to speak. The dramatic conversions set the nature and character of conversion in bold relief, enabling us to appreciate the character of our own experience more fully through an examination of the clearly delineated conversion of another. And it is not merely drama that catches our attention in such a conversion; it is the depth and thoroughness of the conversion, the authenticity and radicalness that subsequently enabled these individuals to play a significant role in the life of the church.

The lives of the saints are given for our encouragement—that we might grow in faith and imitate them even as they imitate Christ and follow him. To this end, consider the narrative of four persons who represent four different eras in the life of the church.

Augustine of Hippo (A.D. 354-430)

Augustine may well be the greatest doctor and theologian of the church after St. Paul. And of all of his writings, his *Confessions* has had a profoundly formative influence on Western culture and thought. This narrative of his own experience, a masterpiece of devotional and also of critical thought, is the first autobiography in the contemporary sense of that term. Because of the *Confessions,* we know more about Augustine than any of his contemporaries.

Malcolm Muggeridge has suggested that the testimony of Augustine is particularly meaningful for the contemporary Christian because his narrative takes account of much that today's church faces: a moral vacuum, apathy regarding justice, and an insatiable passion for new sensations and experiences.[3]

The first nine "books" of the *Confessions* are the primary source for Augustine's conversion narrative. Their underlying theme is the greatness of God's love, our need to know and experience God's love, and the power of divine grace. As Augustine stresses, he provides the narrative of his own experience—from darkness to light—so that he can come to love God and live in God's grace even more (2.1).[4]

Early years. Augustine was born in A.D. 354 in Tagaste, a free village in a Roman province in North Africa, to a prominent though not wealthy fam-

---

[3]Malcolm Muggeridge, *A Third Testament* (London: Little, Brown, 1976), p. 37.
[4]Augustine of Hippo, *The Confessions of St. Augustine,* trans. John K. Ryan (New York: Doubleday, 1960). Further quotes in the chapter are from this edition.

ily. His father was a Roman administrator and a pagan. His mother, Monica, was profoundly influential in his life; it was she who is credited with ensuring that young Augustine received a Christian education and thus an early exposure to Christian thought and practice.

As a young man, while talented and capable, he was lazy and inattentive. Despite his potential, he spent great amounts of time, between his required academic responsibilities, in idleness. More than that, he was taken up with and consumed by sensual pleasure.

He arrived in Carthage (370) at age seventeen and embraced the life of the city—the glory of youth, sensuality, a life lived for pleasure. Eventually (372) he confessed to his mother that he had a son born by a woman with whom he was living, a woman he would live with for the next fifteen years (although later he was quite prepared to send her away if it meant he could make a socially advantageous marriage).

Young Augustine was also consumed by intellectual pleasures. By age nineteen he was reading Cicero, under whose influence he developed a longing for truth that would lead him on a twelve-year search through science, astrology and various philosophies. As some have noted, Augustine's intellectual pursuits reflected a *sensual* desire for wisdom; the longing for truth was part of his passion for life.

This fascination and interest made him susceptible to Manichaeism, a religious movement that affirmed a cosmic dualism in which both "light" and "dark" are eternal, and thus evil is assumed to have eternal existence. The Manichaeans' understanding of the nature and origin of evil made sense to him (he had always been troubled by evil, thinking that the Christian response was not adequate). While a student in Carthage, then, he embraced Manichaeism, drawn not only by the movement's view of evil but also by its asceticism, involving extremely rigorous practices of abstinence and chastity by which he hoped to overcome his inclinations.

The search for truth and the problem of evil. After a period of teaching "grammar" in his hometown of Tagaste, Augustine returned to Carthage as a student and lecturer. Now coming into his mid-twenties, he continued searching. Still plagued with the problem of evil, he grew dissatisfied with the Manichaean solution. The Manichaean philosophy, he decided, was empty: it tore things down but did not build up, it distorted Scripture, and it did not foster a true love of virtue.

At age twenty-nine (383) Augustine went to Rome, where he started a school of oratory. During a visit to Milan he heard the preaching of Bishop Ambrose, which he would later note planted a very significant seed in his heart and mind (5.14). Though Augustine did not embrace the Christian faith at the time, Ambrose's preaching enabled him to abandon Manichaeism and continue his search. His search now had the Christian faith as a point of reference; and he had a preliminary appreciation of Paul's teaching on sin, grace and salvation.

Finally, by September 386, at age thirty-three, Augustine came to a clear conviction of the truthfulness and wisdom of Christian faith. However, he continued to wrestle with the problem of evil, which proved to be an internal obstacle large enough to prevent him from embracing any one religion or system of philosophy. "I believed too that it was in Christ your Son, our Lord, and in the Holy Scriptures, which are affirmed by the authority of your Catholic Church, that you had laid the path of man's salvation . . . but I was still burning with anxiety to find the source from which evil comes" (7.7).

Through readings in Neo-Platonism he came to see that evil really has no positive existence in and of itself. God and God alone has real and eternal existence, and evil is but the consequence of turning away from God. Yet Augustine acknowledged that even as this "barrier" was removed and he was convinced intellectually of truth of Christian faith, he was still hesitant. He had come to mental assent and acceptance; intellectually nothing stood in his way. But he was not yet home.

It is worth mentioning that in later years Augustine would look back and view what he learned through Neo-Platonism as a gift. He affirms in the *Confessions* that the Neo-Platonists had fundamentally Christian doctrines about God, creation and the Word, though in these writers he did not find insight into the incarnation and the gospel of a crucified Christ.

Coming to terms with sinful propensities. Despite Augustine's affirmation of the truth of Christian faith, he did not embrace the truth wholeheartedly. Page after page of the *Confessions* speaks of his struggle with his sinful inclinations. He acknowledges his love of sin—of sensuality—though he knew that his ultimate joy and satisfaction would come in enjoying God.

Knowing this was one thing; experiencing it was another. He describes his continued battle and frustration with sexual temptation and lust in language that echoes Romans 7: he did what he knew he should not do, but could do no other. His will, he would see in retrospect, was incapable of living in truth.

One day he heard a child calling out, "Take and read; take and read." Picking up the Bible, he randomly chose a text and came upon Romans

13:13-14, which in contemporary translation reads, "Let us live honorably as in the day, not in reveling and drunkenness, not in debauchery and licentiousness, not in quarreling and jealousy. Instead, put on the Lord Jesus Christ, and make no provision for the flesh, to gratify its desires."

The impact of the scriptural text was immediate: "I had no wish to read more and no need to do so, for in an instant as I came to the end of the sentence, it was as though the light of confidence flooded into my heart and all the darkness and doubt was dispelled" (8.12). Augustine was flooded with joy as the power of sin was broken. The experience would have a profound impact on his theology of grace, for he came to see the centrality of grace and that everything we have comes as a gift from God.

His immediate inclination then was to embrace asceticism and rigorous legalism. Along with others who chose such a path, he consciously shunned the church, which was viewed as nominal in its faith and compromised in its morality. However, perhaps because of the initial influence of Ambrose, it was not long before Augustine saw his need for baptism (which implied acceptance of the church and its authority). Still in Rome during Lent of 387, Augustine became a candidate for baptism; he was baptized by Ambrose on Easter Sunday, April 24, 387.

Though initially disinclined to join the church, Augustine had carried a burden of uncertainty whether he had indeed repented and was truly forgiven. The resolution came through baptism, which, of course, was offered through the church: "But my faith would not let me feel at ease over my past sins, for they had not yet been forgiven in your baptism . . . [but once we] were baptized . . . all anxiety over the past melted away from us" (9.4, 6). He did not view the sacramental actions as means in themselves of God's saving grace; in book 13 he speaks of the sacraments as necessary and indispensable and yet insufficient if they are not understood and practiced spiritually. However, for him baptism was the critical event by which he came to assurance of forgiveness.

Bishop of Hippo. A year later Augustine returned to his native Tagaste, and following the common custom of the time, he sold all his possessions with a resolve to live out his life in poverty, prayer and study of the Scriptures.

He was not particularly interested in the priesthood and avoided any situation where it might be pressed upon him. While he was on a visit to Hippo to see a friend, however, they were together in prayer at the church when the people demanded that Augustine acknowledge a call into the priesthood. He accepted. This was at age thirty-seven; he was ordained in 391.

In Tagaste he taught theology; these middle years turned out to be very formative as he developed as a scholar and teacher. In 396, at age forty-three, he was installed as bishop of Hippo.

There are many interpreters of Augustine's conversion and religious experience. David Wells, for example, makes the case that Augustine's coming to faith had three distinct phases: (1) an intellectual conversion, the fruit of his pilgrimage from Manichaean dualism to skepticism to Platonism and, through the preaching of Ambrose, to Christian faith; (2) a moral conversion, in which, through the reading of Romans 13, he experienced freedom from the power of sin; and (3) his ecclesiastical conversion, in which he came to accept baptism and the authority of the church.[5] This may be a bit too simple or neat, but it makes clear that Augustine's conversion cannot be set at a particular time or place; it was the fruit of a long search, and it consisted of several distinctive moments, each of which was essential to a thorough conversion, but none of which can be viewed in itself as the conversion of St. Augustine.

Ignatius Loyola (1491-1556)

Ignatius Loyola is best known as the founder of the Society of Jesus, better known as the Jesuits, an order that has had an extraordinary impact in both education and Christian missions. Christians of all traditions have valued Ignatius's *Spiritual Exercises,* a guide to contemplative prayer. But his contribution cannot be appreciated apart from his own experience. It was his own conversion experience that both informed and sustained his work as founder, administrator and spiritual director. The primary source for Ignatius's conversion story is his *Autobiography.*[6]

Early years. Ignatius, born Inigo Lopez de Loyola, was raised a member of a ruling Basque family, loyal to the crown of Castile, active patrons of the church in their hometown. It was a wealthy and prominent family with connections to the royal house.[7]

The structure and context of his life were distinctly feudal. The Loyola family had a keen sense of lineage and loyalty among its members; there was a high stress on obedience to the family head, who ruled with the

---

[5]David Wells, *Turning to God: Biblical Conversion in the Modern World* (Grand Rapids, Mich.: Baker, 1989), chap. 4.
[6]Ignatius Loyola, *The Autobiography of St. Ignatius Loyola,* ed. John C. Olin, trans. Joseph F. O'Callaghan (New York: Harper & Row, 1974).
[7]Candido de Dalmases, *Ignatius of Loyola, Founder of the Jesuits,* trans. Jerome Aixala (Anand, India: Gujarat Sahitya Prakash, 1985), pp. 20-23.

authority of the head of a clan. The setting was rural, with a stress on order and discipline.[8]

The simplicity and robustness of the religious faith of the Basque people would always stay with Ignatius. Basque influence is evident in his language, style and temperament, including, writes Pedro de Leturia, his reflective interiority, personal concentration and firm determination.[9] Leturia suggests that his determination of will was the most lasting effect of Ignatius's Basque heritage.

A new life direction. The second phase of Ignatius's life came when at age sixteen or seventeen he was sent as a page to the king's court to serve Don Juan Velásques de Cuella. He spent more than ten years in this aristocratic setting, becoming formally trained as a courtier. The environment was profoundly formative: the values of the court gradually became part of his character and life orientation. Life at court fed his longing for fame and personal glory, aspirations that were fueled by romantic heroic ideals. But it also instilled in him the qualities of courtesy and politeness typical of the Spanish gentleman—significant only in being critical to the formation of an inner personal poise upon which he drew in later years. The imagery and motifs of royal ceremony would come to dominate his spirituality.[10]

After the death of King Ferdinand, Ignatius (then Inigo) went to Navarre, and there, in the service of the viceroy, he was involved in 1521 in the battle of Pamplona against the French. In a hopeless defense of the fortress, Ignatius was wounded—a cannonball injured one leg and shattered the other. He was seriously hurt; at battle's end the French themselves saw to his medical treatment and arranged for his transfer to his house in Loyola. Sadly, this medical attention was inadequate; the leg did not heal properly. Partly out of a concern for appearances, Ignatius chose to go through the agonizing surgery again, having his leg rebroken and reset. The result was an extended recuperation during which he was forced to remain immobile.[11]

This lengthy period of convalescence was the first crucial turning point in the spiritual development of Ignatius. In his autobiography he says that

[8]Mary Purcell, *The First Jesuit* (Chicago: Loyola University Press, 1981), pp. 10-11.
[9]Pedro de Leturia, *El gentilhombre Inigo Lopez de Loyola en su patria y en su siglo,* rev. ed. (Barcelona: Editorial Labor, 1979), pp. 49-50.
[10]Hugo Rahner, *The Spirituality of Ignatius Loyola,* trans. Francis John Smith (Westminster, Md.: Newman, 1953), pp. 10-14.
[11]Dalmases, *Ignatius of Loyola,* pp. 39-41.

in his early years he had not been known for spiritual zeal. He writes in the third person: "Up to the age of twenty-six he was a man given over to the vanities of the world, and took special delight in the exercise of arms, with a great and vain desire of winning fame."[12] But the time of forced recuperation brought about a radical change. During his immobility, his normal inclination would have been to fuel his imagination with the reading of romantic fantasies typical of the age. But for some reason these were unavailable to him; what was on hand was serious devotional literature. To his own amazement, he read and was captivated by these classics, including two works to which he would make reference later: *The Life of Christ*, by Ludolph of Saxony, and *The Golden Legend (Flos Sanctorum)*, a collection of the lives of the saints. The consequence of this immersion in devotional literature was radical. As an adolescent he had dreamed of glory and honor through military service; through the influence of this reading, he now determined to give himself to a dramatically different kind of chivalry—a life of pilgrimage and penance.[13]

In the account of this convalescence period we have the first inklings of what would eventually develop into the Ignatian notion of discernment—the principle that in an awareness of consolations and desolations we gain a sense of God's presence and activity in our lives. During this period Ignatius had the initial experiences that would eventually form the basis for the *Spiritual Exercises* and the spiritual direction he would one day give others.

As a result of his immersion in devotional literature, Ignatius resolved to do penance for his past life; for him this meant a pilgrimage to Jerusalem (typical of the piety of the time):

> It was at this time that the desire to imitate the saints came to him, and without giving any consideration to his present circumstances, he promised to do, with God's grace, what they had done. His greatest desire, after regaining his health, was to go to Jerusalem, as previously stated, and to observe the fasts and to practice discipline as any generous soul on fire with God is accustomed to do.[14]

His initial decision was to go as far as Montserrat, in eastern Spain near Barcelona, to prepare his soul for his full pilgrimage to Jerusalem.

---

[12]Ignatius, *Autobiography*, p. 21.
[13]Thomas M. Gannon and George W. Traub, *The Desert and the City* (London: Macmillan, 1969), p. 153.
[14]Ignatius, *Autobiography*, pp. 22-23.

On the way, at Aranzazu, he made a vow of chastity. Then at Montserrat he made his confession to a Benedictine, from whom he received spiritual counsel for the next three days. At the conclusion of these days, he consciously and formally made the chivalrous resolution to become a knight with the uniform and insignia of Christ, giving himself as a loyal soldier to his Lord.[15]

Ignatius spent his time at the monastery in fasting and meditation, seeking a generosity of commitment to Christ according to the code of chivalry. That he should choose soldier imagery to describe his relationship with God is not surprising: not only is it an image of the spiritual life found in Scripture, it was a dominant motif of much monastic spirituality of the Middle Ages. And of course it reflected his own experience as a courtier in the king's house and as a soldier in sixteenth-century Spain. He knew the process and the rites for the investiture of knights. Following this pattern, he spent a night in vigil in the chapel and on these terms gave himself in radical commitment to Christ.[16]

Thus two motifs dominated his early spirituality: the pilgrim and the servant-knight. The first was the negative way, the pilgrim way of penance; the second was the positive, the way of the knight with its stress on service for God.

Manresa. Following his three days in Montserrat, still anticipating a pilgrimage to Jerusalem—delayed due to a closure of the port in Barcelona—Ignatius moved on to the village of Manresa, where he ended up spending a total of ten months. What is distinctive to the spirituality of Ignatius had its source in the experience of Manresa.

The pattern of his life in Manresa was likely given to him by the monks in Montserrat. He took Communion weekly (something quite uncommon in the sixteenth century). He practiced mental prayer several hours a day, using the spiritual exercises typical of the "devotio moderna," the spiritual movement that is best known through the work *The Imitation of Christ* (attributed to Thomas à Kempis). *The Imitation of Christ* became Ignatius's preferred devotional reading. He would read a chapter a day and recommend it to all he counseled.[17] Further, he was active in helping the sick at the local hospital and in teaching doctrine to children and beggars.

---

[15]Joseph N. Tylenda, *A Pilgrim's Journey: The Autobiography of Ignatius of Loyola* (Wilmington, Del.: Michael Glazier, 1985), p. 15.
[16]Purcell, *First Jesuit,* pp. 60-65.
[17]Ibid., pp. 66-68.

But these months were filled with emotional turmoil. While it is not certain what exactly was disturbing Ignatius's inner life, it is clear that this was a time of deep temptation and restlessness for him. Resolution came when he experienced what he calls an "illumination" while seated on the banks of the River Cardoner. In his autobiography he describes it as follows:

> While he was seated here, the eyes of his understanding began to be opened; though he did not see any vision, he understood and knew many things, both spiritual things and matters of faith and learning, and this was with so great an enlightenment that everything seemed new to him. Though there were many, he cannot set forth the details that he understood then, except that he experienced a great clarity in his understanding.[18]

Students of visions describe the vision of Ignatius as "intellectual" in character, since it did not involve visual imagery. Through this experience Ignatius came to a new way of understanding and a new way of seeing the world and God in the world. There is a simple phrase that is often used to describe Ignatius and the spiritual tradition associated with him: "seeking God in all things."

In his vision Ignatius came to a point of seeing everything in light of the triune God. All truth could be viewed in relation to divine truth. But it was not a purely cerebral encounter. Throughout his whole life Ignatius drew on this event as an encounter with the triune God, but particularly as a personal and individual encounter with Jesus Christ—not only as One to whom he owed allegiance but as One with whom he had personal communion.

What is not immediately apparent in this recounting, but became more and more evident through the course of his life, was that from this experience Ignatius drew an interior humility that would become the key dimension of his life and work. The encounter altered his whole perspective: the depth of his motivation, his character, the focus of his spiritual experience. He was transformed from a religious eccentric into an apostolic giant. The vision by the River Cardoner was the spiritual event that brought coherence to his life. He came to a profound experience of divine grace and a certainty of his own faith.

Anatomy of a conversion. The full conversion of Ignatius Loyola needs to be seen as something greater than the initial decisions made during his

---

[18]Ignatius, *Autobiography*, p. 39.

recuperation. Although that was clearly a significant turning point, we can speak of Ignatius as thoroughly converted only when we consider at least three distinct moments that formed the foundation of his spiritual experience: the period of convalescence in Loyola, the three days in Montserrat and the time in Manresa that included the experience by the Cardoner River.

The period of convalescence, which is frequently identified as his conversion, was certainly pivotal. Through the reading of spiritual or devotional classics he was immersed in a model of the Christian life that inspired him to follow the example of the saints and give himself in unqualified service for Christ. He would come to speak of his radical conversion as arising from a desire to follow their example.

Certainly the change effected in Ignatius was momentous. He later referred to his early years as those of a man "given over to the vanities of the world" and a quest for heroism fueled by a longing for praise.[19] Through the devotional readings his perspective was dramatically transformed, particularly through the accounts of St. Francis and St. Dominic; through their influence his craving for praise and recognition was replaced with an intense longing for the way of humility.

The three days in Montserrat provided him with a place where he could receive good spiritual counsel at a time in which he was particularly receptive. He also received a benchmark—the moment he made the vigorous decision to be a servant-knight of Jesus Christ. It was also in Montserrat that he learned to pray, a critical skill that in due time cemented his conversion.

Manresa, particularly through the Cardoner River experience, transformed him into an interior man; he became what was later to be called "a contemplative in action." This could not have happened prior to the other two critical moments. He had to make a break from the past; he needed the focus, resolve, teaching and discipline that were offered at Montserrat. But the full working out of the decisions made during his recuperation required both Montserrat and Manresa. Without Manresa he would have been nothing more than a religious Don Quixote.

Ignatius's early spiritual reading gave him a model of the spiritual life. Manresa fleshed it out. He defined his early conversion as a decision to live under the standard of Christ. The Cardoner experience took him further; it was fundamentally an experience of being "in Christ." Christ

---

[19]Ibid., p. 26.

became to him not only a kingly ruler but the point of integration of all truth and a living person in whom he could trust.

Not surprisingly, then, the *Spiritual Exercises* of Ignatius Loyola were designed specifically to serve as a catalyst to an encounter with Christ and to nurture a life that is lived intimately with Christ. For Ignatius, the ultimate goal of the Christian life is a humility defined as knowing, loving and serving Christ, the humility of being in and with Christ.

John Wesley (1703-1791)

John Wesley is best known as the founder of Methodism. He was an extraordinary evangelist who had a remarkable impact on the eighteenth-century English-speaking world, and his influence continues today through the life and witness of the mainline Methodist denominations and traditions with roots in the Holiness movements of the nineteenth century. Like Augustine's and Ignatius's, Wesley's impact and influence cannot be appreciated apart from his own experience. The primary sources for his autobiographical reflections are his *Journal* and certain autobiographical sections of other works.

Early years. John Wesley was born to Samuel and Susanna Wesley in 1703 in the English rectory of Epworth. All biographical authorities agree on the profound influence of Wesley's parents, particularly his mother, in his spiritual formation. Her influence carried on well into his adult life, as the two maintained an extensive correspondence though his university career.

Susanna ran a strict and disciplined household, stressing the need for regularity and order, in part out of a conviction that true piety includes and is only found in mastery of the will. The instruction of the mind was considered secondary to the subjection of the will, for she viewed the essence of evil as rooted in self-will and obedience as the essence of true religion and the basis for joy.

Though his mother's influence was primary, both his parents were committed high-church Anglicans. Further, they had been Puritan Dissenters, and this Puritan influence remained, especially evident in the extensive devotional reading of the Wesley family, which included the Puritan divines Richard Baxter and John Bunyan. And so John grew up with a high appreciation of the value of order and discipline, but also with a reverence for the authority of Scripture and the Church of England.[20]

---

[20]J. Brazier Green, *John Wesley and William Law* (London: Epworth, 1945), p. 21.

Beyond the Puritans, the Wesley family's devotional reading also included devotional works of the mystics, including Scupoli-Castaniza and Henry Scougal, adding another dimension to the formative influences on the young John Wesley. These writers highlighted the vital place of self-denial and the wholehearted love of God, accompanied by a recognition of the efficacious love of God—that is, the transforming power of divine love.[21]

All three of these influences—the Anglican, the Puritan and the mystical—emphasized the critical need for self-denial and self-discipline. Wesley embraced it all, developing what would become a very methodical and ordered pattern of life.

Young adult years. As a young man, Wesley was educated at Charterhouse and eventually proceeded to Oxford University. When he was twenty-two, his parents urged him to enter Holy Orders. While considering the possibility of ordination, he became taken up with a longing for and pursuit of holiness in his life and thought. He chose to monitor with great and detailed care his thoughts, affections, attitudes and keeping of resolutions.

Significantly, during this time at Oxford Wesley was encouraged to read Jeremy Taylor's *The Rules and Exercises of Holy Living and Holy Dying.* Taylor articulates a call to perfection combined with a stress on humility. But perhaps foremost in Taylor is his emphasis on love as the greatest thing we can give to the God who first loved us. In Taylor, love is the fulfillment of the law, and our perfection is thus the perfection of love.

Wesley read Taylor in 1725. Albert C. Outler has observed that Wesley's religious commitment and interests prior to this year had been markedly immature, but during this year, partly as a response to Taylor's work, there was a radical sharpening of his faith and personal commitment.[22] Wesley himself describes this change in his *Plain Account of Christian Perfection* as follows:

> In reading several parts of this book, I was exceedingly affected [by] that part in particular which relates to purity of intention. Instantly I resolved to dedicate all my life to God, all my thoughts and words, and actions; being thoroughly convinced, there was no medium; but that every part of my life

---

[21]Robert Tuttle, *John Wesley: His Life and Theology* (Grand Rapids, Mich.: Zondervan, 1978), pp. 74-76.

[22]Albert C. Outler, in *John Wesley,* ed. Albert C. Outler (New York: Oxford University Press, 1964), p. 7.

(not some only) either be a sacrifice to God, or myself, that is, in effect, to the devil.[23]

Wesley then recounts how in 1726 he came across the *Christian Pattern* (better known today as *The Imitation of Christ*) and the full significance of mystical religion captured his attention. Many years later he would record in his journal that it was through reading this work that he came to see that religion is fundamentally a matter of the heart.

In the following year he read William Law's *Christian Perfection* and *A Serious Call to a Holy and Devout Life*. Through this reading, he would later write, he became thoroughly convinced "of the absolute impossibility of being a half Christian."[24]

The Scriptures were always a primary influence in his life. But these devotional readings taught Wesley something fundamental: that, in the words of Outler, "the Christian life is 'devotio,' the consecration of the whole man in love to God and neighbor in the full round of life and death."[25]

The outcome of this focus and commitment was Wesley's active involvement in a group of men dedicated to spiritual discipline and service. Members of the Holy Club, as they called themselves, encouraged one another toward self-discipline, accountability and service. Later they would become known as "methodists" because of the ordered and methodical character of their association.

Aldersgate Street. We cannot appreciate the significance of Wesley's religious experience without giving attention to his experience of 1738. While the commitments made in 1725 were very significant—they led to the pattern of life and the pursuit of holiness that characterized the Holy Club— something was missing. A vacuum in his life was forcefully brought to his attention in the years leading up to the events of 1738.

In October 1735 Wesley was persuaded to join the Society for the Propagation of Christian Knowledge (SPCK). He responded positively and was presented with an opportunity to take up missionary and pastoral work in Savannah, Georgia. Wesley saw this not only as an opportunity to promote holiness in others but as a means to grow in holiness himself. Yet he could hardly have anticipated how formative this Georgian

---

[23]John Wesley, *A Plain Account of Christian Perfection* (reprint, London: Epworth, 1952), p. 5.

[24]Ibid., p. 6.

[25]Outler, *John Wesley*, p. 7.

experience would be in his own life.

Throughout his early student and ministry days, Wesley had had a pre-occupation with death. This anxiety came to the fore en route to his new appointment. In the midst of a severe storm, while fearing for his own life, he was deeply impressed by the calm manner and serenity of some German Moravians who were traveling with him. He arrived in Georgia even more conscious of his own inner lack.

While in Georgia he came face to face with more of his own limitations. It turned out to be a time of discouragement and defeat, and he returned after two years with a sense of failure at his apparent inability to deal with normal tensions in daily life and interpersonal relationships and the challenges of pastoral ministry. His parishioners did not respond positively to his spiritual leadership, and his leaving was precipitated by a breakdown in a relationship with a woman which led to a thorough alienation from the whole parish.

During this time, however, he continued his spiritual reading. His most significant devotional guide at this time was a biography of the French count Gaston Jean-Baptist de Renty (1611-1649), authored by Renty's Jesuit confessor and published by the Jesuits. What impressed Wesley about this man was the union of a contemplative piety with a life of activity in the world—a bringing together of the contemplative and active lives that Wesley himself longed for. During this period Wesley also read extensively from the works of the desert and church fathers, particularly St. Ephraem—readings that further strengthened his growing desire for the marriage of the interior and exterior life.

These works provided him with a goal: the ideal of the spiritual life. His Georgian experience demonstrated how far short he fell of this ideal. He recognized his spiritual need, evidenced in his constant fear of death and his inability to deal with normal human and parish relationships. He returned from Georgia with the recognition that he lacked a true spiritual center for his life.

On his return to England he came into closer association with the Moravians—those whom he had witnessed on ship on his way to Georgia, and in particular a Moravian leader, Peter Bohler. In the tradition of German Pietism, the Moravians stressed a sentimental awareness of the immediate presence of God and the Lutheran teaching on justification by faith. They also taught the validity of an instantaneous conversion experience. Through his contact with this group Wesley became convinced of the notion of "salvation by faith alone" and came to see that this trust or faith was the element lacking in his own religious experience.

On May 24, 1738, a few weeks after he came to this conviction, he happened to be present at a meeting of a religious society that met on Aldersgate Street in London. His journal records what happened:

> In the evening I went very unwillingly to a society in Aldersgate Street, where one was reading Luther's preface to the Epistle to the Romans. About a quarter to nine, while he was describing the change which God works in the heart through faith in Christ, I felt my heart strangely warmed. I felt I did trust in Christ, Christ alone, for salvation: an assurance was given me that He had taken away my sins, even mine, and saved me from the law of sin and death.[26]

It was an intense experience of the love of God in Christ. Most notably, Wesley felt deeply the assurance that what happened to him was all a gift from God.

Wesley felt disappointed that there had not been more emotional release—a greater sense of joy, perhaps. But not long afterward, he recognized that though the months immediately following Aldersgate were not easy, he was a different person. He recognized a new concern for others; he found he had a greater capacity to resist temptation; and in time joy would become an indispensable part of his spiritual experience and teaching.

Anatomy of a conversion. There are many interpreters of the Wesley experience and of the Aldersgate Street events in particular. But clearly just as Ignatius's conversion needs to be seen as more than the initial resolutions reached during his convalescence, the conversion of Wesley consisted of more than a single decision or experience. Though the experience of Aldersgate was significant, it can only be appreciated and understood within the whole context of Wesley's spiritual formation, including the critical decisions of 1724 and 1725. His decision to enter Holy Orders in 1724 brought a focus to his spiritual formation that led to the resolution of 1725, the decision that his life would be a passionate pursuit of holiness.

Some contend that Wesley was not even a Christian prior to 1738 and Aldersgate Street—that his previous experience was that of a wanderer searching for the saving grace of God. Others see the resolutions of 1725 to be essentially his conversion, with the experience in 1738 as somehow

---

[26]John Wesley, *The Journals of the Rev. John Wesley, A.M.,* ed. Nehemiah Curnock (London: Epworth, 1909), 1:476-77.

completing—or enabling him to live fully within the complete implications of—what occurred in 1725. Some even call the second experience nothing but a "religious spark." These perspectives minimize either 1725 or 1738, something Wesley himself refused to do. Through his life he would refer to 1725 as the time he made the sure resolve to be a follower of Christ. But he never failed to note that Aldersgate Street was the transforming experience.

However, Wesley in time began to see the experience of Aldersgate within the context of each of the early phases of his religious experience. Although Aldersgate was a critical point of integration for him, it could not have happened without the radical decision of 1725, the choice of a young man who, like Ignatius, chose to pursue the holiness of God and not be satisfied with anything halfhearted. More had to happen; 1725 represented an initial resolve, based on reason, expressed in rigid asceticism.[27] That is all. Without Aldersgate Wesley would not have found the joy he longed for, the intimacy with God he desired; nor would he have had the impact in Christian ministry for which he is known today. The year 1725 was a genuine turning point, but Aldersgate, thirteen years later, gave him focus, a renewed orientation and a spiritual center. He came to live by faith.

Dorothy Day (1897-1980)

It is hard to think of the Lower East Side of Manhattan, New York City, and not think of the woman who through much of the twentieth century gave herself in tireless service for the poor there, as the leader of the Catholic Worker movement. While Dorothy Day was a controversial figure, often in tension with the church hierarchy and civil authorities, no one questioned her devotion to Christ and passionate desire to serve him wholeheartedly and sacrificially.

We cannot appreciate Day's impact apart from her conversion. The sources, largely autobiographical, for her story, are *The Eleventh Virgin* (1924), *From Union Square to Rome* (1938; reprint, 1978), *The Long Loneliness* (1952) and *Loaves and Fishes* (1963). *From Union Square to Rome* gives the most explicit account of her experience. As she puts it, this is her attempt "to trace . . . the steps by which [she] came to accept the faith" she believes

---

[27]It is noteworthy that asceticism was a common denominator of all the early major influences in Wesley's thought and a primary focus of his life in the years immediately following 1725, but it never gave him the joy and assurance he sought.

was "always in her heart."[28] *From Union Square to Rome* is more a confession than an autobiography, not so much a life story as a series of glimpses or vignettes into her life, including her coming to faith in Christ.

Early years. Dorothy Day's childhood and early adolescent years were seemingly positive and happy. It is also apparent that as a young person she had deep religious sensibilities. In *From Union Square to Rome* she speaks of the significant spiritual influence of several individuals and of her extensive reading of the Bible: "I must have read it a good deal, for many passages remained with me through my earlier years to return and haunt me."[29] She speaks of an "echo in my heart" when she immersed herself in the Psalms during solitary confinement in jail in her early adult years. Her childhood memories of Sunday afternoons in her home attic, reading the Bible, left her with the abiding impression that God was present to her—even though she did not grow up in a Christian home.[30]

She went to church with the daughter of a neighboring Methodist family and grew to love hymn singing (although she lost this love in her late teens). She was impressed by this family and their faith. Perhaps it was through them that she first heard of John Wesley, for in another context she writes, "What other religious influences were in my life then? I remember coming across a volume of John Wesley's sermons when I was thirteen and being strongly attracted to his evangelical piety."[31]

She also makes reference to *The Imitation of Christ* as a book "that followed me through my days."[32] In her early twenties she read Fyodor Dostoyevsky's novels and later wrote, "I quote him often because he had a profound influence on my life, on my way of thinking."[33] Though she calls her faith "solitary" and considered her late teens a time when faith seemed absent, at the very least Dostoyevsky, and to a certain degree Tolstoy as well, always kept the faith before her. In later years she remembered that she had identified with a Dostoyevsky character who says, "All of my life I have been tormented by God."[34] And so it was with her.

---

[28]Dorothy Day, *From Union Square to Rome* (Silver Spring, Md.: Preservation of the Faith, 1938), p. 1.

[29]Ibid., p. 4.

[30]Ibid., p. 19.

[31]Dorothy Day, *The Long Loneliness: The Autobiography of Dorothy Day* (San Francisco: Harper & Row, 1952), p. 29.

[32]Day, *From Union Square,* p. 7.

[33]Ibid., p. 18.

[34]Ibid.

Two women also had an impact on her, in subtle and powerful ways calling her to faith. A young Jewish woman, despite her lack of faith in Christ, nevertheless had a lasting influence on Dorothy, fostering within her a love of truth and joy. A Miss Adams, a New York hospital colleague, worked with contagious joy and enthusiasm, qualities Day would come to associate with her Catholicism.

Day was always conscious of a sense of hope and expectation. It was not loneliness that drove her to God, she says, but rather joy and thanksgiving, a profound sense of his goodness.[35]

Interest in communism. By age eighteen Day bore a kind of messianic burden for the masses; she felt overwhelmed with pity for those who lived in the slums of the Lower East Side. She moved there, took a room and got a job as a writer with *The Call*, a socialist newspaper, and later for two other leftist periodicals, *Masses* and *Liberator*. Later she would move to Greenwich Village and live a bohemian lifestyle in the company of radicals, writers and artists.

These were days, weeks and months in which she lived close to the predicament of the poor. She worked twelve-hour days, writing, protesting in New York and in other cities, often imprisoned for her public protests. But she was regularly conscious of God. Once while in a saloon with friends she heard the Francis Thompson poem "The Hound of Heaven." The idea of pursuit fascinated her, and as she put it, "the soul recalls to it the fact that God is its destiny." It was one of many times she felt "tormented by God." She would on occasion go to Mass, something she had started doing as a result of the influence of Miss Adams in the hospital.

Yet during this time she consciously identified herself with communism. In retrospect she would write that communism "can be likened to a heresy, and a heresy is a distortion of truth." Through communism she came to appreciate some motifs that would be central to her faith: the collective ideal, a philosophy of labor, and Christ as a worker. "It was the Communists and working with them that made me turn to God."[36]

Even though communism helped her grasp the fundamental reality of human solidarity, in time she saw that "there can be no brotherhood without the Fatherhood of God."[37] She also concluded that the only way for-

---

[35]Ibid., pp. 10-11.
[36]Ibid., p. 10.
[37]Ibid., p. 12.

ward for the oppressed laborer was nonviolence, not violence.[38] Yet these insights did not necessarily lead her to the church. From her late teens she had been convinced that in the church the religion practiced by the majority of people had no vitality and no engagement with the streets of the world. And concern for the poor was her basic commitment and point of reference.

Her turning point was occasioned by two painful relationships. Her primary associations in those days were leftist communist writers and editors, including Lionel Moise, with whom she had an affair and by whom she became pregnant. Moise insisted that she have an abortion and abandoned her as soon as she did. Shortly after this she married, but this relationship lasted only about a year.

Staten Island. Disillusioned and discouraged, she decided in January 1918 to sign up to help at a hospital in response to the crisis of World War I. For a time it was precisely what she needed: heavy manual work in an environment of discipline and order. But eventually "my own immediate desire to write . . . led me to give up my work in the hospital."[39] Several years in her twenties were spent writing short stories, sketches, plays and newspaper pieces. After a stint in Chicago and then New Orleans, she bought a house and property on Staten Island; there she had solitude to write. After a time she began regular Sunday-morning attendance at Mass.

For much of this time she lived in a small rustic cottage on the shoreline in a common-law marriage to biologist Forster Batterham. With Forster she had a child, Tamar Teresa. Day had lived with great guilt because of the earlier abortion, and she was quick to see Tamar as an indication that God was giving her a second chance.

On Staten Island she also met an extraordinary nun, Sister Aloysia, of the local Sisters of Charity, with whom she developed a strong, nurturing friendship. Through this nun Day was brought face to face with a church that was caring for the poor. She became increasingly aware of her need for "religion and God," convinced as much as anything by the testimony of those who cared for and served the poor with generosity. She saw that indeed the Catholic Church could be the church of the poor even as Christ himself is on the side of the poor.[40]

Day spent a winter anticipating the birth of her child. She read and

---

[38]Ibid., p. 13.
[39]Ibid., p. 96.
[40]Ibid., p. 16.

wrote, noting later that she "read the Imitation of Christ a great deal."[41] She enjoyed the season of waiting. Sister Aloysia introduced her to St. Teresa of Ávila and St. John of the Cross to complement her reading of Augustine, the *Imitation* and the Bible; and "three times a week Sister Aloysia came to give me a catechism lesson."[42] Long before she gave birth, Day resolved that her child would be baptized a Catholic.

However, Forster would have no part of this. He was an atheist and an anarchist, and refused to formally marry Day or accept any part of her emerging religious faith. He had no patience with either the official church or the state. Increasingly it became clear that she would have to choose between her newfound faith in Christ and her love for Forster. His delight in their child made it, as Day put it, all the "harder to contemplate the cruel blow I was going to strike him when I became a Catholic."[43]

The birth itself was a moment of great joy for her, as were the days following as she cared for the child and continued her life on Staten Island. But then there were months of inner turmoil as she wrestled with her desire to become a Catholic alongside her continued loyalty to the workers' movement; she feared that in embracing the Christian faith she would betray the poor of the world with whom she had so identified. It was a very intense and long struggle. After more than a year, in December 1927 she finally came to the resolution to be baptized herself. Later she would write of this as a significant benchmark in her life: "A year later my confirmation was indeed joyful and Pentecost never passes without a renewed sense of happiness and thanksgiving. It was only then that the feeling of uncertainty finally left me, never again to return, praise God."[44]

Forster was resolute, and Dorothy eventually ended the relationship. This was not an easy choice for her; she moved to California and later to Mexico partly because she feared her own desires to return to Forster. But the decision was grounded in her growing conviction regarding the truth of the Christian faith, an understanding she could not avoid. The relationship could not continue. Her conversion meant that at least for the time being she was alone; the long-term consequence would be that she would raise Tamar without a husband.

Back in the city. With Tamar, Day returned to New York City and took up

---

[41]Ibid., p. 127.
[42]Ibid., pp. 136-37.
[43]Ibid., p. 141.
[44]Ibid., p. 142.

an active and sacrificial struggle to care for the poor, particularly on the Lower East Side of Manhattan. A long career in generous service of others followed. Crises and problems would come, but she understood that in such times she needed to come back to her original commitment to the service of the Lord Jesus Christ and the poor.

Not long after her return she met Peter Maurin, a French itinerant priest, with whom she founded the Catholic Worker Movement. While she was an activist, Maurin was more a philosopher. Though Day had read Dostoyevsky, Tolstoy and others, it was primarily through the influence of Maurin that she came to accept a faith tradition that could inform her life and work with theological integrity. Day was not one to give herself to theological abstractions; she insisted that she was not a scholar. But she was a keenly intelligent woman and a sharp thinker and needed someone of Maurin's intellectual vigor and deep commitment to the poor to shape her thinking at one crucial point. It was Maurin who enabled Day to see that her vocation could be and needed to be fulfilled in and through the church, that though the church was often adversarial to her concern for the poor, she could not abandon it in Christian integrity. He helped her realize that she could never give up on the church because the church is necessarily part of God's redemptive purposes.[45] She could not accept the faith without at the same time coming to terms with the church.

Day would never be on good terms with the church hierarchy; her care for the poor and the homeless brought her into frequent conflict with the church and its lack of commitment to the poor. But from this time she would always affirm loyalty to the church even if the church hierarchy had little patience with and place for her. Ironically, she was very conservative theologically: her criticism of the church was not for its teachings but for its failure to live by them consistently.

Anatomy of a conversion. June O'Conner makes the observation that "the affective dimension of Day's adult conversion in turn makes possible a cognitive conversion."[46] O'Conner notes the powerful impact of several childhood experiences—the power of witnessing a united Christian response to earthquake victims, the awe of encountering a neighbor woman on her knees in prayer, the wonder of reading the Bible aloud to

---

[45]See a particularly helpful discussion of Maurin's influence in William D. Miller, *Dorothy Day: A Biography* (San Francisco: Harper & Row, 1982), pp. 247-48.

[46]June O'Conner, "Dorothy Day's Christian Conversion," *The Journal of Religious Ethics* 18, no. 1 (spring 1990): 164.

her sister in the attic—along with the romantic encounter with Forster Batterham as a young woman and the birth of her child, Tamar. All enabled her to embrace, affectively, the love of God.[47] Human love enabled her to understand the character of divine love: "the deeply felt affective experiences of friendship, empathy, love, intimacy, caring and community nudged Dorothy a long way in her journey to conversion."[48] So childhood and young-adult experiences of love and intimacy left an imprint on her inner being that stimulated a desire to give herself in generous service for the poor. It was only later that this desire came to be informed by theological truth.

In relation to the church Day intentionally chose a posture of submission, but clearly was not compliant or unthinking in her acceptance of the church's authority. It might seem that Day chose to defer to the theological and doctrinal teachings of the church in an uncritical manner. But we must not conclude that she was unthinking. Rather, she chose to accept what was ancient, reflected her own upbringing and made the most sense to her in the light of the needs of the poor. She did so at great cost—the loss of her relationship with Forster and of all her anarchist and communist friends, including her sister, who could make no sense of her conversion. Day was deliberate, and she chose the posture of humble submission, which probably best reflected how she needed to come to faith. O'Conner calls her "an intensely practical person,"[49] and this is reflected in her resolve to embrace the doctrines and teachings of the church.

O'Conner builds on Walter Conn's contention that one of the critical features of a Christian conversion is a transformation that is cognitive as well as moral. For Conn, a cognitive conversion is more than an intellectual reorientation. It is rooted in the affect and finds expression in moral realignment. A cognitive conversion comes at that point when a person takes responsibility for his understanding of truth *and* for his moral life. One takes personal responsibility for one's own life and work.

Notable in Dorothy Day's experience is that her conversion eventually included a radical and unavoidable identification with the poor and marginalized. Her conversion meant that she gave her life for others, caring for her neighbors and calling others to do the same. Underlying strands in her spirituality were the affective and the penitential; these

---

[47]Ibid., pp. 162-63.
[48]Ibid., pp. 163-64.
[49]Ibid., p. 169.

enabled her to eventually accept the truth of the Christian faith and submit herself to baptism. This, in turn, gave her the freedom to devote all her passion and energies to serve the poor in the name of Christ and eventually to see that this service had to be expressed in submission to and through the church.

As Day tried to make sense of her experience, she captured a reality experienced by many: "A conversion is a lonely experience. We do not know what is going on in the depths of the heart and soul of another. We scarcely know ourselves."[50] But she also described the hope that anchors us through the experience of a Christian conversion: "Gratitude brought me into the Church and that gratitude grows, and the first word my heart will utter, when I face my God is 'Thanks.' "[51]

Concluding Reflections
Augustine, Ignatius, Wesley and Day were all keenly aware of their own conversion process. Also they were aware of how their conversion was linked with their calling—not only to spiritual maturity but also to their service for Christ.

Depth and spiritual passion resulted from each of these conversions. These were thoroughly converted individuals; however, their conversions did not come in a single dramatic moment. Each one was the fruit of a series of events, a complex experience; but the very complexity allowed for a complete conversion experience.

The chapter that follows will examine the revivalist inclination to define and identify conversion by a decision. Evangelism is thus portrayed as preaching for "a decision." Though we certainly cannot read too much into four conversion narratives, the four described in this chapter may not be all that atypical. And none of these conversions came after preaching that called for a decision. Though a decision for Christ was unquestionably involved, for none of the four was this the actual pivot on which the experience turned.

Further, we must celebrate the influence of so many individuals in the lives of each of these persons. No one person could conceivably have claimed to have been the one who brought any of these individuals to Christian faith. No one, to use revivalist language, "won" them to Christ. Rather, each came to Christ through the influence of many others, some

---

[50]Day, *From Union Square*, p. 17.
[51]Ibid., p. 169.

of whom (such as Ambrose with Augustine) never even knew the significance of their influence.

Only the Holy Spirit is the sole defining influence that enables a person to come to faith. And the Spirit's witness and enabling are mediated through any number of persons: parents, peers, religious leaders, devotional writers and sometimes even those who do not confess Christian faith.

We would do well to consider an issue of self-perception. In this analysis of autobiography I have made an ongoing assumption that the authoritative interpreter of a religious experience is the one who had the experience. While such an interpretation can sometimes be misguided or misinformed, the biographical accounts we have surveyed are so compelling largely because of the unflinching honesty that comes through and because of the reality of changed lives. Through these experiences they became new persons. The exercise of attending to the self-interpretations of others is meant to foster our own capacity to interpret our own experience of divine grace. And it can show us how to draw grace and encouragement from the knowledge of our experience.

Our perception of the meaning of our own conversion will probably change over time, as it did for Wesley, who in his later years came to see his Aldersgate experience not as standing alone but as part of a whole. For such mature self-reflection we often need some distance to properly interpret our experience. But we can always start, as long as we remain prepared to rethink our interpretation as we mature in faith and experience.

Finally, none of the conversions we have considered can be reduced to a moment. Each is protracted rather than punctiliar. Each is a series of events, moments and crises that together constitute conversion. Such was the case with Martin Luther as well. Many are inclined to think of Luther's "tower experience" as the moment of his conversion. But Philipp Melancthon's biography of Luther essentially describes what is a series of crises, breakthroughs and phases of experience.[52]

For most if not all Christians, the experience of conversion is similar: a series of events, crises, breakthroughs, moments of joy but also moments of perplexity. Most conversions do not happen in a moment or even in a few days. Rather, they are protracted experiences over the course of many months if not many years.

---

[52]See Marilyn H. Harray, *Luther on Conversion: The Early Years* (Ithaca, N.Y.: Cornell University Press, 1983), p. 178, for a more comprehensive study of Luther's experience and the way his experience shaped his theology.

4

The Evangelical Experience

A Historical Perspective

There is no such thing as generic Christianity or generic Christian theology. All theological reflection is done within the context of particular faith communities and inevitably informed by a particular theological tradition. Whenever anyone contends that they do not follow any tradition, they in effect begin or seek to begin their own.

This introduction to the theology of conversion is intended as an interpretive study from within the evangelical Christian tradition. As will be apparent, I draw heavily on other Christian sources to develop a more comprehensive understanding of conversion. But my point of departure is my own heritage.

If we are to establish a revitalized and comprehensive understanding of Christian conversion, it is helpful to consider how conversion was understood within American evangelicalism in the latter half of the twentieth century. What is the language of conversion that dominates the way American evangelicals think and act regarding conversion? This question is important for two reasons. North America is the immediate context of my own work and that of most of my readers and students. And American evangelicalism, largely through the influence of the media and foreign missions, has had, for good or ill, a profoundly formative influence on other streams of evangelicalism, especially in the language of conversion.

At the beginning of the twenty-first century the majority of evangelical believers are outside of this orbit. Having grown up in Latin America, served as a theology professor and pastor in the Philippines, and lectured and taught in the United Kingdom, Europe and the Middle East, I am conscious that evangelicalism takes on very different expressions. But as we seek to rethink our language of conversion, we all need to come to terms with the influence of the American stream of evangelicalism.

Readers from other settings may wish to read what follows as a kind of case study. I hope that this study will serve as a catalyst for all readers to think critically about their own language of faith and conversion.

The American notion of conversion has been shaped largely by revivalism and crusade evangelism. This perspective and its language of conversion are encapsulated in the idea that you are not "saved" unless you have a conscious conversion that is personal, emotional and decisive. Conversion in American evangelicalism is an event—a definite moment—and the language of conversion is captured in such phrases as "accepting Jesus Christ into my heart." Conversions are often referred to as "decisions." They are seen as punctiliar.

We are in a time of transition. Many evangelicals, let alone those of other traditions, intentionally distance themselves from the language of conversion inherited from revivalism and crusade evangelism. But we are not able to rethink and reconstruct our theology of conversion unless we first come to terms—critically but also appreciatively—with what we have inherited.

Three Classic Perspectives

Prior to examining the evangelical heritage, though, it is helpful to recognize that there are three classic models of the interrelationship between conversion and transformation in the history of the church. The delineation of Rosemary Haughton, a lay English Catholic theologian, is particularly instructive.[1]

Benedictine. First Haughton identifies what she calls the Benedictine understanding of conversion; this model is most readily associated with

---

[1]Rosemary Haughton, *The Transformation of Man: A Study of Conversion and Community* (London: Geoffrey Chapman, 1967).

the Roman Catholic tradition.[2] From this perspective, conversion is a decision to join a community that is seeking salvation. The focus is on the future; but the expression of conversion is a radical choice, a fundamental resolve to follow Christ in obedience. For thousands of Christians over many centuries, the most obvious biblical support for this understanding was the call of the young man whom Jesus bade "sell everything you have and give it to the poor, . . . then come, follow me" (Lk 18:22).

In this perspective, conversion is rarely associated with a particular moment or event. Rather, conversion is more readily linked to the whole of the Christian experience; it is not so much a moment of radical transformation as a lifelong process of growth and change. Within the language of the Benedictine tradition, one is changed and transformed, converted, through a lifelong participation in the forms and structures of the monastic life—the communitarian and liturgical aspects of the Rule.

When this is translated into the common life of the Roman Catholic believer, the language of conversion is often applied to the program or outcome of a program of spiritual formation. A person is converted as they embrace and walk through a program of intellectual or cognitive development, affective growth and maturation, and moral or behavioral change.[3]

Conversion, then, is essentially a decision to choose the way of holiness, to accept the consequences of a path that will eventually lead to justification and sanctification. It requires willingness to pay the necessary price, the vows of poverty, humility and obedience.

This is, then, a distinctly future-oriented model of conversion. The dynamic center of the Christian life is hope—what the Christian believer lives and works for, hope in a transformed life.

The danger of this model—which many would say has always plagued the Roman Catholic tradition—is works righteousness, which easily springs up if there is any doubt that one is loved and accepted by Christ. The sixteenth-century Protestant Reformers eventually rejected this model because in actual experience the goal of conversion is frequently not attained due to anxiety and a faulty foundation for the spiritual life.

---

[2]Roman Catholicism is certainly not monolithic, and in many ways it is simplistic to associate the Benedictine with the whole Roman Church; yet this is the understanding of conversion that has most consistently been *associated* with Roman Catholicism.

[3]See a helpful overview of this model of conversion in Patrick Lyons, "Conversion in the Benedictine and Wesleyan Traditions," *The Asbury Theological Journal* 50, no. 2 (1995) and 51, no. 1 (1996): 84.

The only solution for this, biblically and theologically, is the experience of justification. Justification is the only possible foundation for the Christian life—the assurance that one is forgiven and accepted, loved by God.

Reformed. The second of Haughton's categories is the understanding that has shaped the language of most evangelical Christians. In distinct contrast to—some would say in reaction to—the Benedictine perspective which found primary expression within the Roman Catholic Church, the "Reformed" tradition sees conversion as fundamentally a once-for-all experience, past tense. If in the first model the focus is on the future, a hope of God's justification if one is able to "work out one's salvation," in this model the focus is distinctly on the past. The emphasis is on the assurance one can have that one has been saved. Eternal life, in this sense, is assured; we merely need to wait for it. This experience of conversion is the basis for participation in the life of the church.

The Christian in this tradition longs to testify with confidence to a past event that constitutes her "conversion" and on the basis of which she can be assured that she is "saved." The Christian life involves living out the full implications of this past event. Early in the Reformation a distinction was made between justification and sanctification, with the understanding that justification can be received in an instant but sanctification is experienced gradually. Justification thus became the believer's primary point of reference.

The strength of this model is its unequivocal affirmation of the love and acceptance of God. But here too there are dangers: in practice, this model took spiritual vitality and maturation too much for granted. As often as not the goal of conversion was not attained; people did not become saints with marked levels of spiritual vitality.

If Roman Catholic Christianity has always struggled with the threat of works righteousness, Reformed Protestantism has always struggled with the problem of cheap grace. For many, if not the majority of Protestants, God's love and acceptance do not lead to personal transformation. Evangelical formation often involves seeking to reestablish a pattern of maturing behavior that should be integral to one's conversion. So both traditions can be challenged on whether there is a genuinely helpful connection between conversion and transformation. Is there really a good beginning that in the end enables transformation?

Holiness-Pentecostal. Haughton suggests that there is a third distinctive approach. The perceived problems with the second perspective—the lack of a genuine and widespread experience of sanctification—led to a third way of thinking about conversion and sanctification. It could be described as the Holiness-Pentecostal perspective.

In this way of thinking, conversion itself is conceived of in much the same way as the Reformed model except that sanctification requires a second moment or crisis to complement the first. Conversion is past, but the critical point of reference is actually what came to be termed as the "baptism of the Spirit." This baptism, it was argued, could enable the Christian believer to be not only "saved" but "sanctified."

Later this study will consider the merits of this model, particularly the biblical basis for a distinctive "baptism in the Spirit." What is noteworthy at this point is that it created a two-tiered classification of Christians. Within the traditions where this model gained currency, it was understood that Christians come to Christ through faith and repentance. But this did not inherently lead to transformation. So the contention was that for Christians to lead "the victorious life," they needed a particular manifestation of the Spirit, called by some a "baptism" and by others a "filling."

The strengths of this approach lie in its unequivocal call to mature Christian experience, the abiding assumption that each Christian believer can become a holy person and is responsible to fully embrace the grace of God. Some find this model's weakness in the false assurance of sanctification that resulted if one had the specified experience of the Spirit (though some lived in perpetual anxiety because they had not experienced what seemed normative for others). The other danger, as will be stressed later, was the failure to affirm the incremental character of genuine spiritual formation.

Toward a biblical synthesis. I hope to show that the strengths of each of these perspectives are sustained and the potential weaknesses minimized by a genuine and thoroughly biblical theology of conversion. Each approach is legitimate, but only when the central focus of the other two is affirmed and appropriated. A genuinely biblical theology of conversion must affirm that the ultimate goal of conversion is in the future—that the very purpose of conversion is transformation. The Benedictine-Catholic model rightly propels us forward, calling us to a resolve, a new path, a willingness to lose our lives that we might gain them, to "sell everything" so that we might follow Jesus. If an inquirer were to ask an evangelical, particularly an evangelist, what it would take to know God's salvation, it is virtually inconceivable that the answer would be "Sell everything and give it to the poor, and come follow Jesus." Yet we urgently need an understanding of conversion that takes seriously these words of Jesus, an approach to conversion that affirms the legitimacy of such a response. At present it is much too foreign to the evangelical experience, despite the fact that it is so obviously biblical.

Likewise, our only hope for transformation is that we sustain and embrace a theology of conversion grounded in the limitless grace of God that is evident in justification—the forgiveness of sins, unqualified acceptance by God, the declaration that through Christ we are righteous. There is no other possible foundation than one that leads the Christian to sing, "Amazing grace, how sweet the sound that saved a wretch like me." We must hold on to a theology of conversion that includes this past-tense dynamic in the experience of God's salvation.

And even if there is an exegetical weakness or flaw in their model, those speaking out of the Holiness-Pentecostal tradition have something that we all need: a passion for personal and corporate transformation and a radical dependence on the Spirit for this experience of God's holiness.

In our day we can do theology without having to react to other traditions. I say this because of the propensity of evangelicals to react to Roman Catholicism or Pentecostalism and fail to affirm where there is agreement or to note where evangelical assumptions can be legitimately challenged. Today we have an opportunity to do theology without this posture of reaction. And I will attempt to do it against the backdrop of evangelicalism's understanding and experience of conversion.

A more comprehensive study of the language and experience of conversion would have to follow William James, who looked back to the seventeenth-century Moravians; they were the first to insist that salvation is instantaneous. For my purposes, however, it is sufficient to consider the three major factors that have influenced the understanding of conversion in American evangelicalism.[4] We will first examine the contribution of the Puritans and then that of the Wesleyan and Holiness

---

[4]I have found two analyses of the evangelical experience particularly helpful: Richard F. Lovelace, *Dynamics of Spiritual Life: An Evangelical Theology of Renewal* (Downers Grove, Ill.: InterVarsity Press, 1979), and Bill Leonard, "Getting Saved in America: Conversion Event in a Pluralistic Culture," *Review and Expositor* 82, no. 1 (winter 1985). The latter is a superb essay that considers the understanding of conversion among Southern Baptists. Both authors give particular attention to the American experience. I should note that there are certainly other influences that have shaped the character of North American evangelicalism, such as Continental Lutheran Pietism and the Anabaptist or Mennonite tradition. I focus on Puritanism and Wesleyanism because they have had the most pervasive influence.

movements; then we will review the contribution of revivalism. Throughout, I am working with a simple thesis: the strength of an evangelical theology of conversion lies in a commitment to draw on the strengths of both notions of conversion, those of the Puritans and those of the Wesleyans. I am equally indebted to both streams and am convinced that evangelicalism at its best draws on both sides of its heritage.

The Puritans on Conversion

The Puritan movement began in England in the sixteenth century under Elizabeth I. Deeply dissatisfied with the rate and extent of the English Reformation, the Puritans sought to be a reformation movement within the Reformation. They were convinced that though they had made a formal separation from Rome and identified with the Reformation theology of Luther and Calvin, in actual fact the Reformation had not really happened in the English church. Many in the English church were convinced that it was still too "Roman" in its piety, liturgy and structures of government. They found the Book of Common Prayer's liturgy only half-removed from its Roman Catholic roots because of the continued use of vestments, the liturgical year, formal read prayers and what seemed to many a Roman Catholic view of the sacraments.

Deeply suspicious of symbolic action, the Puritans considered the written and spoken word the only adequate and appropriate means for the Christian faith to be communicated. Further, they called for high ethical standards, convinced that having a state church encouraged laxity in moral transformation. Also, most rejected episcopalian government, which they viewed as a violation of Christian community.

All of this was based on an explicit theology or understanding of religious experience. The Puritans diverged in their theological convictions at many points, but on one matter there was concurrence: an absolute insistence on a conversion experience for every believer. Puritans of status and significance had profound conversion experiences. They recounted dramatic conversion stories; in their preaching they called for momentous conversions, and they validated the faith of a believer by whether he could recount his own experience. That is, the capacity to narrate a conversion experience became the test of authentic Christian faith.[5]

---

[5]See Jerald C. Brauer, "Conversion: From Puritanism to Revivalism," *Journal of Religion* 58 (1978): 230.

The Puritans' fundamental conviction was that the only true foundation for the church is conversion, and the only hope for the transformation of society and the world is through conversions.

The Puritans were fascinated with conversion, and it was a central feature in their theology and preaching. In this respect Jerald Brauer notes a distinct contrast with the theology of older Reformers:

> Because of their focus on the personal experience of conversion and "experimental" divinity, Puritans emphasized the personal appropriation of justification more than its givenness. Under the onslaught of doubt, Luther could say, I have been baptized, and Calvin could rest in the mystery of God's mercy through eternal election, but the Puritan rehearsed the personal experience of conversion. . . . . This, rather than predestination, was the center of Puritan experience and theology. . . . [For the Puritans] the stress on the personal appropriation of salvation tended to outweigh the classical Reformation's emphasis on the givenness, the objectivity of God's action in salvation.[6]

Given this passion for subjective experience, the Puritans very intentionally turned from the sacramental understanding of conversion found in both Catholic and Anglican Christianity. Puritans emphasized an internalized faith that was experienced on the basis of God's electing grace through the work of God's Spirit. Therefore one's baptism was incidental or at best secondary; what mattered was personal faith.

In North America it was the Puritans who broadly affirmed that a conversion experience was normative if one was to be "saved." To claim Christian faith and to be a member of the Christian community, one had to be able to attest to a particular kind of conversion experience. These were distinctive and dramatic conversions; they drew heavily on and were deeply influenced by the conversions of St. Paul and Augustine of Hippo as models normative for Christian experience. Even children, when baptized, were not considered "converted" and were not admitted to the Lord's Supper until they could testify to a conversion experience. A conscious conversion experience was a necessary sign of God's grace in the life of an individual and as such a prerequisite for church membership.

The Puritans did not emphasize so much the punctiliar self-surrender conversions favored by Charles Finney and later revivalism. Rather, their narratives usually pointed to an event that had been preceded by deep inner turmoil and wrestling. Step by step, incrementally, one was con-

---

[6]Ibid., p. 234.

fronted with the horror of personal sin in the face of God's holy law, leading one to despair of ever fulfilling God's requirements and being holy. This would lead to a deep awareness of God's all-encompassing mercy, and one would experience both death and life through a completely new personal orientation.[7]

Two critical qualifiers need to be noted with respect to the Puritan notion of conversion. First, the Puritans emphasized that conversion was to be followed by sanctification. That is, the consequence of conversion was a radical new life orientation and a process of sanctification that would be complete only at death. They tended to use pilgrimage and holy warfare images and metaphors to describe the experience of coming to conversion and then living the faith beyond conversion. Conversion itself was only a beginning; the purpose of the conversion was that a person become mature in Christian faith.

Second, the Puritans emphasized the role of the Holy Spirit, stressing that there is no conversion apart from the Spirit. They were inclined to emphasize as strongly as possible that a conversion is orchestrated by the Spirit and enabled by the Spirit.

The great focus on conversion and conversion narratives left the Puritans with a dilemma: how to resolve the matter of second generation conversions, that is, the experience of those who were the children of believers. We will examine this in more detail at a later point.

Jonathan Edwards was a major influence and interpretive voice for the Puritans, particularly in American piety. He was one of the first theologians to give intentional and extensive attention to a theological analysis of religious experience in general and conversion in particular. He was actively involved in the revivals of the mid-1700s, later known as the Great Awakening, and sought to interpret these events. His *Faithful Narrative of the Surprising Work of God* described the conversion experiences he was witnessing. Then nine years later, in 1746, he published *Religious Affections,* a comprehensive examination of religious experience in which he argues emphatically and clearly that an authentic Christian conversion has distinctive "signs."

With the entire Puritan tradition, Edwards insisted that the goal of a conversion is spiritual transformation. A true conversion leads to lasting and abiding change, or it simply is not a true conversion (regardless of how emotionally intense the experience might have been). Edwards was

---

[7]Ibid., p. 233.

actually skeptical of great emotion if it was not accompanied by true moral and spiritual reform. Not that conversion made a person instantly mature; to the contrary, Edwards assumed maturity might take quite some time. But a true conversion would set a person on the way toward maturity.

On the one hand, conversion *has* a particular order or character; on the other hand, conversion *brings* order to a person's life, an order that orients toward mature Christian experience. Conversion is but a beginning, however; its fruit is to set one on the way. As Edwards puts it, "And the Scriptures everywhere represent the seeking, striving and labor of a Christian as being chiefly after his conversion, and his conversion as being but the beginning of his work."[8] The theological analysis of conversion was for Edwards a pastoral task that ultimately would enable his readers to make sense of their own experience, know their spiritual condition and discern whether their experience was genuine.

Like other Puritans, Edwards was inclined to see conversion as a process of some duration, though he acknowledged that for some it might be a relatively rapid process. Regardless of the length of time, he noted that a conversion is an ordered experience and has the following elements:

☐ a sense of dependence on the power of God

☐ a deep conviction of sin and a sense of helplessness to do anything about it (a sense of horror at one's predicament and destiny) in the face of the justice of God

☐ a recognition that God is gracious and forgiving and that this grace can be known by the individual[9]

Though each Christian conversion would have these elements, Edwards recognized that every conversion is unique. Loath to set norms, he was more inclined to describe what had happened than to prescribe what should occur in conversion. Unfortunately, many who followed him used his descriptions as normative. But for Edwards, the appropriate pastoral response would simply be to describe and identify the signs of conversion and thus enable individuals to know and interpret their own experience. His primary point of reference was the work of the Spirit. Edwards quotes Isaiah 40, "Who hath directed the Spirit of the Lord?" in noting that the specific order of a conversion is not predictable:

'Tis to be feared that some have gone too far towards directing the Spirit of

---

[8]Jonathan Edwards, *Religious Affections*, ed. John E. Smith (New Haven, Conn.: Yale University Press, 1959), pp. 381-82 (pt. 3, sign. 11).
[9]Leonard, "Getting Saved in America," p. 116.

the Lord, and marking out his footsteps for him, and limiting him to certain steps and methods. Experience plainly shows, that God's Spirit is unsearchable and untraceable, in some of the best of Christians, in the method of his operations, in their conversion. Nor does the Spirit of God proceed discernibly in the steps of a particular established scheme.[10]

Beyond these basic elements, and affirming this diversity, there were two other key elements in Edwards's theology of conversion. First, his theological review of conversion integrates head and heart, mind and emotion. Edwards should be credited with affirming both the intellectual and the affective, with sustaining a holistic understanding of conversion. Again, sadly, many who followed Edwards and built on him could easily be accused of romantic sentimentalism. But Edwards himself affirmed that there is no genuine piety that is not informed by truth yet also that the affections are the seat of authentic piety.

Further, Edwards and the Puritans viewed conversion as a matter of discerning what is happening rather than as praying to initiate something. That is, in contrast to later revivalism which essentially viewed God as passive, waiting for the sinner or penitent to act, for the Puritans God is author and agent while the "sinner" is passive. The distinction is crucial and has profound implications. From revivalism and much of contemporary evangelicalism, one could easily get the idea that God's work does not kick into action or take effect until a "sinner's prayer" is said or until we believe and have faith. Then, once we believe and say the prayer, God begins to save. But for the Puritans the fundamental assumption was that conversion does not initiate the work of God; it comes in response to what God is doing. God, then, is the initiator; conversion comes insofar as we recognize and live in the light of this prior work of God.

Conversion, then, is something that one discerns rather than a dramatic or decisive moment. Conversion is recognizing the often subtle ways that God is present and at work in our lives. Rather than placing the locus of God's salvation on our actions—whether a prayer or a response to an "altar call" or any other seemingly decisive moment—conversion must focus on God and his actions. In other words, conversion is about discernment. What is God doing and how has God acted in my life? Indeed, for the Puritans grace could be given to a person well before, if not long before, she actually recognized it.

We must take seriously the human factor in conversion. But Edwards

---

[10]Edwards, *Religious Affections*, pp. 161-62 (pt. 2, sign. 8).

and the Puritans provide an essential anchor to our theological reflections. Where an emphasis on the sovereignty and initiative of God has been lost, it has resulted in an unfortunate pattern of seeking to manipulate conversions through emotional persuasion.

In conclusion, then, Jonathan Edwards and the Puritans made three particular contributions to the theology of conversion. First, they affirmed that there is a discernible pattern to a Christian conversion; though it can vary from person to person, all conversions will have some common elements. Second, the Puritans believed that a conversion experience must be understood through an integration of heart and mind, intellect and emotion. Third, conversion is best understood as a response to God's grace rather than as initiating this grace, and therefore conversion is an act whereby we discern and respond to divine initiative. It is a response to the initiative and superintending work of the Spirit of God.

John Wesley and the Holiness Traditions
I have already described John Wesley's personal experience of conversion; now we consider how his theology and practice shaped subsequent perspectives on conversion. Several elements of Wesley's thought are noteworthy in this regard.

First, while standing squarely within the tradition of the Protestant Reformation, Wesley chose to affirm more fully the significance of human actions than those within a strictly Calvinist or Reformed heritage. Wesley was an Arminian with a greater emphasis on free will and human response. However, this did not imply that salvation is a human endeavor. Wesley rejected George Whitefield's teaching of double predestination—the idea that some are destined for salvation and some are destined for damnation. Wesley insisted that Christ died for all persons and that all are and can be called to experience God's salvation. But Wesley did not defend any idea that the human person is saved through the exercise of free will. In his understanding salvation is entirely the work of God. He had personally experienced assurance and knew that this confidence in God's salvation did not come through an exercise of his will. But he did stress human responsibility and the need to appropriate the grace of God in response to God's love and initiative.

Second, Wesley made an unequivocal call for personal and corporate transformation. He viewed his mission as enabling women and men to become holy, perfect in Christ. He was an evangelist, but an evangelist with a difference: his ultimate goal was that men and women would become perfect. Here we see an echo of the Puritans with their affirmation that the purpose of conversion is spiritual transformation and maturity.

While Wesley stood within the Protestant tradition, his theology and practice came in response to, and somewhat in reaction to, perceived weaknesses in the mainstream of Lutheran and Reformed Protestantism. For Luther, sanctification was simply an outgrowth of justification; it was not a second phase following justification. Since salvation was justification by faith, sanctification was not a second element in salvation; it was nothing more than appreciating our justification and living in its reality. This lies behind the common Lutheran discomfort with the idea of necessary spiritual growth—of anything being "added" to our justification.

The problem with this was that justification became so central and defining to Lutheran thought (some have suggested even to the point of displacing the centrality of Christ) that the notion of spiritual transformation became incidental. Neglecting to develop an emphasis on sanctification, Lutheran theology implicitly negated the fact that the transformation of the believer is essential to the Christian idea of salvation.

Some have suggested that this development arose in part because Lutheran notions of salvation tend to be built almost exclusively on Pauline thought, particularly that found in Romans, 1-2 Corinthians and Galatians. Critics thus suggest that Lutheran and Reformed theology is based on a narrow sector of Scripture. For Wesley, though, the fundamental concern was that Lutheran and Reformed thought and practice did not adequately address and provide for moral and spiritual transformation.

Part of the genius and lasting influence of Wesley was his resolve to never be content to merely encourage someone to be converted; he would have felt a failure if converts did not immediately become participants in a small group of believers designed to foster growth toward spiritual maturity. The very purpose of a conversion was to be set on the course toward "perfection," to use Wesleyan language.

Third, Wesley emphasized the heart: much like Jonathan Edwards, he affirmed the priority of affect or emotion in Christian experience. Wesley's twofold emphasis—the call to holiness and personal responsibility—was balanced by his deep awareness of the preeminence of grace. Spiritual growth is nothing more than growing in grace. And awareness of this grace is felt in the depth of the heart; to use the language he used to describe his own defining moment, it is experienced through the "warmed" heart. And for Wesley an abiding sign of this grace is a lasting and pervasive joy. We experience this grace and joy through the inner witness of the Spirit. While many have presumed to have this inner witness without undergoing authentic religious experience, Wesley insisted that the experience of the Spirit is authentic only if it leads to both inner joy and moral reform.

A treatment of North American evangelicalism necessarily means we consider the teaching on sanctification of Wesley's disciples. One of Wesley's associates, John Fletcher, had a slightly different twist on sanctification from Wesley's own. Fletcher was convinced that each believer can and should have a distinct Pentecostal experience (usually described as a baptism of the Holy Spirit). Wesley differed with but did not censor Fletcher. This could be because Wesley himself recognized the complexity of religious experience. In *A Plain Account of Christian Perfection* he declares, "But we do not know a single instance, in any place, of a person receiving, in one and the same moment, remission of sins, the abiding witness of the Spirit, and a new, a clean heart."[11] This may have, in part, set the stage for the distinction that Fletcher was making.

Regardless, in the century that followed, Fletcher's brand of Wesleyanism was increasingly influential in North America, especially within the revivalism of Charles Finney. Proponents of this position called for a "second work of grace," a "crisis subsequent to conversion," that would make possible a "deeper life" or in some cases a "higher Christian life," all of which was associated with sanctification.

Many church groups and denominations were influenced by this "holiness" movement, largely because the movement itself was interdenominational. Its broad appeal was fostered through the preaching of such people as Phoebe Palmer, a Methodist lay preacher, and D. L. Moody. The Nazarenes, the Christian and Missionary Alliance, the Free Methodists and other groups all continue to be marked, to a greater or lesser extent, by their nineteenth-century Holiness heritage. The most notable religious tradition of the twentieth century that is heir of this movement is the Pentecostal tradition.

Though not entirely indebted to Wesley and the Holiness movement, the initial phase of the Pentecostal movement was influenced by the Wesleyan-Holiness second blessing doctrine. What set the Pentecostal movement apart from the Holiness groups was the assumption and requirement that speaking in tongues is an essential initial evidence of

---

[11]John Wesley, *A Plain Account of Christian Perfection*, in *The Works of John Wesley*, 3rd ed. (Grand Rapids, Mich.: Baker, 1986), 11:380.

the baptism of the Spirit, and that it is expressed in empowerment for service. Earlier Wesleyan Pentecostalism stressed the notion of a second definitive work of grace for sanctification; but in time Pentecostals added a third experience, empowerment for service that was evident in speaking in tongues. Later Pentecostalism, influenced by William Durham in the early twentieth century, was a different variety that emerged from Reformed-Baptist churches. Durham merged the two subsequent experiences into one: empowerment for service and the baptism of the Spirit.

Currently many heirs of the Wesleyan-Holiness movement hesitate to use the language of "baptism of the Spirit," and many are cautious to link this experience directly with sanctification, though most continue to make the link to empowerment for service. But more to the point, many are no longer comfortable speaking of the need for a "second work of grace," largely because they find that it cannot be justified on exegetical grounds and because it is no longer congruent with their experience. They are sincere Christians but find it artificial to seek or pursue some kind of special "baptism" or "filling" subsequent to conversion. To this dilemma we will return in a later chapter.

Nevertheless, the Wesleyan and later the Holiness movement have made significant contributions to the theological understanding of conversion:

☐ the affirmation of personal responsibility for our lives in response to divine grace

☐ the ultimate goal of conversion as sanctification; conversion (like justification) is merely the beginning, for holiness, sought and received by faith, is the fundamental purpose of conversion

☐ the priority of the heart in an integration of heart and mind that takes emotion seriously, as did Jonathan Edwards

☐ the conscious awareness of the gift and presence of the Holy Spirit, especially in later Wesleyan-Holiness movements with their emphasis on a two-stage approach to conversion and sanctification, including the "baptism of the Spirit"

Charles Finney and Revivalism
Now let's backtrack a bit to the beginning of the nineteenth century to consider the influence of Charles Finney and the rise of revivalism. We cannot understand the language of conversion at the beginning of the twenty-first century without a consideration of the influence of revivalism

across a broad spectrum of evangelical denominations.

Revivalist evangelical piety was the fruit of a variety of spiritual movements and influences. The movement was in one sense an heir of Puritanism—perhaps unwittingly—with its focus on conversion as key to being Christian, indeed as the defining event of a person's life (and future life).

However, perhaps more significant was the influence of Charles Finney, who discarded Reformed and Calvinist roots and embraced a more Arminian emphasis on free will and human activity. Finney was the quintessential nineteenth-century evangelist in his emphasis on human responsibility. He stressed both the agency of the preacher-evangelist and that of the "sinner." In fact he spoke against the notion that a conversion is the work of God—and that therefore conversion is necessarily left to God.

Second, Finney emphasized the need for and possibility of an immediate crisis-point conversion. Here he rejected the Puritan assumption that an extensive period of conviction for sin is necessary for conversion, and by implication challenged Wesley's observation that he had never seen all the elements of a conversion occur within a moment.

The third hallmark of Finney and the movement he established was its emphasis on technique. He spoke of conversion not as a miracle but as resulting from the application of the right approach or method. This led to an emphasis on techniques aimed at getting people converted, and eventually to the language of "winning souls" to speak of fostering or encouraging conversions. With the right methods, it was assumed, conversions would follow and souls could be "won."

While there were certainly other voices in American evangelicalism, Finney's influence was pervasive: revivalism became one of the dominant religious forces to shape American piety. It has been institutionalized within many denominations, to the extent that many if not most evangelicals are unwitting children of the movement, associating the language and piety of revivalism with the New Testament.

Part of the strength of revivalism was its uncompromising call for conversion to Jesus Christ. And many are Christian believers today because of the influence of this movement. However, while affirming this positive contribution, we are well advised to note how revivalism has shaped our language and behavior, especially on the theme of conversion, in ways that urgently need to be reconsidered.

The influence can be felt in many ways—first and perhaps most significantly in the emphasis on human volition. Revivalism rightly stressed the importance of human responsibility and the significance of human actions. But this emphasis was one-sided. Growing up in a denomination deeply influenced by revivalism, I gained the abiding impression that if we wanted to be changed, the solution was simple: "submit to the lordship of Jesus." If we were struggling with a problem, if as young people we had behavior or thoughts that needed to be changed, the solution was simple: "put it all on the altar." Life's problems were believed to be directly rooted in a lack of submission; the gospel song "I Surrender All" captures the sentiments of the speakers who shaped our spiritual lives. In wholehearted surrender we would achieve the longing of our hearts.

The problem with such a notion is that it only represents half the truth! Romans 12:1-2 reads: "I appeal to you therefore, brothers and sisters, by the mercies of God, to present your bodies as a living sacrifice, holy and acceptable to God, which is your spiritual worship. Do not be conformed to this world, but be transformed by the renewing of your minds, so that you may discern what is the will of God—what is good and acceptable and perfect." Revivalism ably captures the priority of the first half of this text, the need for unqualified presentation of the self to God as a "living sacrifice." However, in its one-dimensional emphasis on the surrender of the will, it fostered the idea that we are changed through the act of our own will, that our conversion and transformation are fundamentally fruits of our own decisions.

In Romans 12:2 Paul stresses that transformation comes through *the renewal of the mind*. The tragic flaw in revivalism was twofold: there was not only a misguided stress on human volition as the means by which we are saved but also a neglect of the mind as critical in both conversion and transformation, a theme to which I will return later in this study.

In addition to its one-sided emphasis on human volition, revivalism highlighted the immediate, dramatic crisis as the essence of a good conversion. This meant a rejection of the Puritan expectation of a long period of preparation for conversion. Those influenced by revivalism sought dramatic conversions and believed that conversion (and thus salvation) happens in a moment—the moment, of course, being directly linked to one's "decision." Conversion became a discrete event that one could point to— a definitive moment, ideally a climactic moment. The reality, though, is that most people's experience is far more complex. Too many people have been left alienated and perplexed about their own experience by revivalism's pervasive notion that conversion is simple and decisive.

A further unfortunate byproduct of this emphasis was a neglect of the routine and the ordinary. Contemporary expressions of revivalism are filled with palpable longing for dramatic and immediate change. Preachers yearn for the highly emotional event when people are "broken," when all our individual and corporate spiritual problems are brought to the surface and suddenly resolved. And the more dramatic and immediate the experience seems to be, the more "miraculous" the conversion, or so it is implied. This approach neglects the possibility that God might work slowly, through the renewal of the mind, through the ordinary and the routine as Christians observe weekly worship, practice the disciplines of the spiritual life, and grow slowly and incrementally in their capacity to love one another. An emphasis on the immediate and the dramatic also denies the substantial value of the sacramental actions of baptism and the Lord's Supper.

We should not miss another American evangelical assumption inherited from revivalism: the belief that conversion is easy, painless and certainly not costly. Revivalist preachers stress that "salvation" is a free gift that anyone can have if they merely make the decision, pray the "sinner's prayer" and "accept the Lord Jesus into your heart."

Not surprisingly, given such assumptions of the ease of conversion, many lives were simply not changed or transformed as a consequence of "decisions." Those within Holiness traditions found it necessary also to appropriate Finney's notion that conversion is to be followed by the "baptism of the Spirit" and "entire sanctification." While perhaps he made conversion too "easy" or cheap, it can be argued that he complemented this with an emphasis on sanctification.

Further, revivalism nurtured the idea that religion is fundamentally private and personal. The emphasis on human volition implied an emphasis on the individual. For revivalists, much as for the Puritans, there was no such thing as "growing up in the faith." A person was a believer only if as an individual, before God, she personally chose to "accept" Christ. And while the Christian community could encourage and foster such a decision, the focus of attention was and continues to be on the individual.

In contrast, for the Puritans, conversion was nurtured within the church. Conversion was a solitary, individual matter, but it was carefully monitored by the church and its leaders. "Conversion was an intensely personal subjective experience within the context of the convenantal community, and it immediately placed one at work within that community."[12] There was thus a careful balance between the subjective and the objective, the individual and the communal.

But the Puritan emphasis on conversion was a first and major step in the transformation of the church from a nurturing community to a converting community. With revivalism, which inherited so much from the Puritans, the outcome was almost a foregone conclusion. The covenant community was no longer the arbiter of authentic experience. Subjectivism and individualism had gone to seed. Increasingly the only purpose for the church was to foster a particular kind of conversion, so much so that conversion became an end in itself. Conversions were sought without immediate reference to the nurturing community. Everything depended on whether one could answer the question "Are you saved?" In due time this led to the late nineteenth- and twentieth-century phenomenon of mass crusade evangelism, where conversion happened outside the context of the covenant community, divorced from its doctrinal heritage.

Later nineteenth-century revivalists stressed the primary importance of public acts: the sinner must repent and witness to their conversion in some public way, such as "walking the aisle" or "coming forward to the altar." An interesting byproduct of this was that baptism came to be viewed as a means to witness to one's conversion, especially to nonbelievers. There is little if any biblical warrant for this, but many have come to see witness as the fundamental meaning of baptism.

Consistently, and increasingly, conversion was experienced in response to an "altar call," and "souls" were "won" through revival preaching. The would-be convert was often invited to an "inquiry" room or prayer room after the "invitation" was given; there he or she was encouraged to pray a "sinner's prayer." Sometimes, remarkably, the evangelist had already encouraged listeners to "pray this prayer after me."

The emphasis was on the immediate: a decision, a prayer, and with this the experience of "salvation." From then on those who had responded could speak in the past tense: "I have been saved!" Conversion was short, simple and easily accessible to any and all. Again, the emphasis was on the acts of the convert: "You do your part, and God will do his part." "If you pray and believe, repent and confess, then God will do his part to regenerate." For Jonathan Edwards and the Puritans, conversion was a matter of discerning what God was doing. For Finney, and later for D. L. Moody, most twentieth-century crusade evangelists and other evangelists,

---

[12]Brauer, "Conversion," p. 240.

one's "conversion" involved doing something that precipitates the work of God.

Many have noted that this understanding of conversion had one positive component—the emphasis on personal responsibility. But even this potential strength is weakened when viewed alongside the glaring flaws in the movement: the emphasis on human actions as precipitating the work of God; the use of technique to get people to become believers; the inadequate emphasis on transformation as the fruit of conversion; and failure to affirm the renewal of the mind, the role of baptism and the Lord's Supper, and the disciplines of the spiritual life.

A pervasive theme in revivalist evangelism is *subjectivity*. The Puritans, with their emphasis on religious experience, had brought a new emphasis on subjectivity to Protestantism. But with Finney this focus went awry. The Puritans had emphasized conversion within the context of Reformed theology; revivalism emphasized conversion outside of this doctrinal context. Further, it emphasized a subjectivity no longer rooted in the context of a covenant community of faith.

Evangelicals and Conversion at the Beginning of the Twenty-first Century
What then can we say about the evangelical experience as we make sense of this complex heritage? Conversion continues to be normative for participation in congregational life, for membership—formal or informal— in our faith communities. But we are faced with some sobering realities, each representing not only a problem but also an opportunity.

Theological confusion. First, there is considerable theological confusion about the nature of religious experience and conversion in particular. Bill Leonard's astute observation about Southern Baptist Christians applies equally to most evangelicals: whether they know it or not, they are heirs to both Reformed and Arminian traditions (we are all Calvinists and we are all Wesleyans!). The problem, Leonard contends, is that we have borrowed from both sides of our evangelical heritage in ways that are neither discerning nor consistent.[13]

Consider how Finney's Arminian model is adopted when it comes to evangelism and conversion: we become Christians by an act of our will, and God's work comes in response to our work (a "decision" and a "sinner's prayer"). We are "in" by virtue of our work. But then we embrace a Calvinist model when it comes to perseverance: if we are Christians we

---

[13]Leonard, "Getting Saved in America," pp. 120, 123.

can be assured of what is called "eternal security"—thus implying that everything depends on God's work. Most evangelicals have bought into a Finney-Arminian notion of conversion as a punctiliar event, once and for all; the process is initiated and maintained by the sinner, that is, by one's actions. We become Christians by an act of our will. We do this and we are saved—a decisive and singular event of which we can then speak in the past tense and say we are "saved." However, evangelicals have generally retained the Calvinist "once saved, always saved" belief. Now that we are "in," we can rest in the reality that we are kept by the grace of God. In other words, we got "in" by virtue of our work, but we are "kept" by the work of God. This is a very tenuous theological state of affairs.

Another irony is that most American evangelicals bought into only half of the Finney conversion package. Finney himself acknowledged that he presented conversion as easy; but he compensated for this by calling for a further work of sanctification, along similar lines to the experience advocated in the Holiness movement. Many streams of evangelicalism reject such a "second crisis," though they have accepted Finney's notion of a "first crisis," the initial salvific event. The consequence has been a widespread emphasis on easy conversion without an attendant emphasis on sanctification. Tragically, then, those outside the Holiness movement have often viewed holiness, spiritual maturity and the work of the Holy Spirit as entirely incidental or secondary within the Christian experience.

Ambiguity about the experience of conversion. Many Christians harbor a profound and widespread ambivalence about the experience of conversion itself, for at least two reasons. First, there is a general lack of a consistent and meaningful theology of conversion that people can draw on to make sense of their experience. The available theological models are usually not congruent with their experience; the popular model of conversion that is preached from pulpits, sung in hymns and assumed in Sunday school classes is not their own. Some even wonder whether their conversion is illegitimate or inauthentic. They do not have the "testimony" that would authenticate their life in the Christian community. The language of the pulpit and of gospel songs does not reflect their experience. They did not become Christians instantly and dramatically. Their faith community gives them no language with which to speak meaningfully of how they did come to Christ. Sadly, then, their conversion holds little or no personal significance; it is not a meaningful spiritual experience or benchmark from which they can consciously live their lives.

Increasingly, though, evangelicals are recognizing that there is an extraordinary diversity to our experience and that we cannot tell our stories in the simple and unambiguous language that is normally associated with the motif of the "testimony."

Second, evangelicals often feel an ambiguity about experience because the tradition is as yet profoundly ambivalent about the children of Christian believers. Neither the Puritans nor the revivalists had a place in their constellation for second-generation Christians. The children of believers were expected to move through the same process in becoming a Christian. But the spiritual, social and emotional dynamics are profoundly different when one's parents are Christians.

Most second-generation Christians simply cannot identify with preaching and hymnody that assume punctiliar conversions. As young adults they may be comfortable with affirming that "I have always believed in God and always loved Jesus." Because the dominant language implies that a conversion is a crisis or a punctiliar moment, the children of believers are often left ambivalent about the significance of their spiritual experience. Many are confident they are Christian believers; but because the evangelical tradition does not have a thorough and consistent theology and language of conversion incorporating second-generation Christians, they often feel that their experience of conversion is incidental—not a significant source of meaning and strength for their Christian lives. This poses a dilemma for both the children of believers and their parents, who lack meaningful and helpful language with which to describe the spiritual journey of their children when they are still "on the way."

For reasons like these, many within evangelical faith communities live with a marked unease about their experience of conversion, evident in their lack of confidence in faith, worship and witness. Some lack assurance—a deep confidence that they are indeed believers, accepted, forgiven and filled by God's Spirit. Without such a benchmark, without a clear sense of beginning, many feel aimless spiritually and are unsure how to proceed toward spiritual growth and discipline.

Within our churches there is pervasive doubt, a profound lack of confidence that prevents many from being able to say, "I am a child of God." This is a sure consequence of the approach that emphasizes simple human actions to get "saved." It is reinforced by revivalistic hymns that people sing enthusiastically and somewhat nostalgically but with which they do not truly identify. The "old-time religion" does not reflect their experience, only their perception of what others have experienced. They feel as though they are singing about someone else; thus they feel increasingly alienated from their own experience. I hardly dare think about the long-term consequences and implications of this for the life of the church.

Formulating a Response to This Evangelical Dilemma

For rethinking the character of conversion, there is probably no factor so significant as the changing face of evangelicalism—a change that is global and permanent. The twentieth century's extraordinary missionary movement has born fruit: the majority of evangelicals are no longer found in North America, and there is a consequent demand that we rethink our understanding of conversion in light of diverse cultural dynamics. For perhaps two centuries American evangelicalism dominated both the theology and the language of conversion; now we are in a momentous transition that represents an equally momentous opportunity for the church to rethink the nature of religious experience in general and conversion in particular.

Hopefully, we will be able to embrace new metaphors and images of the spiritual life and religious change. This time of transition offers us the opportunity to consider how culture shapes and influences religious experience. In regard to conversion, it will be necessary to examine how particular cultural contexts will inevitably establish a climate that either fosters or impedes conversion—given that culture is an inevitable factor in religious change.

To respond effectively to the circumstances we face will require several simultaneous actions and agendas. First, we need a fresh reading of the Scriptures, to allow us to hear as clearly as possible the New Testament call for conversion. We must do all we can to allow the Scriptures to speak for themselves, and we must avoid diluting the force of the text by theological rationalizations. What I mean by this will be clearer when we come to a reading of the various models of conversion in the New Testament.

Second, in reading the text we must also embrace afresh our evangelical heritage—Puritan and Wesleyan—and its strengths. But we embrace this heritage with discernment; our primary criteria for an authentic theology of conversion must be gleaned from Holy Scripture. I am convinced that our only hope is to abandon the ways revivalism has infiltrated our language, our patterns of thought and affect. Yet here there is an irony: within the contemporary church the denominations and movements that are heirs to Edwards and Wesley and were least influenced by revivalism are the least likely to take conversion seriously. Revivalism at least took seriously the need for conversion, and thus in one sense this very study of conversion stands within that heritage. However, while we emphasize the need for conversion we must do so in a way that calls forth the best of our evangelical heritage.

As we reread the New Testament text, we must do so conscious that we are situated within a spiritual tradition, allowing the tradition to be a lens to the text while the text is always a corrective to the tradition. I am not suggesting that we first read the text and then consider insights from our predecessors; rather, our spiritual heritage enables us to read Scripture afresh even as Scripture challenges the assumptions we carry out of our spiritual traditions.

Third, we need to trust our own experience and learn from the experience of others, those outside the evangelical tradition and those from other cultures. So as we affirm our own theological and spiritual heritage and build on it, we consciously choose to learn from other cultures and traditions—especially from their witness to their experience. Many do not believe that trusting in experience is part of formulating true Christian theology. But as already suggested in the first chapter, I am convinced that experience is a vital means by which the Scriptures can be understood and a critical lens through which we read and embrace the Scriptures. One of the objectives of this study is to come to a greater appreciation of our own experience of conversion within our spiritual tradition—and in the process both to strengthen the tradition and to transcend its inherent limitations.

Finally, our only way forward is to articulate a doctrine of conversion as a beginning rather than an end—to develop a theology and language of conversion that fosters spiritual maturity.

Our critical task is to formulate a renewed language of conversion—a language that describes and interprets, that mediates the power of biblical theology to our understanding, that effectively interprets our own experience, and that is formative.

Divine Initiative and Human Response

As we learn from and draw on the evangelical heritage to understand conversion, there is probably nothing so crucial as affirming both divine initiative and the significance of human activity. We draw on the breadth of our evangelical heritage when we refuse to compromise on either score.

Conversion is fundamentally the human converse of God's saving work in the life of an individual. Thus the theological focus is on human action in response to divine initiative. But though conversion represents human endeavor and responsibility, the Scriptures consistently speak of conversion as a gift of God. Conversion is an act of the will, in other words; but it is not, in the end, a human achievement. It involves human decision and actions; thus one might superficially conclude that it is a matter of persuasion and human response. But actually conversion is initiated and sustained by God. First, this is so because God is Creator and Redeemer. God saves. Because of the depth of the human predication, human beings are incapable of self-transformation.

But further, God's grace is sovereign in the lives of individuals and in the world. If we experience conversion it is all of grace, and no merit can be claimed or sought. This is captured cogently in the words of Paul: "For by grace you have been saved through faith, and this is not your own doing; it is the gift of God—not the result of works, so that no one may boast" (Eph 2:8-9). Even faith is a gift. As will be stressed later, we are responsible to exercise faith; but the very faith we are called to exercise is a gift. Even baptism, which seems so clearly to be a human action, is in Pauline theology a work of God.

The Holy Spirit superintends the process of conversion; in fact conversion is always directly attributable to the work of the Spirit in the life of an individual and a community. And since the Spirit is like a wind that "blows where it chooses" (Jn 3:8), there is always something mysterious, unpredictable and distinctive to the experience of each individual and community. But though we must affirm this diversity, there is one Spirit. This means that all conversions will have some common elements.

The Spirit's initiative and work are not necessarily tangible nor observable. The work of the Spirit is often mysterious and cannot be quantified; in some respects it cannot even be traced. Further, the work of the Spirit is often simultaneous with our response to the Spirit, so that one might speak of the Spirit's work as behind our actions and responses—invisible, but nevertheless the sustaining dynamic of our actions. This is not to minimize the significance of human actions and responsibility; it is merely to recognize the priority of the work of the Spirit.

Stanley J. Grenz identifies four dimensions of the activity of the Spirit.[14] First, the Spirit convicts of sin, so that we take personal responsibility for our lives and our behavior, aware that our lives are inconsistent with the

---

[14]Stanley J. Grenz, *Theology for the Community of God* (Nashville: Broadman & Holman, 1994), pp. 538-41.

holiness of God and God's love for justice and peace (Jn 16:8).

Of course, the conviction of sin includes the awareness of our need for conversion—we recognize that in sin our lives are characterized by death and darkness and that in sin we have no hope. Therefore the convicting ministry of the Spirit has two distinctive dimensions: we are enabled to see our hopelessness, but we are also enabled to see that there is hope in Christ. The Spirit grants us the capacity for both simultaneously. While we may go through a time of despair as we wonder if there is any possibility of acceptance by God, given the gravity of our sin, the Spirit never so abandons us to our predicament that we cannot also eventually recognize our need for Christ and the reality of life and hope in Christ.

Second, the Spirit is the means by which we hear the call of God. Deeply woven into the biblical theology of salvation is the notion that God calls us to himself and to his salvation. Jesus pictures this as an invitation to a banquet—to a meal in the company of Jesus and ultimately in the presence of the whole of heaven at the consummation of time. God calls us out of darkness and into light (1 Pet 2:9). This calling is, explicitly, an invitation to enter into and enjoy fellowship with God through Christ, symbolized in many instances by a meal.

It is by the Spirit that this call is issued and heard. For many it comes through the preaching of the Word, as was the case on the day of Pentecost (Acts 2). Scripture suggests this is the normal way the Spirit enables us to know the call of God—through Spirit-anointing proclamation of God's Word, however and wherever it is heard.

But for some the convicting and illuminating ministry of the Spirit comes through other means and in other contexts and settings. Augustine, as we saw, had his mind arrested by the words of a child at play, which he recognized to be the call of God to his own heart. For Ignatius Loyola, this work of the Spirit came through the writings of devotional authors. John Wesley's heart was stirred as he heard a reading from Luther's commentary on Romans. That is, while the Scriptures are a key means by which we hear the Spirit's call, the Spirit's testimony has often come in ways that have been both surprising and effective.

Third, the Spirit's work includes illumination—the enlightening of the mind. As Grenz notes,[15] sin works to darken and blind our minds, so that without the illuminating work of the Spirit there would be no comprehension of truth (2 Cor 4:4, 6). The Spirit illumines our hearts and minds with

---

[15]Ibid., p. 540.

truth (Jn 16:13); the Spirit guides us into truth, enabling women and men to hear and understand and appropriate God's truth. Apart from the gracious work of the Spirit, we cannot know the truth that sets us free.

Fourth and no less important, the Spirit enables our response. The power of the Spirit overcomes the deep antipathy of the human heart to obedience to the truth. The human will, apart from the Spirit, is in sin and bondage. Only through the Spirit are we freed to hear and then to obey, to act on what we have heard, to live in the light that has shone into our hearts. The Spirit enables us to believe and repent.

For this reason the Puritans considered it more appropriate to speak of conversion as discernment of the work of God (and response to that work) than as actions that we hope will solicit a response from God. God most assuredly is a God who responds; when we seek forgiveness, he forgives. But conversion is never this simple. It is in fact a complex series of events, each of which comes as a response to various movements and initiatives from God, who both solicits and enables our response.

One of the reasons I enjoy reading biographies is to see the distinctive and diverse ways the Spirit wooed and won the heart of an individual—how the Spirit convicted, called, illumined and enabled. We must affirm human agency and responsibility, but always with a recognition of the priority of divine initiative and the reality of God's grace.

Finally, it is important to highlight the means by which the Spirit's influence is known: the Word. The New Testament often speaks of the Word of truth as the means through which salvation comes. In two cases it is explicit: in James 1:18 we are reminded that we experience new birth by the word of truth; in 1 Peter 1:23 we are "born anew . . . through the living and enduring word of God" that is preached or announced to us. Consequently, many have stressed that conversion (and transformation, for that matter) is through the Spirit and the Word, and rightly so. And though the chapters to come will stress that the Spirit and the Word work in the context of the community of faith, it is in the end the Spirit that brings about our transformation.

However, while it is essential to speak of the divine initiative and prerogative of the Spirit in superintending the process of conversion, Scripture never portrays the experience of conversion in a manner that would negate or neglect human agency. Within our theology of religious experience we need to maintain a clear sense of human agency, incorporating the full force and significance of such texts as Malachi 3:7: "Return to me, and I will return to you." God does not repent for us, believe for us or obey for us. And conversion is never forced or coerced. God takes the initiative, but what makes the biblical narrative so compelling is that God takes the human response so seriously, both our yes and our no.

The genius of a genuinely biblical theology is the capacity to hold to a clear vision of both the sovereignty of God and of God's grace (the classic Reformed contribution) and the responsibility and even power of human agency (the Arminian-Wesleyan contribution). Human agency is the focus of this book; while acknowledging the work of God and the supremacy of grace, this book particularly considers the human element, as reflected in such questions as "What must I do to be saved?" "What must I do to inherit eternal life?" "What can and must we do, as individuals and as communities, to experience the transforming grace of God fully and completely?" Such an affirmation of human agency must always come within the context of a continued appreciation of the prior and the providential work of God's Spirit.

Affirming the significance of human agency has several implications. First, we affirm the reality of human responsibility. The implications are sobering: though the gift of faith is intended and offered to all, and though all are invited to "return" to God—that is, the call of conversion is made to all—not all will respond in the affirmative; not all will be converted.

In asserting human agency we also highlight the consequent diversity in the nature and character of conversion. Conversions differ in many respects because people are different and experience conversion differently. Contexts are different; personal histories and personalities differ. Consider, for example, the rich young ruler and Zacchaeus, whose stories are told in Luke 18 and Luke 19. Even in the same cultural context Jesus related to these two men of means in dramatically different ways.

For a conversion to be truly Christian, it must have certain basic elements. But because of human agency, there will also be diversity in our responses to God. There is no one form or way a person must be converted to faith in Christ Jesus. There are common denominators or elements to each conversion; but each conversion is unique, a distinctive union of intellectual, experiential and social factors.

Any study of conversions in the history of the church will of necessity look at those that are particularly dramatic, decisive and determinative. These are better laboratory material, so to speak. But they should not be understood either as prescriptive or even ideal, but merely as viable models to highlight the dynamics of conversion. As we have seen, conversions can be decisive and determinative without being dramatic or sudden.

5

Models of Conversion in the New Testament

What does a conversion look like? What are its critical components, the elements that make a conversion truly Christian? All conversions are unique; each person's experience of conversion is a product of a distinctive union of intellectual, experiential, cultural and social factors. Nevertheless a reading of Scripture suggests that there are common critical elements or factors that make a conversion a *Christian* conversion. Further, it is the presence of these elements that make a conversion the basis for a transformed life.

However, the New Testament actually offers different answers to the question What does a conversion look like? There are distinctive models of conversion within the New Testament—models that reflect diverse circumstances and perhaps different phases in biblical revelation. The question we ask is simple: What does a person need to do in order to become a Christian? But the answer varies; within the New Testament there are at least four different answers to this question. This does not imply contradiction. Each answer represents a different though complementary model of conversion that needs to be heard and appreciated on its own terms. Once we have considered all of them, we can stand back and identify the essential elements of a Christian conversion.

As we consider various texts, it will be important to keep the following questions clearly in mind: Who experiences the grace that justifies and regenerates? What is the way they enter into Christian faith and come to a knowledge of Jesus Christ? What does it mean to become a believer? The answers will not be found by doing a word study of Greek words relating to conversion. Conversion is a larger concept than can be found in the meaning of any single word. It is more fruitful to ask of the New Testament texts: What does it mean to become a Christian? How does one become a Christian? What does a person need to do to experience the saving grace of Jesus Christ?

But we are not seeking the bare minimum. Rather, we are asking what it is that enables a person to begin well, to establish a foundation to their Christian experience so that they will ultimately experience a significant degree of spiritual transformation.

We will consider (1) the answer of the Synoptic Gospels, (2) the answer of Acts, (3) the answer of Paul's writings and (4) the answer of the Gospel of John. For each we will examine a representative text.

Conversion in the Synoptic Gospels

The Gospels of Matthew, Mark and Luke profile Jesus as one who lived and preached the presence of the reign of God. Jesus proclaimed a new age in which the reign of God would bring truth, justice and freedom. Conversion is a conscious and intentional response to this proclamation, for the announcement of the kingdom included a call to repentance and an invitation to live in the kingdom under the liberating reign of Jesus. Inherent in this announcement is a distinctive pattern or model of Christian conversion. A Christian, quite simply, is a *disciple* of Jesus, which is another way of saying that a Christian is one who *follows* Jesus Christ. This culminates in Matthew 28, where Jesus' mandate to his followers is to make disciples. They will make disciples by "baptizing them . . . and teaching them." Thus if someone were to ask, "How do I become a Christian?" the Synoptic answer would be "Become a disciple or follower of Jesus."

For a representative text to give us more insight into what it means to become a disciple, Luke 5 serves us well by portraying the initial call of the disciples.

It is not easy or even helpful to ask when the first disciples actually became Christians, when they were converted. Their circumstances were unique. Their initial response to Jesus was as Jews responding to a Jewish prophet;[1] only over an extended period, as we see from the conversation between Jesus and the disciples in Mark 8, then later through the experience of the transfiguration and the resurrection, did they come to see and appreciate the full significance of Jesus. Still, this representative text sheds critical light on what it means to become a follower of Jesus.

> Once while Jesus was standing beside the lake of Gennesaret, and the crowd was pressing in on him to hear the word of God, he saw two boats there at the shore of the lake; the fishermen had gone out of them and were washing their nets. He got into one of the boats, the one belonging to Simon, and asked him to put out a little way from the shore. Then he sat down and taught the crowds from the boat. When he had finished speaking, he said to Simon, "Put out into the deep water and let down your nets for a catch." Simon answered, "Master, we have worked all night long but have caught nothing. Yet if you say so, I will let down the nets." When they had done this, they caught so many fish that their nets were beginning to break. So they signaled their partners in the other boat to come and help them. And they came and filled both boats, so that they began to sink. But when Simon Peter saw it, he fell down at Jesus' knees, saying, "Go away from me, Lord, for I am a sinful man!" For he and all who were with him were amazed at the catch of fish that they had taken; and so also were James and John, sons of Zebedee, who were partners with Simon. Then Jesus said to Simon, "Do not be afraid; from now on you will be catching people." When they had brought their boats to shore, they left everything and followed him. (Lk 5:1-11)

This passage does not give us a comprehensive description of a conversion and what conversion meant. But it does give seeds that are elaborated on in the chapters that follow, filling out what it means to become a disciple of Jesus.

The elements of a conversion. This passage includes several key elements.

1. *Repentance and belief in Jesus.* First, conversion comes as a consequence of an encounter with Jesus Christ—particularly with an appreciation of the uniqueness and wonder of the Lord. When Simon Peter exclaims that he is a sinful man, this is not so much a declaration of his need for repentance (though repentance must come) as an awareness that he stands in the presence of one who has come from God. In this case the mercy, grace and goodness of God's presence were evident by the abundance of the catch of fish. In other cases throughout the Synoptic Gospels there are a variety of manifestations—in Jesus' words and

---

[1]R. T. France, "Conversion in the Bible," *The Evangelical Quarterly* 65, no. 4 (1993): 302.

deeds—by which people recognize the exceptional character, glory and power of Jesus Christ and see that they have no choice but to respond.

If we become disciples, then, it is because we believe something about Jesus; we come to an understanding, at least on some basic level, that Jesus Christ represents divine presence in our world. Eventually, of course, the disciples would come to see that he was the Messiah—the Son of the Living God. But the main point is that Jesus was recognized as a unique person, one sent from God and representing the grace and presence of God in the world.

Within the Synoptic Gospels it is sometimes the actions of Jesus that are viewed as significant; in other cases it is his preaching—particularly his announcement that the kingdom of God is at hand. We see this in the Gospel of Mark, for example, where Jesus comes announcing the kingdom of God (Mk 1:15). Clearly the appropriate response is to repent and believe the good news. This encounter involves repenting, turning from sin and falsehood because one acknowledges that Jesus is unique and his words are to be believed. A follower is one who believes in Jesus and his teaching and repents of a previous life course.

Jesus is clearly seeking followers. As becomes clear through the Synoptic Gospels, Jesus is calling for people who will turn from their way of sin and embrace his way, the way of life and holiness. Thus within the Synoptics the essence of conversion is a response to the person of Jesus (not just truth, but Jesus himself, the one who is seeking followers). And as people meet Jesus and respond in belief and repentance, they are no longer the same. The encounter leads to transformation.

2. *Renunciation.* In the Synoptic Gospels conversion involves not only repentance and belief in response to an encounter with Jesus; it also includes renunciation, portrayed in radical terms. In Luke 5:27-28 Levi responded to Jesus with a resolve to "leave all" in order to follow him.

A disciple is a follower; to be a disciple is to be a follower of Jesus. But this following cannot happen without renunciation. What "leaving all" can mean is dramatically depicted later, when a young man asks Jesus, "What must I do to inherit eternal life?" And Jesus replies, "Sell all that you own and distribute the money to the poor, . . . then come, follow me" (Lk 18:18-22). The example of Zacchaeus in the following chapter makes it clear that Jesus does not ask everyone to sell everything and give it to the poor. But he does ask everyone to "come, follow me." "Come, follow me" is the essence of being a disciple. Although the terms vary, each person is asked to give it all up, to take up their cross, to deny themselves and if necessary family, friends, everything, and as Jesus puts it to us, "Come, follow me."

Conversion is costly; discipleship is not cheap. It costs us everything we have. To become a Christian means recognizing the cost of turning from everything for the sake of something of eternal value. Luke emphasizes the demands of faith even more than Matthew and Mark, stressing that conversion is necessary (13:3-5) and urgent (13:6-9), requires renunciation (14:33), means that one does not turn back (9:62) and entails self-denial (9:23).

Not that this theme is absent from Mark and Matthew. In Matthew 4:19-20 we read that the disciples left everything and followed Jesus. Matthew also records the encounter with the rich young ruler (Mt 19:16-30). Nevertheless, it is in Luke that the theme of renunciation comes through most pointedly, particularly in Luke 14: "So therefore, none of you can become my disciple if you do not give up all your possessions," which echoes the words earlier in the same passage: "Whoever does not carry the cross and follow me cannot be my disciple" (vv. 33, 27). The point of this whole text is that we need to count the cost, for we cannot become disciples without renunciation.

3. *Call to service.* It is common among evangelicals to make a distinction between conversion and a call to service. But in the Synoptic Gospels the call to service—for Christ and for his kingdom—is inherent in the very call to, and experience of, conversion.

Jesus made an extraordinary statement in his first call to discipleship: "Do not be afraid; from now on you will be catching people" (Lk 5:10). These words must have amazed the first disciples as they wondered at what Jesus could possibly mean. Clearly the image of "fishing" implies some kind of continuity with their former tasks and occupation. But as disciples of Jesus their loyalty would change. Their orientation would now be toward Jesus and his kingdom purposes. And their lives would be oriented toward service, the service of Jesus.

In coming to Christ, in becoming his followers, we are invited to participate in the work of his kingdom. For the first disciples, the Twelve, their work would be the evangelization that led to the formation of the early church. But the call of Zacchaeus is a reminder that many who were called would remain within their occupations. Some like Levi (Matthew) were called to leave their tax-collecting tables; some, indeed most, remained in the line of work they had before conversion. But all underwent a fundamental change of orientation.

The elements of belief and repentance, renunciation and a call to service are found within Luke 5. Although not featured in this chapter, there are two other vital themes essential to the Synoptic notion of conversion.

4. *Joy and consolation.* In the Synoptic Gospels there is a distinctly *affective* element in conversion; repeatedly we see that joy is the fruit of conversion. Joy is an inherent consequence of the encounter with Christ.

In Matthew 11:28-30 joy is described as rest for the weary; those who come to Jesus have the burdens of their souls lifted. But many have noted that Luke is the Gospel of joy. This is perhaps most powerfully evident in Luke 15, where in the parable of the lost son joy is depicted not merely as restoration but as a homecoming where one finds rest, acceptance, forgiveness and the blessing of God. This parable is one of three in Luke 15, each of which has as its underlying theme the joy of being found. And this joy is not restricted to the one who is found; we read in the same chapter that there is great joy in heaven over just one sinner who repents.

5. *Water baptism.* There is also a sacramental component to conversion within the Synoptic Gospels. This is most explicit at the conclusion of Matthew, with Jesus' specific mandate with regard to how disciples are made: "All authority in heaven and on earth has been given to me. Go therefore and make disciples of all nations, baptizing them in the name of the Father and of the Son and of the Holy Spirit, and teaching them to obey everything that I have commanded you" (Mt 28:19-20). Baptism is clearly an integral part of what it means to *become* a follower of Jesus. One might even conclude from a simple reading of this text that one actually becomes a follower by being baptized. While such a one-to-one link would be inappropriate, it is clear that the Christian understanding of conversion must take account of a connection between baptism and conversion.

In summary, then, in the Synoptic Gospels conversion comes in response to an encounter with Jesus Christ—either to his deeds or to his words or both—a response that is characterized by belief and repentance. And we can follow Christ only when we turn from ourselves and from all that might keep us from a full and radical commitment to him. To follow is to choose the way of renunciation—to leave everything, if need be, so that we truly do follow. When we turn to Christ, we enter his "kingdom," which means that we come under his reign or authority (Mk 1:14-15). Further, conversion includes accepting the call of God to serve him—to participate in his kingdom purposes. And when we come to Christ we come "home." We find joy and rest for our souls, as though we were lost children being received once more into the arms of a father. Finally, this act of coming to

Christ is marked by baptism, which in some significant way symbolizes all of these components of conversion.

Before we move on to the next model of conversion, note something critical here in the Synoptic Gospels. The word *disciple* is a noun, not a verb. "Disciple" is something that someone *is;* it is not something we *do* to another person. In the language of the Gospels one does not "disciple" another person; rather, a person *is* a disciple, a follower of Jesus who has been baptized in the name of the Father, the Son and the Spirit, and who has chosen to become a learner—to be taught everything Jesus has commanded (Mt 28:16-20).

It is common to make a distinction between converts and disciples. In Richard Peace's extensive study of the Gospel of Mark, for example, he speaks of the need to make converts into disciples and notes that American evangelicalism has been "quite good at creating *converts* . . . but not nearly as good at generating *disciples*."[2] But making that distinction is part of the very problem he identifies. It is a false distinction; for in the Gospels a convert is a disciple or there is no conversion. In other words, if we are not good at making disciples, we are not good at making converts! Mature disciples are the fruit of thorough and authentic conversions.

But we continue to make the distinction and to use *disciple* as a verb to describe something that is done to Christian converts. What does it mean when we use the term *discipleship* to describe something that is done *to* Christians rather than to speak of enabling people to *become* Christians? I cannot but conclude that this is a subtle but powerful way in which the church has minimized the character and especially the costliness of conversion.

Conversion in Acts

The book of Acts was authored by Luke, the writer of the third Gospel. Nevertheless, the model of conversion found in Acts varies from that within the Synoptics, largely because it represents a different phase in the redemptive work of God. The model in Acts comes with the day of Pentecost and finds important expression as the church is established. This should not for a moment mean that we discount the model found in the Synoptic Gospels. Instead the Synoptic model and that described in Acts give us different perspectives on what it means to become a Christian.

---

[2]Richard V. Peace, *Conversion in the New Testament: Paul and the Twelve* (Grand Rapids, Mich.: Eerdmans, 1999), p. 304.

A representative text is readily at hand: many New Testament scholars see Acts 2:36-42 as intentionally paradigmatic. Through the words of Peter, the Spirit-inspired author presents a clear, concise outline of what one must do to become a Christian.

> "Therefore let the entire house of Israel know with certainty that God has made him both Lord and Messiah, this Jesus whom you crucified."
>
> Now when they heard this, they were cut to the heart and said to Peter and to the other apostles, "Brothers, what should we do?" Peter said to them, "Repent, and be baptized every one of you in the name of Jesus Christ so that your sins may be forgiven; and you will receive the gift of the Holy Spirit. For the promise is for you, for your children, and for all who are far away, everyone whom the Lord our God calls to him." And he testified with many other arguments and exhorted them, saying, "Save yourselves from this corrupt generation." So those who welcomed his message were baptized, and that day about three thousand persons were added. They devoted themselves to the apostles' teaching and fellowship, to the breaking of bread and the prayers. (Acts 2:36-42)

On the day of Pentecost those who heard Peter's proclamation—the gospel of the Lord Jesus Christ—responded enthusiastically and asked, "What should we do?" The answer is clear, straightforward and compelling, essentially a paradigm of conversion: "Repent, and be baptized every one of you in the name of Jesus Christ so that your sins may be forgiven; and you will receive the gift of the Holy Spirit."

The elements of a conversion. Three thousand heard the message, believed and were baptized. They chose to respond to the preached word by doing specifically what Peter called them to do. The model of conversion presented has the following elements.

1. *Belief and repentance.* The first act of conversion in this event was believing the word preached about Jesus. The people were "cut to the heart" because they recognized the truth, particularly the truth concerning Jesus of Nazareth, whom they knew to have been crucified. They recognized the truth that he had come from God. They recognized their own guilt and sinfulness. And so it comes as no surprise that Peter called them to repentance. If we believe, we repent.

2. *Baptism and the forgiveness of sins.* Peter's words are unequivocal: his hearers must be baptized. Baptism is clearly linked to their conscious awareness that their sins are forgiven. Baptism, as we will see, means more than the forgiveness of sins, but on this occasion forgiveness is highlighted. Through conversion they would experience assurance of forgiveness.

It is noteworthy that in the book of Acts *every* conversion narrative or explicit reference to a conversion makes mention of baptism. Baptism is consistently associated with conversion: always, whether the new converts are the Samaritans (8:12) or Simon (8:13) or the Ethiopian (8:35-38) or Cornelius (10:44-48) or Lydia (16:14-15) or the Philippian jailer, who was baptized "without delay" (16:33), or the Corinthians (18:8) or the Ephesians (19:1-6). So baptism is clearly normative, not incidental to the conversion experience. It is viewed as integral to coming to faith. The Ethiopian knew instinctively that if he believed the gospel, then it only made sense that he should be baptized (Acts 8:35-38).

3. *Reception of the gift of the Holy Spirit.* In Acts 2:38 Peter makes explicit reference to the gift of the Holy Spirit. He speaks of the Spirit as a gift his hearers could confidently assume would be granted to them; they would experience this as part of the experience of believing, repenting and being baptized.

Many students of the New Testament have noted that this gift of the Spirit is linked directly with the affective life of the early Christian community. In Acts 2:46 we read of the gladness that characterized the first Christians' common life. In descriptions of the early church that follow, joy pervades their lives, worship and witness, a joy that was clearly not incidental but an essential element of their common life. In this regard, two things should be noted: the affective or emotional dimension of Christian faith is not only mentioned but highlighted in the initial chapters of Acts, and this pervasive and confident joy is linked to the gift of the Spirit.

In the Synoptic Gospels the defining feature of conversion is one's new identity as a disciple; in Acts the defining feature of conversion is the presence of the Spirit in the life of the new believer.

4. *Incorporation into congregational life.* In Acts 2:42 we read that those who believed and were baptized came together and devoted themselves to three activities. First, they were learners who gave attention to the apostles' teachings. This would follow, of course, from the commission at the end of Matthew where those who were baptized were to be taught. Second, they devoted themselves to "the fellowship," which means they entered into a commitment to one another and to their common life. Third, they devoted themselves to "prayers," a common worship that included "the breaking of bread," a reference to the Lord's Supper or Holy Communion.

Those who came to believe and were baptized joined themselves together as a fellowship of learners and worshipers. While from this text it is not clear whether this incorporation into congregational life is inherent in conversion or the consequence of conversion, clearly conversion is both an individual and a communal experience. This commitment to a common life becomes even more apparent when we read this text in the light of the other models of Christian conversion portrayed in the New Testament.

These elements are the common strands in a Christian conversion as portrayed in Acts. Peter's words provide a model of conversion that is both concise and specific; it includes belief, repentance, baptism, assurance of forgiveness and reception of the gift of the Spirit. But it is important to note that an examination of the conversion narratives in Acts indicates that rarely was conversion actually experienced in this precise order.

Acts 8:35 tells of an Ethiopian who believed the Word as it was explained to him by Philip. He was baptized, at his own initiative, and he went on his way in joy—rejoicing in what he had experienced. His experience echoes the order of Acts 2:38. But his experience would seem to be the exception rather than the norm!

The experience of Cornelius was different. Cornelius, a God-fearing man committed to truth and righteousness, believed the Word spoken to him by Peter (Acts 10:34-43). Then, without further ado, he was baptized with the Spirit, and Peter's only possible conclusion was that nothing should prevent them from proceeding with a baptism in water. It should be pointed out that before their meeting Cornelius already identified in many ways with Peter in both belief and practice; he was not a pagan.

Thus while the elements and the order in which they would logically occur are outlined in Acts 2:38, the actual experience of many—through the working of the Spirit—varied and in some cases varied dramatically. Clearly, then, a true conversion required all of these components but did not need to have them in the order specified in Acts 2:38.

Conversion in the Pauline Epistles

As a representative text in Pauline thought I have chosen Romans 6. This passage was written to make clear the *foundation* of the Christian life, to establish precisely what it means to come to Christ to gain power to break out of a pattern of sin or immaturity. Paul elsewhere makes it plain that believers are to grow up in their salvation (Eph 4:11-16); conversion is to lead to maturity. In this text he speaks of the foundation that makes this possible.

What then are we to say? Should we continue in sin in order that grace may abound? By no means! How can we who died to sin go on living in it? Do you not know that all of us who have been baptized into Christ Jesus were baptized into his death? Therefore we have been buried with him by baptism into death, so that, just as Christ was raised from the dead by the glory of the Father, so we too might walk in newness of life.

For if we have been united with him in a death like his, we will certainly be united with him in a resurrection like his. We know that our old self was crucified with him so that the body of sin might be destroyed, and we might no longer be enslaved to sin. For whoever has died is freed from sin. But if we have died with Christ, we believe that we will also live with him. We know that Christ, being raised from the dead, will never die again; death no longer has dominion over him. The death he died, he died to sin, once for all; but the life he lives, he lives to God. So you also must consider yourselves dead to sin and alive to God in Christ Jesus.

Therefore, do not let sin exercise dominion in your mortal bodies, to make you obey their passions. No longer present your members to sin as instruments of wickedness, but present yourselves to God as those who have been brought from death to life, and present your members to God as instruments of righteousness. For sin will have no dominion over you, since you are not under law but under grace.

What then? Should we sin because we are not under law but under grace? By no means! Do you not know that if you present yourselves to anyone as obedient slaves, you are slaves of the one whom you obey, either of sin, which leads to death, or of obedience, which leads to righteousness? But thanks be to God that you, having once been slaves of sin, have become obedient from the heart to the form of teaching to which you were entrusted, and that you, having been set free from sin, have become slaves of righteousness. I am speaking in human terms because of your natural limitations. For just as you once presented your members as slaves to impurity and to greater and greater iniquity, so now present your members as slaves to righteousness for sanctification. (Rom 6:1-19)

The elements of a conversion. Paul is not exhaustive in his depiction of conversion in this text. But from this passage we can identify at least three crucial elements to an authentic (and complete) conversion. We will then look to other texts to flesh out the model of conversion found within Paul's letters.

1. *Identification with Christ.* For Paul, conversion is fundamentally an encounter with Christ through which an individual comes into union with Christ. While this reflects his own experience, Paul is clear that such an encounter and union are essential for all. The outcome of a conversion is

a mystical and dynamic identification with Christ. But further, conversion is the act of identification itself. To become a Christian is to identify with Christ—the person of Christ, the life, death and resurrection of Christ, the mission of Christ in the world. And this identity becomes the single most important fact of a person's existence.

2. *A transfer of allegiance.* This union with Christ is reflected in freedom from sin (Rom 6:7); but it is *not* an experience in which the new believer is entirely passive. We are freed from sin by virtue of our union with Christ. But the apostle also assumes that there is an *intentionality*—in some way the Christian believer takes responsibility. Belief in Christ has a distinctly volitional element: a Christian is one who consciously accepts a new paradigm of personal loyalty and allegiance. This entire chapter of Romans is based on the assumption that in becoming a Christian one accepts that one no longer lives in sin but in righteousness. To become a Christian is to choose the way of obedience, an obedience that is freedom.

3. *Water baptism.* Both the identification with Christ and the transfer of allegiance are symbolized by water baptism (Rom 6:3-4). Baptism is the mark, the definitive evidence or benchmark, indicating that a person is one with Christ, a believer in Christ and loyal to Christ. Paul uses baptism as his point of reference because he assumes that every believer is baptized. But he also uses baptism because in his mind it is closely linked with the foundational act of becoming a Christian.

In the Synoptic Gospels and Acts baptism symbolizes repentance and forgiveness of sins; here in Romans it represents union with Christ (in his death and resurrection), a union that reflects a transfer of allegiance. In Colossians 2:12 the apostle reminds his readers that they "were buried with [Christ] in baptism." Thus it is clear that in Paul's mind baptism represents a turning from one way of life to another; those who are baptized are made alive in Christ and have chosen the way of loyalty to Christ.

While these three elements of conversion are evident in this representative text, it is important to highlight other aspects of Paul's notion of conversion, and for this it is appropriate to lean heavily on the book of Ephesians, particularly Ephesians 2.

4. *Faith.* Faith is clearly central to Paul's concept of what it means to become a Christian believer. It is a dominant theme in the earlier chapters of Romans, before he comes to the matters discussed above, and it is also evident throughout his other letters: we know the saving grace of God through faith. Without faith there is no experience of God's grace (Rom

3:26). Faith is the fundamental expression of the heart that seeks to know God.

From Ephesians we know that such faith results in good works—a change of orientation or purpose, a change that is experienced in Christ. The good works are the fruit of faith (Eph 2:8-10). This faith presumes repentance. However, faith remains the distinctive or critical element.

5. *Receive the promised Holy Spirit.* The apostle also teaches that in and through conversion we receive the gift of the Spirit. This is spoken of as a kind of down payment: "In him you also, when you had heard the word of truth, the gospel of your salvation, and had believed in him, were marked with the seal of the promised Holy Spirit; this is the pledge of our inheritance toward redemption as God's own people, to the praise of his glory" (Eph 1:13-14).

It is important to highlight that "believed in him" is synonymous with the faith mentioned in Ephesians 2 and then later in Ephesians 3:12. This belief or faith is complemented by a gift or a mark, spoken of here as a "seal": the Holy Spirit given to those who believe. We see this also in Galatians 3:2, where Paul sums up the whole act of becoming a Christian by asking, "Did you receive the Spirit by doing the works of the law or by believing what you heard?" Clearly, the Galatians began their Christian life with the Spirit. In coming to Christ, in believing, they received the Spirit.

A vital sign of the reception of this gift is emphasized in Romans 8:16, where we are advised that the Spirit witnesses with our spirit that we are children of God. In other words, a fundamental assurance of one's new identity in Christ is given by and through the presence of the Spirit.

6. *Incorporation into the family of God.* Though this element is not emphasized in Romans 6, we would be remiss if we did not note that for Paul conversion included incorporation into the community of faith— another theme vital to the discussion of conversion in Ephesians. Here Paul stresses that when we come to Christ we are no longer alienated from the people of God; in Christ we become full members of this body, this family, this people. And the apostle's assumption is that this membership finds expression in congregational life, where we experience what it means to be members of the household of God (Eph 2:19). This house is spoken of as the temple of the Spirit—the dwelling place for God that is formed as we are joined together in the Spirit.

For Paul, the experience of conversion is superintended by the Holy Spirit. The earliest reference to conversion in the New Testament comes in 1 Thessalonians 1:4-6, where Paul appeals to his readers' conversion as a means of encouragement in a time of suffering.[3] He stresses that their conversion is an example of religious experience in response to Spirit-inspired preaching and that their joyful response is overseen by the Spirit. And this is a reminder that we have a truly biblical understanding of conversion only when we sustain an awareness of the presence of the Spirit throughout the whole experience.

Conversion in the Gospel of John

In considering the meaning of conversion in John's Gospel, we are drawn to John 3 and the remarkable encounter between Jesus and Nicodemus. While the text in one sense speaks of God's unilateral work of regeneration—new birth through the work of the Spirit—we can discern elements of a human response to this divine initiative, and thus the elements that make for an authentic Christian conversion.

> Now there was a Pharisee named Nicodemus, a leader of the Jews. He came to Jesus by night and said to him, "Rabbi, we know that you are a teacher who has come from God; for no one can do these signs that you do apart from the presence of God." Jesus answered him, "Very truly, I tell you, no one can see the kingdom of God without being born from above." Nicodemus said to him, "How can anyone be born after having grown old? Can one enter a second time into the mother's womb and be born?" Jesus answered, "Very truly, I tell you, no one can enter the kingdom of God without being born of water and Spirit. What is born of the flesh is flesh, and what is born of the Spirit is spirit. Do not be astonished that I said to you, 'You must be born from above.' The wind blows where it chooses, and you hear the sound of it, but you do not know where it comes from or where it goes. So it is with everyone who is born of the Spirit." Nicodemus said to him, "How can these things be?" Jesus answered him, "Are you a teacher of Israel, and yet you do not understand these things?
>
> "Very truly, I tell you, we speak of what we know and testify to what we have seen; yet you do not receive our testimony. If I have told you about earthly things and you do not believe, how can you believe if I tell you about heavenly things? No one has ascended into heaven except the one who descended from heaven, the Son of Man. And just as Moses lifted up the serpent in the wilderness, so must the Son of Man be lifted up, that whoever believes in him may have eternal life.

---

[3]These observations on 1 Thessalonians 1:4-6 follow the commentary of Gordon D. Fee, *God's Empowering Presence: The Holy Spirit in the Letters of Paul* (Peabody, Mass.: Hendrickson, 1994), pp. 41-47.

"For God so loved the world that he gave his only Son, so that everyone who believes in him may not perish but may have eternal life." (Jn 3:1-16)

The text's primary stress is that the radical renewal of human life comes through divine initiative; it is the work of God. But it is clearly the intent of Jesus not only that Nicodemus accept and believe this but also that he take personal responsibility for his response to the work of the Spirit.

The elements of a conversion. Beginning at the end of this representative text, then, the following elements of a Christian conversion can be identified.

1. *Belief in Jesus.* Nothing is so central or determinative to John's portrayal of conversion as this simple fact: a convert is one who *believes in Jesus.* Those who believe "have eternal life" (3:16). We know the grace of God by believing in Jesus Christ. In believing (1:12) we receive Christ. Indeed, to believe in Christ and to receive him seem to be synonymous in John 1:12. In John 4:39, conversion is captured simply in the statement "Many . . . believed in him." In John 6:29 we read that "this is the work of God, that you believe in him whom he has sent." And again, John 12:44 affirms that to believe in Jesus is to believe in the One who sent him.

Importantly, it is not merely that "belief" is an element of conversion but specifically that belief in *Jesus* is required. Jesus is the object of this belief.

It seems very simple, and such simplicity is what makes John's Gospel different from the others. On first reading, conversion in John's Gospel does not *seem* complex or costly—it is merely a matter of believing in Jesus. But such an assumption misses the full meaning of the call to believe—believing is inherently both complex and costly. To believe clearly has, in John's use of the term, an *intellectual* component—it presumes an understanding of Christ Jesus and his work. Those who believed recognized the uniqueness of Jesus; they were responding to truth that had been revealed to them, and they accepted or believed, or better yet embraced, that truth.

But it also has an *affective* dimension. This comes through clearly in John 14, when Jesus speaks directly to his disciples: "Do not let your hearts be troubled. Believe in God, believe also in me" (Jn 14:1). In other words, to believe is to trust such that our hearts are no longer troubled. In John 14:27 he speaks of such belief as peace. "Peace I leave with you; my peace I give to you. I do not give to you as the world gives. Do not let your hearts be troubled, and do not let them be afraid." To believe is to move from being afraid to knowing the peace of God.

This peace is complemented by *joy*. The place of joy is a recurring theme not only in the Synoptic Gospels (especially Luke) but also in the Gospel of John. At the conclusion of his ministry, Jesus emphasizes joy as the critical outcome his work for the disciples (Jn 15:11; 17:13). While one could conclude that for Jesus these references are not to conversion per se but to the maturing Christian experience, my counterargument is that these remarks of Jesus are not peripheral but central to his stated mission. It is also clear that the foundation of the Christian experience (a full conversion) has within it the capacity for and thus the seeds of this experience of joy.

There is also a *volitional* dimension to the call to believe in Jesus. We know from John 8 that we truly believe in Jesus as his disciples only if we know the truth (which can set us free) and if, as Jesus says to his disciples, "you continue in my word." Clearly, then, it is not merely a matter of intellectual assent; belief also includes turning from sin and embracing the way of freedom (for sin is identified with slavery in John 8:31-36). Jesus' purpose, we read in John 12:46, is that in believing in him we should no longer remain in darkness but live in the light. To believe in the Word is not only to hear but also to understand and to obey (or, as Jesus sometimes puts it, to "keep" his words).

The consequence of conversion—of believing—is that we are in union with Christ. If we believe, we are one with Christ and grafted as branches into the vine (Jn 15).

In one sense this model of conversion is simply *believe in Jesus!* But there are two other aspects of conversion in John's Gospel that are also significant and that necessarily complement the call to believe.

2. *Receive new life "from above."* A convert is one who is "born from above," which Jesus equates with being born of the Spirit (Jn 3:8). While evangelicals tend to use the "born again" metaphor, there is good reason to believe that "born from above" more accurately captures the intent of Jesus. His very point in this text is to establish that this is the work of the Spirit; it is not something we do but something that God does. A convert is one who experiences renewal and regeneration (new birth) *"from above."*

The phrase "born again" has established itself in the English language and particularly within evangelical language for conversion so firmly that one hesitates to question its usage. But while John's word here, *anothen,* could mean "again," a more literal rendering would be "from above." Beverly Roberts Gaventa thus concludes that Jesus' point was that Nicodemus had it all wrong in suggesting that he had to do something "again," return to his mother's womb. Jesus was correcting this false perception and explaining that conversion is about being born "from above" rather than being "born again." As Gaventa notes, "The irony continues in contemporary Christianity, since the meaning of *anothen* that Jesus rejects has become a dominant way of describing conversion."[4]

The point is not that something happens a second time or in a particular timeline; the emphasis of the text is that conversion is an experience of the Spirit's regenerating grace. From Nicodemus's perspective, conversion meant recognizing his inability while at the same time appropriating God's work which would be done unilaterally for him.

In this connection, it is also important to recognize that in John's Gospel the Spirit is spoken of not only as the One who would effect this birth from above but also as the One whom believers would receive.

> On the last day of the festival, the great day, while Jesus was standing there, he cried out, "Let anyone who is thirsty come to me, and let the one who believes in me drink. As the scripture has said, 'Out of the believer's heart shall flow rivers of living water.'" Now he said this about the Spirit, which believers in him were to receive; for as yet there was no Spirit, because Jesus was not yet glorified. (Jn 7:37-39)

This text does not specify that the Spirit will be received at conversion. Yet it is clearly the case that conversion will either include or at least lead to a reception of the Spirit. That is, those who believe in Jesus will receive the Spirit (after Pentecost, namely, after Jesus is "glorified").

3. *Born of the Spirit and of water.* A person who believes in Jesus is born from above, "born of the Spirit" (Jn 3:8). But in the first reference to being born of the Spirit, Jesus speaks not only of the Spirit but also of water: "No one can enter the kingdom of God without being born of water and Spirit" (Jn 3:5).

Students of the New Testament are divided on the meaning of water in this phrase. Some see a reference to water baptism; others categorically reject such a suggestion, adamant that this could not be a reference to literal water. Usually those who resist the tie to water baptism strongly oppose any notion that baptism is linked to new birth. This is a legitimate concern. However, if Jesus is indeed speaking of water baptism, it would not violate the tone or focus of the text: regeneration is "from above" and the work of the Spirit, but it is effected in an act that is very tangible and

---

[4]Beverly Roberts Gaventa, *From Darkness to Light: Aspects of Conversion in the New Testament* (Philadelphia: Fortress, 1986), pp. 133-34.

down to earth—water baptism.

Oscar S. Brooks, in *The Drama of Decision: Baptism in the New Testament*, sees this reference to water as part of a critical underlying theme in John's Gospel, the relationship between baptism and witness. The witness of John the Baptist is embodied in his water baptism: "Baptism," Brooks insists, "is an integral part of his commission and proclamation."[5] The baptism of Jesus reflected and stood in continuity with the baptizing ministry of John, for "the coming and submission of individuals to this water rite presuppose a proclamation and an acceptance of it."[6] This, Brooks notes, is the context in which Jesus meets with Nicodemus and presents him with the challenge of accepting Jesus' identity. To accept that Jesus is the revealer sent from God necessarily means that Nicodemus would submit to water baptism. Brooks contends that in this context Nicodemus would have no doubt what Jesus means in saying that he would have to be born of "water and Spirit"; it is an allusion to the need for water baptism.[7]

Even if we cannot be definitive on what this phrase means, at the very least we must note the mention of water. Given explicit references to baptism in the other three conversion models, it would seem that we should remain open to the possibility, if not the likelihood, that Jesus did in fact refer to baptism.

Bringing the Models Together

Four perspectives and four models of conversion: the Synoptic Gospels, the book of Acts, the letters of Paul, the Gospel of John. These four models represent four distinct but complementary perspectives on the Christian experience of conversion. All is therefore essential for a comprehensive or thorough appreciation of the foundation of the Christian life. None of these models takes priority over the others.

In *The Normal Christian Birth*, an important contribution to the conversation about conversion, David Pawson builds a case almost entirely on the book of Acts, arguing that the Gospels show a kind of pre-Christian conversion. He argues that we do not find *Christian* conversions in the Gospels.[8]

---

[5]Oscar S. Brooks, *The Drama of Decision: Baptism in the New Testament* (Peabody, Mass.: Hendrickson, 1987), p. 82.
[6]Ibid., p. 82.
[7]Ibid., p. 83.
[8]David Pawson, *The Normal Christian Birth* (London: Hodder & Stoughton, n.d.).

But this argument fails at one critical point: The Gospels were written by a mature and established church, and there is every reason to believe this perspective did shape their understanding of their own life in Christ. Certainly we would not have a full concept of Christian conversion without the book of Acts. But Pawson makes a false distinction in giving it priority over the Gospels. Further, we cannot come to a Christian understanding without incorporating Pauline perspectives. Consequently, it could make sense to begin with the book of Acts and get an overall structure or model for a conversion experience. Then the Gospels and Paul will inform and shape what we discover in Acts and help to clarify its meaning. Truly we need a comprehensive model of Christian conversion that takes account of each of the perspectives of New Testament theology.

My own reading of the New Testament, particularly the four models outlined above, considered in light of the conversion experience of Paul, leads me to conclude that Scripture calls for and assumes a conversion to Jesus Christ that includes seven distinct but inseparable elements. When taken together, the four models of conversion in the New Testament either explicitly call for or assume the following:

- [ ] belief in Jesus Christ
- [ ] repentance
- [ ] trust in Christ Jesus
- [ ] transfer of allegiance
- [ ] baptism
- [ ] reception of the gift of the Spirit
- [ ] incorporation into congregational life

What gives unity to these elements is that conversion is an encounter with Jesus Christ, an encounter in which the posture of heart and mind is humility before God.

The Conversion of Paul

Before this overview of models of conversion in the New Testament concludes, it must address the conversion of St. Paul and its theological significance.

In Holy Scripture, Paul's conversion is prominent and surely shapes a biblical understanding of conversion. It stands alone in large part because of the frequency with which it is recorded (three times) and because it is so frequently alluded to.

Now as he was going along and approaching Damascus, suddenly a light from heaven flashed around him. He fell to the ground and heard a voice saying to him, "Saul, Saul, why do you persecute me?" He asked, "Who are you, Lord?" The reply came, "I am Jesus, whom you are persecuting. But get up and enter the city, and you will be told what you are to do." . . . Saul got up from the ground, and though his eyes were open, he could see nothing; so they led him by the hand and brought him into Damascus. For three days he was without sight, and neither ate nor drank.

Now there was a disciple in Damascus named Ananias. The Lord said to him in a vision, "Ananias." He answered, "Here I am, Lord." The Lord said to him, "Get up and go to the street called Straight, and at the house of Judas look for a man of Tarsus named Saul. At this moment he is praying, and he has seen in a vision a man named Ananias come in and lay his hands on him so that he might regain his sight." But Ananias answered, "Lord, I have heard from many about this man, how much evil he has done to your saints in Jerusalem; and here he has authority from the chief priests to bind all who invoke your name." But the Lord said to him, "Go, for he is an instrument whom I have chosen to bring my name before Gentiles and kings and before the people of Israel; I myself will show him how much he must suffer for the sake of my name." So Ananias went and entered the house. He laid his hands on Saul and said, "Brother Saul, the Lord Jesus, who appeared to you on your way here, has sent me so that you may regain your sight and be filled with the Holy Spirit." And immediately something like scales fell from his eyes, and his sight was restored. Then he got up and was baptized, and after taking some food, he regained his strength.

For several days he was with the disciples in Damascus, and immediately he began to proclaim Jesus in the synagogues, saying, "He is the Son of God." (Acts 9:3-20)

Though it is prominent, the conversion of Paul does not in itself constitute a model or a prototype of Christian conversion, as it has often been seen to be. Many have noted that this experience is dramatic, decisive and determinative, and rightly so. But this conversion is in no sense portrayed as ideal or prescriptive in any respect other than that it describes an encounter with Christ. Not all conversions recorded in the New Testament are as dramatic or sudden; yet, ironically and perhaps unfortunately, Paul's conversion has been a point of reference for religious experience for two millennia—a kind of standard by which conversions are judged or measured.

Some propose that Paul's experience be seen as a prototype of a punctiliar conversion. Richard Peace, for example, presents what he sees as two models of conversion in the New Testament—that of Paul, which he contends is punctiliar, and that of the twelve disciples, which he suggests, through a study of the Gospel of Mark, is a protracted, extended process.[9] However, there is no solid basis for concluding that Paul's conversion constitutes a model of Christian conversion. It is never presented as such by Paul or by any other biblical author.

Further, and just as critical: was Paul's conversion actually punctiliar? At the very least his conversion lasted three days. And even though it was decisive and dramatic, there is a great deal about which we are not informed. We do not know the full meaning of his time in the desert following the Damascus experience. Indeed, it could be argued that we actually know relatively little about his conversion. We know something of his experience on the road to Damascus and then in Damascus itself. But it could be argued that we have this information for another purpose. There is ongoing debate about the actual significance of this conversion— whether Acts or the Pauline letters are primary and which is more authoritative; whether we really can know much about Paul and his experience. Biblical scholars like F. F. Bruce say we can know a great deal; S. Kim even

---

[9]Peace, *Conversion in the New Testament*. The account of Acts 9 is taken by most to imply that Paul's conversion was a punctiliar event. But at the very least it lasted three days. Furthermore, Galatians 1:16-18 makes reference to a three-year period. In other words, Paul's conversion may not necessarily have been so punctiliar. Nowhere is it portrayed as a model of conversion. Rather, Paul describes his conversion only with reference to his transformation under mercy and his call to preach to the Gentiles. Consequently, it could well be that we do not have access to his full conversion narrative, but only have it described for us for these particular purposes, which means that he is naturally selective and not comprehensive. We can only, therefore, conclude that it is not to be taken as a model of Christian conversion.

However, Peace uses it as a model and indeed goes so far as to use Paul's conversion as the template by which he interprets other conversions, notably that of the Twelve (using the Gospel of Mark). One naturally wonders: Why did Peace begin with Paul and not with the Twelve; why did he not use the experience of the Twelve as a template by which he would interpret the experience of the apostle Paul? By beginning with the experience of Paul, he creates categories that are not obvious from the text (see his three elements of insight, turning and transformation). Further, he places all three of these events as having happened right there in a moment, on the road to Damascus. But though he certainly received insight, do we know that Paul then and there repented and turned? Do we know that he was immediately transformed? As noted above, are we not reading into the Damascus Road scene more than the existing narrative gives us, without having in hand a description from Paul of what actually happened over the next three days (and over the next three years)? It is noteworthy that Peace uses Paul's conversion as example of a punctiliar conversion for seemingly no other reason but that it has been viewed that way at various points in the history of the church.

argues that Paul's whole theology came out of his experience of conversion. Others, in contrast, wonder whether we can know much about the conversion itself.[10]

Thus we would be wise to not overstate the significance of this conversion account. However, we can confidently draw two conclusions from the apostle's experience that have significance for Christian thought and experience.

First, there is a clear connection between Paul's conversion and his apostolic service. Paul's theology of God's saving grace to both Gentiles and Jews arose out of his own experience of that grace. He viewed his conversion as a critical point of reference in his ministry. His encounter with Christ (a Christophany) on the road to Damascus was the source of his gospel—his message or theology—as well as his own apostolic call to the Gentiles. Thus his conversion and his call constituted fundamentally one occasion.

Through this experience the apostle almost became an immediate leader within the Christian community, if not the de facto founder of the movement in its outward orientation, especially to Gentiles. His conversion represents that of the founder of a religious movement more than that of a person whose conversion includes incorporation into an established religious community.[11] It is thus reasonable to conclude that the primary significance of Paul's conversion lies in his theological impact on the history of Christianity and his mission to the Gentiles.[12]

Second, there is something in Paul's conversion experience that is necessarily integral to every conversion: a profound awareness of the overwhelming mercy of God. This comes through very powerfully in many texts in Acts and in Paul's letters, but especially noteworthy is Philippians 3:7-11, which stresses the encounter with Christ, and Titus 2—3, where the

---

[10]Two helpful resources on the conversion of St. Paul: Gaventa, *From Darkness to Light*, pp. 22-25; and Richard N. Longenecker, *The Road from Damascus: The Impact of Paul's Conversion on His Life, Thought and Ministry* (Grand Rapids, Mich.: Eerdmans, 1997), particularly Bruce Corley, "Interpreting Paul's Conversion—Then and Now," pp. 1-17. Also, I should mention that contra those who say the Damascus Road experience was not a conversion, in that he was a Jew and this encounter made him more faithful to his Jewishness, I am defining *conversion* as an encounter with Christ that leads to a new orientation that is Christ-centered. This is surely what happened Paul; it was a religious experience—of Christ—that led to a radical redirection of his life.

[11]See Larry W. Hurtado, "Convert, Apostate or Apostle to the Nations: The 'Conversion' of Paul in Recent Scholarship," *Studies in Religion* 22, no. 3 (1993): 281.

[12]Corley, "Interpreting Paul's Conversion—Then and Now," p. 16.

focus is on the mercy of God. Any number of other Pauline texts could be cited to make the same point. Paul's conversion radically transformed him and fundamentally altered the contours of his life and work. He had met Christ; he had experienced mercy.

This awareness of God's mercy was the dynamic of Paul's life. He lived always conscious that he was a man who had known mercy and who would always live under that mercy. He was a forgiven sinner—a sinner who had seen forgiveness. He came to Christ because the grace of God had been revealed (Tit 2:11). And this experience of grace became the point of reference for the rest of his life:

> But when the goodness and loving kindness of God our Savior appeared, he saved us, not because of any works of righteousness that we had done, but according to his mercy, through the water of rebirth and renewal by the Holy Spirit. This Spirit he poured out on us richly through Jesus Christ our Savior, so that, having been justified by his grace, we might become heirs according to the hope of eternal life. (Tit 3:4-7)

The motivating and guiding force of Paul's life was the "goodness and loving kindness" of God and the awareness that he was saved by God's mercy, justified by God's grace and thus an heir to the hope of eternal life.

It is imperative that in a theological and critical analysis of conversion we not lose sight of this central and defining principle of the character of religious experience: *It is the goodness of God that motivates and sustains the spiritual growth that arises out of a conversion experience.*

Based on this, we acknowledge that there is a crucial posture of mind that undergirds the Christian experience of conversion and arises out of the awareness of God's mercy: it is humility.

Humility as the Posture and Fruit of Conversion

Humility is both the posture of the heart that makes conversion possible and the outcome of such a conversion.

The way of the disciple is the way of humility, and thus it is appropriate to speak of conversion as a reorientation of one's life to the way of humility. In humility we walk in the fear of the Lord. From this posture of humility we are able to love God and receive God's Word, which both cleanses and transforms. Humility serves as the ultimate test of whether we truly live with faith, hope and love.

This perspective on humility is reflected in the Scriptures at many points. The New Testament speaks of the humiliation of God in Christ for the redemption of the world (Phil 2:1-11), a redemption from pride and its consequences. Those who live in response to Christ and his work are participants in his kingdom. We enter the kingdom only when we come as children; and we live the authentic kingdom life only when we live in humility expressed in obedient service (Mt 5:3; 18:4; see also Phil 2:3). When we enter the kingdom we receive a new heart—a heart transformed by grace, renewed in the power of the Spirit.

The classic liturgical line "Lift up your hearts" reflects the biblical injunction that we receive Christ in our hearts, which requires a fundamental humility of spirit. It is the humility of acceptance of God's Word and obedience to it. Such humility was personified in Mary, the mother of the Lord, the first disciple and model of authentic discipleship. Baptism too is an act of humility, regardless of what mode is practiced (though perhaps most apparent in believers' adult baptism)—the humility of accepting the grace of God toward us.

Humility is a classic Christian principle, repeatedly confirmed by the church's spiritual masters. It stands at the heart of the Rule of St. Benedict; the twelve steps of humility (RB 7) represent the transition from fear to love. Patrick Lyons, in a review of Benedictine monasticism, notes that a monk was to respond to God in humility and obedience; however, the priority clearly lies with humility. Humility is fundamental in the Rule.[13]

St. Gregory the Great referred to humility as "the mother and mistress of all virtues": "Since humility is the very source of virtue, it follows that a virtue will spring up and endure if it is rooted in humility, but if it is cut off from this root, it will wither away because it lacks the life-giving sap of charity."[14]

Later Calvin affirmed the words of St. Augustine: "If you ask me [what is the first, second and third precept] of the Christian religion, I will answer, first, second and third, humility. . . . By humility," Calvin writes, "[Augustine] means not when a man, with a consciousness of some virtue, refrains from pride, but when he truly feels that he has no refuge but in humility."[15] Elsewhere Calvin affirms that "there is no access to salvation

---

[13]Rule of St. Benedict—The Twelve Steps of Humility (RB 7); Patrick Lyons, "Conversion in the Benedictine and Wesleyan Traditions," *Asbury Theological Journal* 50, no. 2 (1995), and 51, no. 1 (1996): 87.

[14]Quoted in Joseph De Guibert, *The Theology of the Spiritual Life,* trans. Paul Barrett (New York: Sheed & Ward, 1953), pp. 279-80.

[15]John Calvin *Institutes of the Christian Religion* 2.2.11, trans. Henry Beveridge (reprint, Grand Rapids, Mich.: Eerdmans, 1979).

unless all pride is laid aside and true humility embraced; . . . [humility] is the unfeigned submission of a mind overwhelmed by a serious conviction of its want and misery."[16]

A more contemporary spiritual master, Thomas Merton, remarked that it is virtually impossible to overstate the value of authentic humility in the Christian life, since "humility contains in itself the answer to all the great problems of the life of the soul."[17] But it is not merely the goal of the Christian life. In Teresa of Ávila's metaphor of a building to describe the Christian life, humility is the foundation. "If humility is not genuinely present, for your own sake the Lord will not construct a high building lest that building fall to the ground."[18]

At this point the formative influence of language becomes critically apparent; for it is imperative not only that we speak of the vital place of humility in authentic Christian religious experience, particularly conversion; we must also be clear about what humility means within the context of the Christian faith. Humility is, in the first place, living in the truth—an eager acceptance of the Creator as Creator, of a theocentric universe and of oneself as a dependent creature.

But further, humility is also a freedom from the creation—a holy indifference to the created order and the order of things. This is not the indifference of apathy but rather the gracioius affirmation of the provisional nature of all things aside from God, which means that as creatures we find ultimate life and meaning only in the Creator.

Then also, humility is the acknowledgment of the reality of sin in the world and in one's life, that to live in sin is to live falsely, and that our only hope is found in living under and in the mercy of God. This also includes a recognition that human moral systems are vacuous and empty; Christian spirituality is not a spirituality of morality or success or fulfillment. It is the humility in which we acknowledge need, the humility that rejects the way of pride and self-sufficiency. It is the humility that acknowledges responsibility for sin and wrongdoing and one's absolute dependence on God's mercy. It is the humility of receptivity and responsiveness—of submission of our wills to the will of God. It is only through humility that we can live under and be embraced by the mercy of God.

---

[16]Ibid., 3.12.6-7.

[17]Thomas Merton, *New Seeds of Contemplation* (London: Burns & Oates, 1961), p. 140.

[18]Teresa of Ávila *The Interior Castle* 7.4.8, in *The Collected Works of St. Teresa of Ávila*, trans. Kieran Kavanaugh and Otilio Rodriguez (Washington, D.C.: ICS, 1980), 2:447.

But most important, the way of humility is the way of Christ and his cross. For the Christian, the principle of humility cannot be conceived of apart from the humility of God in Christ Jesus. To become Christian is to identify with the self-humiliation that eventually took the Lord to the cross. Thus humility is a conscious identification with Christ in his humility; the goal is union with Christ, not humility as an end in itself.

It is only as we are found, through humility, in Christ that we are freed from longings for praise, honor and prestige, freed from longings for material well-being and freed from longings for power and influence. Wealth, the praise of others and influence are not wrong in themselves; it is merely that the human person is prone to seek satisfaction in God's creation and God's gifts rather than in God himself.

When the ancients chose the way of poverty, it involved both a conscious denial of the longing for sensual gratification and a quiet acceptance of humility. This way called them to abhor anything that would have the taint of pride or that might feed their propensity for pride. The way of poverty was not merely a denial of wealth; it was also a rejection of the pursuit of honor, prestige and the praise of others.

Throughout the church's history its spiritual masters have also warned against false humility. This is the supposed humility of pretension and hypocrisy. One form of false humility, already mentioned, involves viewing humility as an end in itself, the goal of the spiritual life. This inevitably leads to a self-consciousness that violates the very heart of what it means to be spiritual. For humility is never an end; it is always the means by which we live in him in whom we have our being. The end is Christ himself.

The outcome of true humility is that we are capable of love toward others; the virtue of humility enables us to turn from self-centeredness and pride and embrace the way of love. Only in humility of identification with Christ is there an enduring strength and peace in life and work, a freedom to love others without fear of rejection and to serve with generosity without fear of failure. In humility we are not crushed by failure or criticism; but neither is the ego inflated by success or praise. In humility alone is there an identification with Christ that frees us to live in joy.

In this study I stress the value of a clear conversion narrative. To some this may seem to encourage self-centeredness or an unhealthy focus on self. I hope to show, however, that there are many benefits to knowing one's conversion narrative, one of them being that it frees us, paradoxically, from self-centeredness. It is surely possible that for some developing their narrative would merely be an exercise in self-importance and narcissism. But generally it is by making our story both conscious and "public" that we come to see that our story belongs not merely to us but to all; it demonstrates God's mercy not just to one person but is a window through which we appreciate the depth of mercy to *all*. In Paul's writings, references to his own experience are anything but arrogant. His conversion was rather the lens through which he saw, and through which he helps all of us see, God's merciful work for the whole of the creation. And this is a humbling exercise.

6

Elements
of a Christian
Conversion

Within evangelicalism there is a propensity to think of conversion in minimalist terms: What is the very least that a person needs to do in order to be freed from the horrors of hell and assured of the glories of heaven? But when we take this approach, the outcome is hardly a genuinely Christian theology of conversion. C. S. Lewis makes the sobering observation that in conversion, he had "never seen how a preoccupation with [immortality] at the outset could fail to corrupt the whole thing."[1]

Rather than positing minimalist questions, we should be asking, What is the foundation necessary for a transformed life? How can we experience justification in such a way that sanctification will follow? Or, putting it differently, what kind of conversion sets the stage for the kind of spiritual transformation we long for? What needs to happen, foundationally, for us to have a comprehensive experience of the transforming grace of God? What kind of conversion will foster real maturity, so that we become men and women of spiritual depth and wisdom? What kind of conversion will make it likely and possible that we will truly live under the reign of

---

[1]C. S. Lewis, *Surprised by Joy* (London: Geoffrey Bles, 1955), p. 185.

God, in but not of the world? Saints are made by good conversions. If this is true, what does a good conversion look like?

Paul Helm makes a helpful comment regarding the character of authentic conversion. He rightly stresses that a Christian conversion comes in response to divine initiative. Thus, he contends, it is a gift of new life that occurs deep within the human psyche, "below the level of self awareness."[2] Yet Helm also insists that this gift gives rise to "an experience with a distinctive structure" and that "the experiences of conversion are infinitely varied but they all have the same structure."[3] In other words, "the elements of the experience are the same."[4]

He concludes: "This is not peculiar to conversion or to religious experience. No two football games or illnesses or courtships are the same. But this does not mean that just *anything* could count as a football game or that a football game could be confused with a courtship."[5] So just as there are some essential elements to a football game, there are some essential elements to a conversion, even though the experience of these elements will be immensely varied.

Some may be concerned that if we are overly analytical regarding religious experience we will somehow undermine its wonder and mystery or even its power. On the contrary, to build on Helm's analogy, the appeal of a football game is not destroyed when we are attentive to the rules of the game, when we insist that it be played within particular boundaries and under a specific set of guidelines. The rules of the game preserve it as a game.

Similarly, only when we are clear about the parameters of conversion can we truly embrace the experience as one of wonder, grace and transformation. Thus what follows is an examination of the *elements* of a Christian conversion, the critical components of an intentional response to the initiative of God, who has acted and is acting for us through Jesus Christ. These elements are human actions in response to divine initiative, with the understanding that conversion is being defined as the converse of God's work of salvation. This is an attempt to enumerate the actions by which we appropriate God's grace in a manner that we can with some

---

[2]Paul Helm, *The Beginnings: Word and Spirit in Conversion* (Edinburgh: Banner of Truth, 1986), p. 22.
[3]Ibid.
[4]Ibid.
[5]Ibid.

degree of confidence say will lead to transformation.

I have already stressed the value for each Christian believer of developing a deep, self-conscious awareness of his or her own conversion narrative. Just as there are rules to a game or guidelines to the writing of a sonnet or a haiku poem, what follows are the essential features of a conversion. No two haiku poems are identical; no two conversions are identical. But both have some essential features that make the one a haiku poem and the other a conversion. Attention to these features enables us to know and give critical and reflective thought to our own experience of coming to faith in Christ.

Many theologians have recognized that there are some essential elements to conversion. According to E. M. B. Green, these are repentance, faith and baptism. They are identified by James Dunn as repentance, water baptism and the gift of the Spirit. J. Dupont highlights what he calls a sense of sin, an awareness of the mystery of Easter and a change of life. Bernard Lonergan, in his *Method in Theology*, speaks of three aspects of conversion: the intellectual, the moral and the religious. Walter Conn, building on the thought of Lonergan, has developed a theory of Christian conversion that considers four categories: affective, cognitive, moral and religious. Richard Peace suggests there are three elements: insight or perception, turning, and transformation (the beginning of a new life).[6]

Gordon D. Fee identifies five elements of a Christian conversion: conviction of sin (which he says leads to conversion); repentance and the experience of forgiveness; the regenerating work of the Spirit; an empowerment for life and obedience to mission; and baptism in water. He views the empowerment of the Spirit as the crucial element.[7] Fee's perspective is more comprehensive than that of Helm, who speaks of three elements: conviction of sin, faith and repentance.[8] And to add yet another voice, John Stott suggests, "The norm of Christian experience, then, is a cluster of four things: repentance, faith in Jesus, water baptism and the gift of the Spirit. Though the perceived order may vary a little, the four belong together and are universal in Christian initiation."[9] Hav-

---

[6]Richard V. Peace, *Conversion in the New Testament: Paul and the Twelve* (Grand Rapids, Mich.: Eerdmans, 1999), pp. 24-25.

[7]Gordon D. Fee, *Gospel and Spirit: Issues in New Testament Hermeneutics* (Peabody, Mass.: Hendrickson, 1991), p. 117.

[8]Helm, *Beginnings*.

[9]John R. W. Stott. *The Spirit, the Church and the World* (Downers Grove, Ill.: InterVarsity Press, 1990), p. 305.

ing said this, though, Stott elsewhere contends that "true conversion also issues in church membership."[10]

Borrowing Stott's word, I suggest it is most helpful to think of an authentic Christian conversion as a *cluster* of seven distinct elements—if we want a conversion that reflects the full expectation of the New Testament rather than just the minimalism of only wondering if one will "go to heaven." A generation of scholars has suggested that conversion is indeed a complex experience that includes several distinctive elements; it is time to acknowledge that taken together we have a remarkable congruence of opinion.

Conversion is best thought of as a protracted experience that involves several distinct element or events. But these events or elements are not to be referred to as steps or stages in a conversion. This cannot be stressed too strongly. These are not "hoops" that one goes through to get converted; they are not hurdles along the way that one must jump in order to get the reward at the end of a course. Rather, these are elements of conversion that each person will experience in a different way and in a different sequence, reflecting the unique manner in which the Spirit of God is at work in his or her life. The order of their presentation here, then, has a certain *theological* logic, but this may not be reflected in actual experience.

Seven Elements of a Good Conversion

1. *Belief: the intellectual component.* First, a Christian conversion will have an intellectual component—intellectual in the sense that something distinctive happens in a person's understanding. There is a change of mind, an illumination in one's thinking. To become Christian we must *believe* the gospel. Such belief usually comes through hearing the gospel preached or spoken in a manner that enables us to see its truthfulness.

This belief is in certain facts or truths concerning Jesus Christ. Later I will explore the idea that a Christian conversion is not merely belief *about* Jesus but actually a belief *in* Jesus. But for the moment I am affirming the reality that one element of conversion happens in the intellect: a new orientation in our understanding. We believe the gospel; we believe that Jesus is the Christ, the Son of the Living God. We believe that he died for our sins and that through him we have forgiveness and hope.

Different readers of the New Testament will differ on the minimum level of belief needed to call oneself a Christian—what specifically one

---

[10]Ibid., p. 178.

must believe about Jesus and how comprehensive that belief needs to be. However, I suggest that all readers of Scripture would concur that something fundamental about Jesus must be believed—intellectually, as truth— if we are to know the saving grace of God.

2. *Repentance: the penitential component.* In a Christian conversion there is also an intentional acknowledgment of and confrontation of sin, a penitential element. As comes through so forcefully in the words of Peter in Acts 2:38 and is clearly present in each model of conversion found in the New Testament, belief in Jesus Christ must be complemented by repentance for our sin—for our current and former way of life.

Repentance in this sense is not merely remorse (feeling sorry or bad for our sins). It is a radical and unequivocal rejection of the way of sin and the pattern of life that leads to sin. But it is admittedly rooted in an awareness that we are sinners in need of grace. We know forgiveness because we repent. We acknowledge our sin; we acknowledge our guilt, without making excuses. And in humility we ask for mercy.

Thus the act of repentance includes both remorse and a rejection of the way of sin.

3. *Trust and the assurance of forgiveness: the emotional or affective component.* A Christian conversion has a distinctly emotional element, an affective strand or component that is not incidental but essential to an authentic and complete Christian conversion. It will be expressed differently by different people, depending on culture, personality and the circumstances of the conversion. In the New Testament models we can discern three expressions of this emotional component when a person comes to Christ.

First, there is assurance of forgiveness. We do not only confess our sins; we move forward with an assurance that our sins are no longer counted against us. This is wonderfully exemplified in Wesley's experience of the heart "strangely warmed" and the deep, heartfelt assurance that he was loved, accepted and forgiven.

Second, there is trust—which comes through most obviously in Paul's language of "faith" and John's language of "belief." Clearly these words for these writers mean more than intellectual assent to a truth or a conviction. What is at stake in the faith of which Paul speaks and in the language of John when he speaks of believing in Jesus is a radical abandonment of self to another, to the Lord Jesus Christ. There is no faith and there is no belief if there is not this radical trust in God.

And third, joy runs through each of the New Testament models of conversion. It is the joy of those who have found "home." They have found life in Christ and thereby have found hope. And the sign of this is joy. Joy is not merely a nice "topping" to a conversion; it is not secondary or incidental or even merely derivative of conversion. Rather, joy is essential—a critical and irreplaceable element of an authentic Christian conversion.

4. *Commitment, allegiance and devotion: the volitional component.* Conversion includes a transfer of allegiance. Jesus' words in the Synoptics are dramatic: we must "leave everything." And there is nothing equivocal about the words of Paul. When we become Christians, we are no longer slaves to sin; we are slaves to righteousness. There is a fundamental change of loyalties.

In and through his death, resurrection and ascension, the Lord Jesus Christ assumes the position of ultimate and final authority in the universe. Christ says, "All authority in heaven and on earth has been given to me" (Mt 28:18). In coming to Christ we inevitably come under the authority of Christ. A transfer of allegiance, then, is a necessary and defining element of conversion.

This transfer of allegiance, the resolve to live in obedience to Christ, is evident in two ways. First, it becomes evident in the quality of our lives— the moral standards by which we live. We choose to live lives congruent with the character of God as reflected in God's holy will.

But second, the transfer of allegiance is also evident in the focus of our energies. We reject the way of sin and darkness and choose to live in the light; we no longer live for ourselves but for Christ, and we accept his call to participate in his kingdom purposes in the world. In both cases, the critical question involves obedience; conversion includes a distinctly volitional component.

It is important, though, to stress that this volitional component is rooted in devotion—a love for Christ that comes in response to his love for us. We obey and serve because we love the Lord who has first loved us.

5. *Water baptism: the sacramental component.* While some Christian traditions view water baptism as essential, others are more inclined to view it as optional. But the weight of the evidence from the New Testament is that baptism is an integral component of the experience of coming to Christ and incorporation into Christian community. Whether we are looking at the character of conversion in the Synoptic Gospels, Acts, Paul's letters or the Gospel of John, baptism plays a critical and indispensable role (though admittedly it is only alluded to in the Gospel of John).

The chapters that follow will argue that those who stress the priority of faith need not fear that affirming the integral place of baptism would be caving in to what is known as "baptismal regeneration." We can maintain the priority of faith yet also recognize the integral place of this sacramental action. We affirm that the external act of baptism is commanded, linked directly to conversion in each of the models of conversion in the New Testament. We can appreciate that this command is given because we human beings need an external ritual action that complements and confirms what is happening to us internally. I hope to show in the pages that follow that baptism and faith stand in close relationship with each other, but they are distinct and never to be identified with each other.

6. *Reception of the gift of the Holy Spirit: the charismatic component.* The charismatic element of conversion is the appropriation of the gift of the Spirit, of God himself residing within the Christian believer. Later I will explore in greater depth the idea that receiving the gift of the Spirit is integral to and inseparable from the conversion experience. But this is not inherently a contradiction to the Reformed and Baptist belief that we receive the Spirit at regeneration, nor to the Holiness and Pentecostal insistence that this gift is received after one is already converted. I will make the case that the gift of the Spirit is integral to conversion but that nevertheless it can be viewed as an experience distinct from initial faith, repentance and water baptism. Thus it is legitimate to speak of the reception of the Spirit as a distinct though inseparable element of Christian conversion.

7. *Incorporation into Christian community: the corporate component.* Finally, most powerfully exemplified at the conclusion of Acts 2:38-42 and also outlined as a fundamental theological axiom in Paul's letter to the Ephesians, conversion of necessity includes a corporate component: incorporation into Christian community.

Contemporary evangelicalism is still coming to terms with the radical individualism that has so thoroughly shaped the movement. Consequently, it is often very difficult for us to appreciate that an authentic understanding of conversion must include a corporate component. When we come to faith, we become members of the people of God. And it is fair to say that *until* we are incorporated into Christian community, our conversion is incomplete and we lack the necessary structure and context that would enable us to grow toward spiritual maturity. We are not designed to live the Christian life in isolation from others. True conversion necessarily brings us into Christian community.

The Seven Elements as a Whole

I conclude that there are seven essential elements of an authentic Christian conversion. No doubt others reading the New Testament would come to a different conclusion, perhaps adding to my list or combining some elements. This list is given as an attempt to be comprehensive and to reflect the complexity of conversion. It may be helpful as a point of departure as others read the New Testament in a dissimilar cultural context or setting.

In the chapters that follow each element will be examined in detail. But first I will attempt to describe these elements as a package, as components of a single experience, the act of becoming a Christian.

The central place of belief and repentance. Belief and repentance stand as a pair at the center of the Christian experience of conversion, as the fundamental or essential core. Together, belief and repentance represent the act of faith by which we know and are confident of the justifying grace of God. One might even say that this was the basis for the whole phenomenon of evangelicalism—the conviction of the central place of faith, the faith of belief and repentance. When belief and repentance are understood as the *core* within the conversion experience, this is the fundamental strength of evangelicalism. But when they are understood as the *whole* of the conversion experience, people have been led to a truncated and one-dimensional understanding and experience of conversion that are neither faithful to the New Testament nor effective in fostering spiritual maturity and strength.

Some will protest that the outline of seven essential elements of a conversion undermines the conviction so central to the Protestant evangelical heritage that we are justified by faith *alone.* In response I would insist that a distinction must be made. Faith alone justifies; through faith alone we can know the saving grace of God. But faith is never alone. My outline is meant to identify those elements that necessarily *accompany* true faith.

Conversion is both a complex experience and a simple experience. Its simplicity is captured in the two actions of faith and repentance. In Mark 1:15 Jesus makes his pronouncement and his call: "The kingdom of God has come near; repent, and believe in the good news." Although conversion is a complex experience, this call profiles the core actions of faith (or belief) and repentance. In repentance we turn from sin, darkness and death; in faith we turn to holiness, light and the life of God. In this way, repentance makes obedience possible; it is the necessary foundation for true Christian discipleship.

While there may be a logical basis for concluding that repentance must precede faith, in actuality the two are mutually dependent acts—distinct but inseparable. There is no faith without repentance; no repentance without faith.

The central place of faith and repentance is the basis for the biblical understanding that conversion is a *turning*, a change, a *metanoia*. This turning reflects a change of mind, but much more than that, it is a radical change of orientation. One's face is turned from one fundamental orientation to a radically new direction. The "turning" of faith and repentance means a change of loyalty and allegiance.

These two acts stand at the center for a simple reason: a Christian conversion is radical (going to the core or root of our being) or it is no conversion at all. Jesus condemned the Pharisees for having made conversion a matter of externals. It is not that externals do not matter; Jesus asserts in the Sermon on the Mount that the righteousness of his disciples must exceed that of the Pharisees. But Jesus is calling for a change from *within*—a change that arises from faith and repentance. The New Testament writers used the language of *metanoein* to stress that the call to conversion is radical: it is not merely an external turnaround but a change of mind and heart, a change of attitude and inner posture.

Each conversion is unique, but all involve a deep change of direction. We move from self-centeredness to other-centeredness focused on Christ. We move from living for ourselves to living for another. We move from moralism to the dynamic of a holy life lived in response to and in relationship with Christ.

Donald Bloesch, in *Crisis of Piety*, notes that different traditions have had different conceptions of where the focus point really lies.[11] For sacramental traditions, the locus is baptism, the sacramental event. Revivalistic traditions point to the surrender of the will, often expressed in the "altar call" and the intentional response to a preached word. Still others, such as Karl Barth, place the locus of human conversion in the objective truth of the cross. In covenantal traditions, the emphasis is on incorporation into the covenant community; attention is less on individual conversion experiences than on the reality that people join a covenant community by being born to Christian parents. Yet others see the critical matter to be engagement with the heart and will of God, perhaps in the struggle for justice, as liberation theologians emphasize. Others point to the intellect and understanding. For them the essence of conversion is response to the proclamation of the Word (kerygma); conversion is cen-

---

[11]Donald Bloesch, *Crisis of Piety* (Grand Rapids, Mich.: Eerdmans, 1968), pp. 80-81.

trally the Word heard, embraced and obeyed.

Each of these is essential to an authentic conversion. But the center of gravity in the conversion experience is found in the interplay between repentance and faith, a simultaneous movement away from sin and toward trust in Christ. This is evident from Paul's definitive focus on faith in the doctrine of justification, Jesus' simple words announcing the kingdom and the apostles' preaching recorded in Acts.

Rather than simplifying conversion, this discussion has aimed to identify its focal point. Conversion remains a complex event, with a variety of factors and elements that make repentance and faith meaningful and effective in personal and corporate transformation.

The elements are distinct but inseparable. The New Testament, taken as a whole, assumes and expects all seven elements to be foundational for spiritual growth and maturity. Yet the seven are distinct, not synonymous. Believing in Christ leads to repentance but is distinct from repentance. Receiving the Spirit is distinct from water baptism, but as we see in Acts, it is important to affirm that they go together. Cornelius received the gift of the Spirit prior to water baptism; but Peter's assumption was that if you had the one, the other should also happen. In Acts 19:3 Paul questions the validity of water baptism if it is not accompanied by Spirit baptism— thus assuming that they are distinct but also that they are inseparable. Or better said, the one without the other is abnormal, and the assumption in such cases is that the situation needs to be rectified.

The elements of a conversion, then, are distinct but inseparable, mutually reinforcing. In some cases one element enables a person to encounter the need for and be open to the possibility of another.

Each element of a conversion can represent the whole of the conversion experience. No New Testament text lists all seven elements. While there are summaries of elements, in every case one or more of them is taken for granted. Indeed often the whole conversion process is spoken of by reference to one of them. It is as if any one of these elements can be used as the lens through which the whole conversion is viewed. Each element can be used as a kind of verbal shorthand to speak of the whole.

For example, baptism represents the whole of conversion in the opening verses of Romans 6. Paul is speaking of conversion, but he mentions only baptism to identify this critical spiritual transition.

In Galatians 3:2 the gift of the Spirit is used to refer to conversion as a whole. Paul asks his readers: "Did you receive the Spirit by doing the works of the law or by believing what you heard?" The question, which refers to their conversion, or their initial coming to God or faith, could have been worded in any of various ways. "Did you receive forgiveness by observing the law?" "Were you baptized because you did the works of the law?" Paul speaks of the whole conversion experience through a single dimension of it—in this case the reception of the Spirit.

In the same way, it would not be inappropriate to speak of becoming a Christian as *joining the family of God*. If someone were to say that she has joined the family of God, we would know that she has become a Christian believer.

I can also speak of becoming a Christian as transferring my love and allegiance to Christ—as a decision to follow him. Here faith and repentance are understood and taken for granted, and the focus is on a resolution to live in obedience to God.

Consequently, when the Bible refers to the conversion experience through *one* of the components, we must not be reductionist and conclude that that particular element is all that is necessary "to be saved." While conversion is complex and has many different elements, any one of these elements can represent the whole of the experience.

When the Philippian jailer asked how he could be saved, Paul simply advised him, "Believe on the Lord Jesus Christ, and you will be saved." Some use this to argue that we can ask no more of a potential convert. But try making a similar deduction from Acts 6:7: "a great many of the priests became obedient to the faith." Could we say that all we should ask for is obedience? Surely the priests in question also believed. The focus is simply different from that of the Philippian account. In each case a different dimension of conversion is used to summarize the whole.

These elements are not stages or phases of a conversion. As already noted, while each of these elements or components is important, we cannot call them "stages" or "phases" of conversion. They may be experienced as such, but they can actually come in virtually any order; each conversion is different. The more conversion narratives I read, the more it seems the experience of conversion could begin at just about any point in the spectrum. The wonder of this is that different people experience conversion in dramatically different forms. The order in which the elements are experienced varies. And the degree to which particular elements are pivotal in a conversion also varies, depending on previous life experience, religious upbringing, personality and temperament, and cultural, social and other circumstances.

It seems logical that water baptism would precede the reception of the gift of the Spirit and that a prayer for the gift of the Spirit would be made *after* a person has been baptized in water. But Cornelius's experience is a reminder that the order is secondary to the need for all dimensions to be in place eventually, and it further displays that water baptism and Spirit baptism are complementary but distinct.

The goal of all of this reflection is to encourage a way of speaking about conversion in our Christian communities that fosters thorough conversions and leads to spiritual maturity. But we also need a language of conversion that frees us from forcing one pattern of experience on everyone. We do not need to. In fact when we try to force a particular pattern, we are seeking to manipulate something that is, and should be, entirely under the control of the Spirit of God.

Paul Helm stresses that conversion's elements are not stages; he prefers to speak of them as *strands* in a conversion: "To talk of conversion in terms of strands rather than stages has the advantage of making clear that these strands are conditions in the logical rather than the causal sense. They are not conditions which have to be fulfilled in order for a person to be converted; rather they are what being converted *means*."[12]

The elements are not all of the same "kind." The seven elements are not all components or elements of conversion in the same way. The following distinctions need to be made.

First, as already noted, belief and repentance stand at the center and form the core of the experience.

Second, some elements are located or find their foci within the person: belief, repentance, trust and the transfer of allegiance. These are dispositions, attitudes or actions that lie at the center of every person and find expression in mind, heart and will.

Third, these four dispositions or actions are complemented and sustained by three more external realities that constitute the very grace or the means of grace that enable these inner dispositions and actions to be effective: reception of the gift of the Spirit, water baptism and incorporation into Christian community.

All seven elements are essential. We do a disservice to ourselves and others when we minimize what it means to be a follower of Jesus. Sometimes we find that either in our own pilgrimage or in the experience of another, one dimension takes on special prominence. One person may initially come to God primarily through a discovery of truth; for another the piv-

---

[12]Helm, *Beginnings*, p. 88.

otal element is coming into fellowship with the Christian community, or choosing radical submission to the lordship of Christ, or experiencing new freedom through a knowledge of God's forgiveness. Well and good. But eventually, for a person to be fully converted and have a good foundation for a continued experience of the transforming grace of God, all seven elements need to be encountered and experienced. Each element is essential. If any is missing, a person's conversion, while meaningful, lacks thoroughness, at least with respect to that particular element.

Further, and perhaps more to the point, if a person is missing resolution in one area, that lack has the potential to sabotage the whole and thus becomes a weak point in the conversion experience, a point of real vulnerability.

For example, a lack of genuine emotional conversion will eventually sabotage the intellectual and the moral. A failure to learn and practice obedience will eventually undermine our understanding. Lack of a corporate connection will eventually leave us without the vital sustaining grace of the community.

Moral transformation without a renewal of affect will generally lead to rigid legalism and intolerance or lack of patience with others. A conversion that is purely intellectual (and thus one-dimensional) creates a cerebralist; often these kinds of converts become one-dimensional crusaders for "truth." Donald Gelpi, working with the Lonergan framework for conversion, speaks of a fundamentalist as one who has had an intellectual conversion but not a religious transformation.[13]

Thus those who are responsible for the spiritual well-being of others, whether as pastors, teachers or spiritual mentors, might consider undertaking a spiritual diagnosis when beginning a relationship with a new Christian. Start by determining if there is a good foundation on which to build. Has the person experienced every dimension of Christian conversion? If not, what is missing and needs to be appropriated? For if even one of the seven dimensions has not been appropriated or acted upon, the spiritual growth of the Christian will be crippled.

We are instruments of God through which others come to knowledge of God and are led into Christian faith. Integrity in our task demands that we not determine our success by the numbers of people who through us become followers of Jesus. We are true to our calling only when we are

---

[13]Donald L. Gelpi, *Charism and Sacrament: A Theology of Christian Conversion* (London: SPCK, 1976), p. 21.

faithful to the gospel in all of its demands. Then we will preach a costly discipleship. Fewer will respond favorably to our message. Some will turn away. When people make an initial faith decision to follow Jesus, we will not be skeptical, but neither will we assume more has transpired than has actually happened. We will recognize that if the decision is not followed by repentance, submission to Christ, baptism, the filling of the Spirit and incorporation into congregational life, the decision will mean little and perhaps nothing in the end. Indeed it may be worse than nothing, for that initial movement of faith could become a kind of inoculation, leaving the person with an impression of having come to Christian faith but actually impeding progress toward a full experience of the transforming work of God's grace.

We must, then, emphasize a thorough notion of Christian conversion in all of its dimensions. Only then are we faithful to the gospel and to those we assist toward a knowledge of the gospel. Only then can we, in our own experience and as pastors and teachers, ensure that the Christian community is established on a strong spiritual foundation on which renewal and ongoing transformation can be built.

As noted in a survey of conversion narratives in an earlier chapter, the seven dimensions of conversion are rarely if ever experienced in a single, dramatic event. Emotionally and spiritually we are complex creatures. It takes time to come into a radical reorientation of our lives—to understand the character of the gospel, the nature and extent of the demands of Christ and their implications, and to find the emotional capacity to experience such a comprehensive reorientation.

Some dimensions of the gospel we may not be able to appreciate fully until we make an initial step of repentance. Some cannot submit to the lordship of Christ until they have been assured of his love, and assurance of the forgiveness and love of God is not gained in a single moment. *Ideally* we should be able to believe with certainty that we are loved. But if a person has had a difficult childhood or later experiences that have left emotional scars, he may find it very hard to believe with confidence that he is loved. And the assurance that we are loved is essential if we are to surrender all that we have to God. So confidence that we are loved and surrender to the will of God could be separated in time. Both are essential to a full conversion, but they are not necessarily appropriated easily and simultaneously.

For Wesley, who made a radical commitment to holiness and to the will of God, thirteen years passed before he felt an assurance of God's love and forgiveness. And Wesley is by no means unique. Most Christian believers recognize that their coming to Christ was a series of events, decisions and actions. Sometimes there was an initial decision followed by a time of spiritual apathy. Others speak of their baptism, perhaps as young teens, as having foreshadowed a mature commitment to Christ that came years later. None of these sequences or time delays are problems if we recognize that conversion is a series of events in which different dimensions of conversion are appropriated.

The tragic fact is that many are misevangelized and misinitiated into the Christian faith and community because some approaches to evangelism leave people with only bits and pieces of what it means to come under the reign of God. The result is a poor foundation for growth and maturity in the Christian life.

It is worth noting, however, that sometimes a person will be incapable of embracing one of the seven elements. Generally the obstacle is emotional and psychological, perhaps as serious as clinical depression. This does not mean that all seven elements are not needed in his or her conversion; rather, such an obstacle may indicate a need for professional psychological care.

Each element of conversion is the fruit of the Spirit's work. Throughout the series of events that constitute a conversion, the Spirit of the Living God remains sovereign, and each element in the conversion comes from the Spirit's work. This means of course that we necessarily experience conversion in response to God, but more: each element of conversion comes in response to the illumination or convicting ministry or comfort or call of the Spirit of God.

We need to recover something of the Puritan notion of conversion as discernment of and response to the prompting of the Spirit. We can rightly assume that the Spirit is at work in our lives; a conversion is a response to that work, rather than the initiation or trigger of it. It comes in response to divine initiative; it is neither initiated by human will nor sustained by human effort.

The Spirit works differently in each life. Each person is a complex being, and our lives are complicated. We are complex creatures; religious experience is multidimensional, multifaceted. And the Spirit does not work in the same way in all people. In the exercise of articulating a conversion narrative we come to terms with the complexity of our own lives and then identify how the Spirit of God has chosen to work and woo us within *our* particular circumstances, opportunities, difficulties and possibilities.

This also means that conversion is not merely a matter of checking seven items off a list. It involves discerning how the Spirit is operative in our lives and how these elements have been or are being woven together in a unique pattern of experience.

Conversion is essentially an adult experience. All of this means that conversion is essentially an adult experience. This is not to discount or minimize the significance of the spiritual experiences of children. There is no doubt that children can make profound and significant spiritual choices in response to a genuine awareness of the love, grace and goodness of God. Many have testified of how in childhood they were deeply conscious of God's presence with them and the assurance of God's love and care.

However, we must not confuse this with the New Testament idea of conversion. When it comes to choosing to be a disciple of Jesus—deciding that we are going to walk in radical obedience, as slaves of righteousness and not of sin, and as women and men who in the fullness of the Spirit will live in union with Christ—we are necessarily speaking of an adult resolve and experience.

If a young child were to tell her mother that the Lord told her to go to bed at 9:30 when her mother had just informed her that it was 7:30 and thus bedtime, the mother would assuredly remind the daughter that for now she is living under parental authority and there will be tangible consequences if that authority is not obeyed!

Some young people are adults prematurely, due to the fractured or conflicted nature of their family experiences. Some relatively young persons are prematurely forced to bear adult responsibility for their own lives and the lives of others. But this is not the way we are designed to live. Rather, we are designed as children to live under and dwell secure in the love and spiritual protection of our parents.

I hope my sons will mature into young men who will in one sense no longer view me as father but recognize that I am their brother in God's family. I hope they will know that they have one Father, one Lord, to whom they owe allegiance, loyalty and in whom they ultimately find their identity and security. This transition is the same process by which an adolescent becomes an adult. Thus coming to faith may be part of the adolescent experience of becoming an adult.

Conversion, then, is an essentially adult experience. This has great significance for baptism in traditions where believers' baptism is practiced: how old should a person be to receive baptism? Much more will be said in the chapters that follow about this and other questions surrounding second-generation conversions.

Assurance is found in the interplay of the elements. A vital theme of conversion within the evangelical heritage is the principle of assurance. Evangelicals have consistently argued that Christians should be able to experience a heartfelt assurance that they are "saved." For some this means certainty of understanding or knowledge: I know I am a Christian if I have a deep conviction that Jesus is indeed the Son of the Living God. For others, assurance is found in an experience; many Puritans, for example, had confidence that they were children of God, among "the elect," only if they had had a particular kind of religious experience. Others seek assurance in the quality of their lives—they are indeed God's children because they can testify to their identification with the purposes of God.

Yet genuine Christian believers can be vulnerable at any of these points. I grieve when I meet Christians who doubt that they are God's children because they have failed God in some way, or because they have not had what they perceive to be the right kind of conversion experience, or because they live with doubts. I would argue that the assurance we seek depends not on one element or one particular experience, nor on the fact that one has prayed a particular prayer or appropriated a particular biblical promise. Instead our inner confidence rests on the interplay of all the elements as they support and reinforce one another. This is particularly the case in the interplay of the four subjective elements as they are reinforced and sustained by the three external elements. More will be said on this when we come to a more comprehensive examination of these elements.

No particular element is necessarily linked directly to God's justifying grace. With this understanding of conversion, we cannot link the justifying grace of God with any particular element or even, perhaps, any particular time in our lives. As I noted earlier, building on Helm's thought, the work of God is by its very nature beyond human consciousness. God's work is subtle and often mysterious. All we can attest to is the structure or character of our response to the divine initiative.

This means that we can only and finally give witness to the underside of the tapestry of God's work in our lives. Though we can see the threads of God's grace woven through the contours of our experience, in the end all we can really identify are our own actions, responses, feelings and attitudes.

Therefore we resist the inclination to say that when we did this or that, God in response did something. We resist the thought that "God saved us" in response to our prayer or our commitment or our baptism. Rather, our actions came in response to God's gracious initiative. And though we cannot claim to know God's saving grace apart from our actions, God's actions necessarily precede our response.

Spiritual formation is the outworking of a conversion. If there are elements in a conversion, it follows that there are elements in a program of formation. Indeed spiritual formation is in reality nothing more than the outworking of our conversion. We begin well, and then we embrace a pattern of formation that fosters spiritual transformation. And the elements of a program of spiritual formation will ideally be in continuity with the elements of conversion.

First, transformation requires the renewal of the mind. Just as conversion takes the mind seriously and calls us to an encounter with truth, formation will include teaching that builds on belief as the point of departure. Christian growth is sustained by a lifelong program of study, learning and meditation. It is an encounter with truth. We begin with belief, but then in coming to Christian faith we become learners.

Second, transformation requires comprehensive turning from sin. Conversion includes repentance—but this is only a beginning. An effective program of formation enables people to understand the character of sin in their lives and to practice the discipline of confession, remaining constantly in a posture of turning from sin.

Third, transformation comes as we grow in faith and in capacity for unqualified trust and dependence on God, most evident in our capacity to live with joy in a painful world. Conversion includes an affective component; spiritual formation then builds on this beginning and seeks to foster our capacity to live in radical dependence on Christ as we grow in joy.

Fourth, conversion includes submission of the will. And then throughout our Christian walk we are regularly confronted with our need to obey and to find freedom in obedience, the freedom that comes in saying, "Your will be done."

Fifth, just as there is a sacramental action that we associate with our initiation into Christian faith, there is a sacramental action of nurture that sustains the Christian faith: Holy Communion.

Sixth, conversion includes reception of the gift of the Spirit. It follows that spiritual formation includes enabling women and men to grow in their capacity to respond intentionally to the voice of Jesus heard through the inner witness of the Spirit.

And finally, if conversion includes becoming a participant in the common life of the community of faith, the whole of our Christian life will be marked by our desire and ability to love one another, to grow in our capacity to love and be loved, to forgive and to serve others.

Conversion is never an end; it is a beginning and a means to an end. Thus it must be followed by a program of spiritual formation that should mirror the very nature and contours of a Christian conversion.

Conversion as a Complex Experience

Conversion is a series of events that in isolation may not seem to be particularly significant, but that when taken together have great personal significance. The seven elements, experienced over time and interconnected with each other, reach a certain critical mass at which point their sum constitutes something that is radical, life-changing and transforming.

This is wonderfully expressed in the biographical reflections of Anne Lamott, particularly in her image of lily pads:

> My coming to faith did not start with a leap but rather a series of staggers from what seemed like one safe place to another. Like lily pads, round and green, these places summoned me and then held me while I grew. Each prepared for me the next leaf on which I would land, and in this way I moved across the swamp of doubt and fear. When I look back on some of these early resting places—the boisterous home of Catholics, the soft armchair of the Christian Science mom, adoption by ardent Jews—I can see how flimsy and indirect a path they make. Yet each step brought me closer to the verdant pad of faith on which I somehow stay afloat today.[14]

Lamott's experience and imagery capture the reality that conversion for most, if not all, is a series of events and moments. Some of these events move us forward; but just as significant are times in which we are hardly conscious of the Spirit's presence in our lives.

Some, while accepting my thesis that conversion is complex, an extended series of events, will nevertheless resist this critical analysis of specific components of religious experience. But we must give analytical attention to conversion. As Helm suggests, no two football games are alike, even though we certainly know when something is or is not a football game. In the same way, though no two conversions are alike, conversion is a matter of life and death; we need to know with certitude that we are speaking of and experiencing a *Christian* conversion.

---

[14]Anne Lamott, *Traveling Mercies: Some Thoughts on Faith* (New York: Pantheon, 1999), p. 3.

Further, no one would suggest that a clear and intentional precision regarding rules destroys a football game or even makes it less unpredictable or exciting. On the contrary, the rules of the game ensure that the game happens in a way that is both entertaining and fair. Referees are very precise about adhering to the boundaries and rules in order to protect the integrity of the game. Similarly, we must be clear about the boundaries and nature of a Christian conversion to protect the integrity of the experience.

The outline of the elements gives those who are not sure of their experience, or who are in process of conversion, reference markers to guide, encourage and show them what they need to be attentive to as they respond to the prompting of the Spirit. It also can provide Christian communities with a clear idea of what they need to attend to as they foster and facilitate conversions. Christian communities need to respond carefully and intentionally to those who seek to know Christ Jesus and respond to his love. To do this, we need to have a clear biblical understanding of what makes for a Christian conversion.

Inevitably, though, the question arises, particularly for evangelicals: When is a person in? How do we know if someone is in or out? If conversion is a series a events—lily pads, to use the Lamott image—then when is a person actually "saved"? This question is usually driven by an anxiety to know if a person is on their way "to heaven." Such a concern reflects the assumption that conversion is a simple decision to follow Jesus, and this idea of conversion is equated with the gospel. When can we know for certain that a person is a child of God? What happens if a person has only six of the seven components? Are they saved? Is such a person a child of God?

First, a multifaceted concept of conversion seeks to appropriate the whole New Testament teaching on conversion. As we consider the teaching of our Lord in Matthew, Mark and Luke, and the example of the early church in Acts, it seems clear that conversion involves much more than just a simple decision.

Second, we must recognize that the church is often weak and lacking in spiritual depth and vitality, with little impact on society and culture. The number of people who claim to have been Christians for years but who lack spiritual depth and maturity is reason for alarm. Consider the possibility that at least part of the root of this problem is a weak understanding of Christian conversion.

Third and most important, the gospel, rather than being weakened by the perspective I have outlined, is actually preserved. This understanding of conversion strives to underline the radical change that occurs in the life of a new believer.

So then, how do we respond when asked whether a particular person is "saved"? I contend that we are not in a position to make such a decision or come to such a verdict. First, the question is based on the assumption that our great concern is to be sure that people are going to heaven. While this is a legitimate concern, when it is our *only* concern we are left with a one-dimensional, misguided notion of conversion. It is better to recognize that conversion is the first stage in the Christian way. If the first stage is experienced to the full, it will be a good foundation for vital spiritual development. If it is bypassed, then the rest will suffer.

Within that first stage, we can assume that we are on the road and truly accepted by God and granted his salvation. But if the initial act of faith or the initial decision is not completed by all the dimensions of conversion, then it will die like a seed in rocky soil.

God alone ultimately knows whether we are on the way. Our need is to move as intentionally and fully as possible through all seven dimensions. An evangelist or pastor who does not lead a person to all seven fails in his or her calling. By neglecting to lead a person through the whole experience of conversion, a pastor, in effect, allows rocks and thorns to crowd out the initial decision of the new believer.

An individual who refuses a particular dimension of conversion needs to be asked some tough and honest questions. If he resists baptism, or a full surrender to the lordship of Christ, or the gift of the Holy Spirit, then the initial decision is put into question. But if he is moving toward an appropriation of all seven elements, there is no reason to hurry or push or force the matter. When he is ready, he is ready.

Only when all seven elements are in place will a young believer be capable of spiritual growth and maturity. A full and thorough conversion is the essential foundation for a full experience of the transforming grace of God. Conversion is the prerequisite for transformation.

The question "But when and at what moment is someone saved?" assumes our capacity to know empirically that another person is a child of God. Rarely do actual life circumstances give us the freedom and confidence to state definitely when someone was regenerated or born from above. This information is known ultimately only to God.

When I was in seminary, theology professor Dr. James Cheung gave us a helpful image. He compared a conversion to an air flight across an international border, perhaps between Canada and the United States. A passenger approaches the pilot midflight and asks at what exact moment the airplane will be crossing the border. But assuredly the pilot cannot know the precise moment. And if the passenger insists that she absolutely *must* know when the border is crossed, the pilot will say in frustration, "I cannot tell you the exact moment, but when we have landed you will know for certain that you have crossed the border."

In the same way, I suggest that the actual moment of our justification is not known to us; yet we can know when we have crossed from death to life, from being a people of no mercy to a people of mercy (1 Pet 2:10). We know it because we see the markers that are *behind* us. Still, even in retrospect we may not ever know the exact moment when we were justified.

There is a point at which we recognize that we have become Christians—at the end of the process, or perhaps at some point in the process, when life events and the decisions we have made reach a certain critical mass and we know that we have turned a corner. When we come to this point, the response should be joy, of course, but not somehow thinking that we have "arrived." Rather, thankful for God's grace to us thus far, we can accept that we have had a good beginning, a good place to start.

7

Four Internal Actions of the Christian Convert

Intellectual, Penitential, Affective & Volitional

We come now to a more extensive examination of the seven elements; each of them will be considered in its own right. The prevailing question will be how conversion establishes a foundation from which a person will mature in Christian faith.

Though each element will be considered individually, none of them stands alone. They are distinct but inseparable, and thus at regular points we need to consider how each is dependent on the others, how each reinforces and intersects with the others. For example, teaching is essential for growth in understanding; there is an intellectual dimension to both conversion and spiritual growth. However, Matthew 28:19-20 says teaching is *toward obedience*. There is no authentic intellectual growth that does not nurture genuine obedience, a transformation of behavior enabling us to live out our allegiance to Christ. Similarly, in Romans 6 baptism is linked to the transfer of allegiance. So though each of the following elements will be considered individually, they are to be understood as inseparable.

Taking Our Minds Seriously

The gospel is good news, liberating truth that intersects our lives and potentially gives us a radically new way of thinking, seeing and responding to our world. As good news, it is truth: an encounter with reality—truth without illusion or misunderstanding—that affects the very ground of our being. Conversion thus has a distinctively cognitive dimension; true evangelism includes a proclamation of truth.

Conversion comes in an encounter with truth—the gospel of the Lord Jesus Christ. A basic New Testament assumption is that only in coming to a new understanding, centered in Jesus Christ, can a person know God's saving grace. There is no conversion without a fundamental change of mind—or, at the very least, an understanding of the truth of the gospel that can be owned and embraced.

Belief, worldview and transformation. Evangelicals commonly assume that it is possible to become a Christian on hearing one simple presentation of the gospel. Is this possible? Paul Hiebert, having asked this question regarding a Papayya Hindu, worshiper of Vishnu, responds, "This depends, in part, on what we mean by the term Christian."[1]

Hiebert affirms that the Hindu certainly has experienced regeneration and become a member of the family of God, and so the answer would be yes. But if we are asking whether the person has the capacity to communicate his or her newfound faith effectively to another, the answer is surely no. Hiebert's conclusion: in establishing new Christian communities, we must distinguish between the essential minimal understanding required for an authentic conversion and the understanding that is necessary for mature Christian discipleship.

The ultimate goal of such mature understanding, Hiebert says, includes a thoroughly Christian worldview. Thus for a Papayya Hindu to become a Christian means not only belief that Jesus Christ is God incarnate who has died for sin and freed humans from condemnation; it means that in time the structures, categories and assumptions of his or her thinking need to be changed. That is, the ultimate goal is that the convert come to think Christianly. If the gospel does not ultimately transform this person's worldview, it "remains surface and transitory."[2] And in that case it is a "conversion" only in a very limited and individual sense; it does not

---

[1]Paul G. Hiebert, "Conversion and World View Transformation," *International Journal of Frontier Missions* 14, no. 2 (1997): 83.
[2]Ibid., p. 84.

lead to transformation in either the individual or communal/societal sense.

For Christian faith to take root in a society, it must come as the result of a comprehensive transformation of understanding. Hiebert contends that we must go beyond mere beliefs and behavior to a radical Christianization of worldview: "If we convert only beliefs and behavior, in time the world-view will take the Christian beliefs captive."[3]

The importance of the mind in evangelism and witness. Worldview transformation begins with a clear and decisive wedge of knowledge and understanding through conversion, a wedge that will ultimately transform the whole. That is, the way our minds are engaged through conversion establishes the tone and base from which our whole understanding is ultimately transformed.

People will not experience ultimate transformation unless we take the human mind seriously, affirming from the beginning that understanding matters, that truth makes a difference and that therefore true conversion includes, and is inconceivable without, a clear and decisive intellectual encounter with the gospel.

By taking the mind seriously in evangelism we establish a beachhead from which the individual is encouraged to take her mind seriously throughout her Christian pilgrimage. In Matthew 28 Jesus calls his followers to make disciples by baptizing them and teaching them obedience. It follows, then, that true evangelism enables a person to become a learner, one who responds to teaching; conversion establishes the basis from which this learning will happen.

Christian faith is a response to truth proclaimed and heard. We cannot know God apart from an encounter with truth and a consequent change of thinking that is reflected in a belief in truth. Conversion necessarily pivots on this element; it is a prerequisite for the other dimensions of conversion. But we are seeking not merely initial belief but a belief that will lead ultimately to the embracing of a biblical worldview; to what Lesslie Newbigin calls a conversion of the mind as well as of the will and the heart.[4]

When I say that this is a prerequisite for conversion, I do not mean that every conversion begins with an encounter with truth. Dorothy Day's cognitive conversion, for example, was made possible by what was already

---

[3]Ibid.
[4]Lesslie Newbigin, *Foolishness to the Greeks: The Gospel and Western Culture* (Grand Rapids, Mich.: Eerdmans, 1986), p. 94.

happening to her affectively. Rather, what I intend to stress is that a Christian conversion pivots around a change of mind, and apart from this change of mind all other aspects of the conversion experience would be anchorless. Newbigin is not minimizing the place of will and affect, but stressing that most basically conversion has to do with the way that we make sense of the world, with understanding.[5]

Conversion is believing certain things to be true. But what constitutes the minimum intellectual understanding, the essential understanding without which a genuine conversion is not possible? It is not that we want to be minimalists; it is merely that we need to affirm our point of departure. We want to begin well. What does a person need to know, understand and believe in order to know the saving grace of Jesus and open up to a full conversion of the mind?

If we are too minimalistic, the potential convert merely incorporates new truth into an old and faulty worldview. Hiebert points to Simon the converted sorcerer (Acts 8:9-24), the sons of Sceva (Acts 19:11-16), the people of Lystra (Acts 14:8-13) and Malta (Acts 28:3-6) as examples of potential converts who merely turned their new "Christian" understanding into another form of their previous belief systems.[6]

At the same time, if we overstate what a new Christian needs to know, becoming a Christian becomes equated with nothing more than absorbing comprehensive catechistical instruction. We need to affirm the minimum as the point of departure from which a worldview is ultimately transformed.

The bottom line is found in an understanding of who Jesus is. Christians generally agree that the crucial point of departure must be defined in light of the person of Christ. So conversion comes with some level of intellectual understanding and acceptance of the unique identity and contribution of Jesus Christ. Everything rests on hearing, understanding and believing that Jesus Christ is Lord, the One who was uniquely sent by God and who, as the Son of God, provides life and hope through the cross and resurrection.

Reason, tradition and faith. This is the minimum then, the essential point of departure in the conversion of the mind. But we must also con-

---

[5]See George R. Hunsberger, *Bearing the Witness of the Spirit: Lesslie Newbigin's Theology of Cultural Plurality* (Grand Rapids, Mich.: Eerdmans, 1998), pp. 159-61, for an insightful analysis of Newbigin's theology of conversion.
[6]Hiebert, "Conversion and World View Transformation," p. 83.

sider how a person comes to belief. What makes belief possible? Some, for example, would assume that this understanding comes in response to a rational presentation or apologetic: one believes because one has been presented with clear and irrefutable evidence.

But increasingly we are appreciating that reason operates neither alone nor autonomously. Our understanding of truth cannot happen apart from a context that enables us to see, appreciate and respond to truth. As Newbigin says, "Every kind of systematic thought has to begin from a starting point. It has to begin from taking some things for granted."[7] In other words, something is accepted as a given before we can come to understanding. There is no such thing as a purely objective stance from which we can consider truth—any truth, let alone the truth of the gospel. Again, Newbigin writes, "reason does not operate in a vacuum. The power of the human mind to think rationally is only developed in a tradition which itself depends on the experience of previous generations."[8]

Reason, then, functions in the context of a tradition. If this is so, then conversion, properly speaking, includes not only affirming the unique identity and work of Christ, as noted above, but also accepting the tradition that has borne and is bearing this gospel. That is, we accept not only the central message of Christ Jesus but also, of necessity, the tradition that bears the knowledge and experience of Jesus. We place our trust—our faith—in the tradition, for, as Newbigin puts it, "no learning takes place except within a tradition whose authority is accepted as guidance for exploration."[9]

William J. Abraham offers a noteworthy insight regarding the interplay of the church and evangelism. He suggests that Christian initiation cannot avoid central and defining theological proposals. Further, these proposals are not worked out individually—each person considering divine revelation to seek to know the truth. Rather, the church has wonderful resources for evangelism and conversion in its ancient creeds. Thus "it is the church's responsibility to hand on the substance of its intellectual heritage in the form of a creed; moreover, the creed to be handed over is that of the councils of the early church."[10]

---

[7]Lesslie Newbigin, *The Gospel in a Pluralist Society* (Grand Rapids, Mich.: Eerdmans, 1989), p. 8.
[8]Ibid., pp. 8-9.
[9]Ibid., p. 12.
[10]William J. Abraham, *The Logic of Evangelism* (Grand Rapids, Mich.: Eerdmans, 1989), p. 145.

When we pass on the confessional tradition of the church, we enable a new convert to own the truth in community and embrace the understanding of Christ that is rooted in the tradition—the only way that message can be known and embraced. Thus, says Abraham, "handing over the Scripture as the sole content of faith is inadequate. The Bible cannot do what a creed does, nor was it ever intended to do so. . . . It is much too big and unwieldy as a summary of the faith."[11]

What is needed is something concise, simple, accessible and clear, open to minimal levels of interpretation, having the capacity to anchor faith and enable the growth and development of the intellectual life. "The creed," Abraham argues, "provides a basic summary of the intellectual structure of the Christian mind: it supplies a map that lays out the fundamental contours of how the Christian thinks about God, about Christ, and about the Holy Spirit."[12]

I would go so far as to say that baptism should come only after an encounter with the Apostles' Creed, for example, and that it should include an affirmation of the creedal faith. In so doing we would, incidentally, return to the way the creeds were used in the early church.

It is not that our traditions cannot be challenged, at least as they find expression in the diverse denominations that make up the contemporary church. We often need to urge one another to think more carefully about the spiritual traditions that have shaped our understanding and practice. In many cases the traditions in which we have been raised need to be reformed. But we seek the grand theological and spiritual tradition of the church, particularly as expressed in the ancient church creeds. And these cannot be known and embraced except through actual, visible and tangible church communities. These may be less than perfect expressions of the tradition, but they are the means by which we will come to know the truth. They are the means by which we are enabled to engage the ancient Christian faith.

If this understanding of the interplay between evangelism and the ancient creeds is valid, the implications are profound. First, it means that the early creeds should be a primary point of reference in our preaching. Many contemporary Christian congregations neglect the Scriptures, which is tragic, of course. But there are others that claim to preach nothing but the Scriptures. They would insist that their preaching is nothing but the exposition of scriptural texts. While this practice is surely com-

---

[11]Ibid., p. 150.
[12]Ibid.

mendable, the potential problem is that the congregation sees only the trees, only the text of Scripture, and never learns how to worship, serve and live in the light of the big picture, the creedal faith of the Christian community. Ideally, then, we would preach the texts of Scripture quite intentionally through the lens of our confessional heritage, the ancient tradition from which these very sacred texts come.

Second, in drawing on the creeds the posture of our learning and understanding is humility—the grace and meekness of attending to the wisdom of a previous age. We recognize that we do not have rational power over the gospel and that our understanding never comes through either our own investigation (scientific) or mystical encounter (direct revelation). Rather, we all know the truth through another, and particularly through the teachings of a community of faith.

Third, the link between evangelism and the early creeds has another implication: the credibility of the message is linked to the credibility of those who bear the message. An intellectual presentation of the gospel never happens within a vacuum; it does not stand alone. Understanding is possible only when we trust in the tradition that bears the message; and this by definition means trust in the ones who bear the tradition and proclaim its message. We cannot present the truth of the gospel with integrity unless and until we are living it out credibly. The integrity of the verbal proclamation is sustained by the integrity of the community of faith that bears the truth, lives the truth and from that context proclaims the truth.

The Christian tradition has credibility only if it is embodied in communities of faith that bear, at the very least, four distinctive marks. (1) We witness to the truth not only in word but also in deed. Our actions authenticate our words and become the context in which our words are heard. (2) Our words are authenticated by our common life together, our capacity to love one another within Christian community. (3) In the midst of a messy and broken world, the Christian community is marked by joy. This persistent joy makes it impossible to avoid the truth that is proclaimed by such a community. (4) The Christian community visibly demonstrates what it means to be wise. Western urban societies are marked by an urgent desire for wisdom. It is wise men and women who will, through their life and behavior, point to the viability of the Christian gospel.

An encounter with Jesus. We need to acknowledge one essential qualifier to everything that has been said thus far. In the end, conversion is never simply a matter of believing something to be true; it never comes merely from comparing two sets of beliefs in order to embrace the one that seems to have the most logical coherence. The heart of Christian conversion is a personal encounter with Jesus Christ. It is not merely an encounter with a system of beliefs or propositions. It is an encounter with a crucified and risen Christ who calls for our worship and submission. From such a beginning, our minds are engaged with truth that forms and reforms our thinking, enabling us to live truthfully.

The Freedom of Confession

We cannot speak of the gospel or of conversion without reference to repentance and, following that, the forgiveness of sins.[13] While there is debate among Christian theologians regarding the order of faith and repentance (Calvin, for example, contends that faith precedes repentance),[14] none question the vital place of both.

The New Testament assumes that conversion includes a penitential dimension—repentance and a repudiation of sin. Conversion is as much a turning from sin as a turning to Jesus. For it to be a genuine encounter with Christ, it must involve true repentance. Repentance is more than remorse; it is also a resolve to turn from sin out of genuine grief over sin. It necessarily includes a rejection of sin as a habit of life. Repentance enables conversion to be truly radical—a conversion of the whole person, making change and transformation possible.

We will not appreciate the crucial place of repentance unless we take sin seriously. In fact we must begin with the assumption that conversion is necessary because of sin. For conversion to be authentic, then, there must be a confrontation with sin and turning from it. In repentance we acknowledge sin, receive forgiveness and repudiate sin. This is what makes conversion a *turning;* it is a turning from sin.

Dissecting repentance will help us appreciate it more fully. Repentance begins with conviction. The first part of repentance is the realization that we are sinners in need of grace. In the graphic phrase of Acts 2:37, Peter's hearers were "cut to the heart" when they heard his proclamation of the gospel. Their consciences were stricken. It was not an emotional impulse or irrational feeling; rather, as Paul Helm stresses, they were struck by the realization that they were guilty before God.[15] Every conversion includes

---

[13]On repentance and conversion see John Calvin *Institutes of the Christian Religion* 3.3.1.
[14]Ibid., 3.3.2.
[15]Paul Helm, *The Beginnings: Word and Spirit in Conversion* (Edinburgh: Banner of Truth, 1986), p. 30.

conviction of sin. Where this is not explicit in a New Testament conversion narrative it may be inferred.

Further, true repentance includes confession. In confession, usually but not necessarily through verbal acknowledgment before God, we take responsibility for our sin, our behavior, our rebellion. We acknowledge that we are convicted of sin and that we are responsible in the face of God and God's truth for our behavior. We reject excuses; we do not claim extenuating circumstances. We acknowledge our guilt.

Then also, repentance includes repudiation. Helm asks, "Conviction of sin is a necessary element in Christian conversion, but is it sufficient?"[16] He goes on to show that the Scriptures offer some compelling examples of persons who though convinced of their sin were not truly converted. The rich young man of Matthew 19, though acknowledging his need for Christ and for eternal life, walked away from the Lord when he heard the call to discipleship; Felix (in Acts 24), trembled before the apostle Paul, deeply troubled by this man, his message and his own conscience. Helm says Felix knew that Paul was speaking truth—indeed the very word of God—but it had no lasting impact:

> Felix was impressed by the word of God. He realized, at least fleetingly, his own shortcomings when measured against the righteousness of God. He recognized these matters not as speculative possibilities but as truths which made him tremble. But then he put them to one side. His old nature reasserted itself. He became interested only in the money which he could make out of having Paul released.[17]

So Felix was convinced of his sin; but he was not converted. It is tempting to say that both of these men felt some sorrow for sin; but actually the rich young ruler's sorrow was for what it would cost for him to follow Jesus. In other cases people are not truly sorry for sin; they are sorry for the consequences of their sin. Felix feared judgment; it was judgment that stirred sorrow in his heart, because he saw in Paul's words the truth that he would have to face God with his guilt. But this did not lead him to turn from his sin. It is probably not incidental that money was an issue in the case of both the rich young man and Felix.

Therefore we must stress the vital place of repudiation of sin. As Helm emphasizes, "Conviction involves an awareness of what sin is in God's sight coupled with a resolve to hate it and to forsake it because it is dis-

---

[16]Ibid., p. 32.
[17]Ibid., p. 35.

pleasing to God." Without repudiation "all other conviction of sin is likely to prove temporary and abortive."[18] True conviction of sin moves past sorrow over the consequences of sin to a deep desire and resolve to turn from sin, to repudiate it, to move contrary to it.

And this may be the actual genius of a conversion experience, at least in regard to this essential element. Many speak of conversion as though it has brought complete transformation, such that a person is no longer a sinner and no longer needs to be concerned about sin. It is far more helpful and consistent with the biblical testimony to affirm that a convert remains a sinner. Conversion is not instant transformation. In a fully genuine Christian conversion the sins of a person may well remain; however, as Jonathan Edwards notes, they will be "altered." Repentance does not eliminate the convert's sin; rather, as Edwards puts it, "true repentance . . . turns [a] man against his own iniquity."[19]

Helm provides an appropriate caution here. When we do not see what we consider evidence of genuine repentance—conviction along with repudiation—we might be tempted to dismiss someone's professed conviction of sin as having no legitimacy whatsoever. However, even though conviction must be coupled with repudiation, we are never in a position to make a definite judgment. "The fact that a person has undergone a period of conviction of sin, even if it seems to be or has proved to be temporary, provides no conclusive evidence for supposing that God will never grant His regenerating grace to that person in the future."[20]

God works in ways that will continually surprise us; we must not underestimate the power of a seed planted in a heart and mind through a word spoken; at first it may lead to sorrow with no repentance, but in the future it may yet bear fruit. So, Helm insists, we are to be very cautious in making judgments about the spiritual condition of others. We do not know what God is doing and how God is doing his work in his time; "God's regenerating grace often has small beginnings."[21] To dismiss a person because their behavior does not fulfill our expectations is to place ourselves in a position of judgment that belongs only to God.

Many times conversion is spoken of as an experience wherein our sins

---

[18]Ibid., p. 38.
[19]Jonathan Edwards, *Religious Affections*, ed. John E. Smith (New Haven, Conn.: Yale University Press, 1959), p. 342.
[20]Helm, *Beginnings*, p. 39.
[21]Ibid., p. 40.

are forgiven—past, present and future. While we must certainly celebrate the reality that in the cross our sins our forgiven, it is probably most accurate to say that our past sins are forgiven and our whole being is now set against sin. We will sin in the future; and when we recognize our sin, we cannot for a moment think that confession is not necessary because all our sins are already forgiven. Far better is the realization that our being is set against sin and through confession we come back to this fundamental posture of mind and heart. We confess; we are forgiven and once more align ourselves against all that is contrary to the life of God in us.

It is imperative that we do not think of repentance as merely a stage or phase of conversion. If we treat repentance as a phase or stage, the tragic consequence is that after we have once repented we will think we can move on from it. Instead, true conversion leads us to be always conscious of sin and our need to turn from it. Repentance is a strand in our conversion that remains a continuing and vital element of the spiritual life. For without its abiding presence, there is no transformation.

Surprised by Joy

Leo Tolstoy noted that his search for God could not be attributed to his rationality: "This search after a God was not an act of my reason, but a feeling, and I say this advisedly, because it was opposed to my way of thinking; it came from the heart. It was a feeling of dread, or orphanhood, of isolation amid things all apart from me, and of hope in a help I knew not from whom."[22]

For some who come to God, the affective aspect of the experience is the engine that drives the whole conversion process. In fact, though it finds different expressions in various cultures and temperaments, affect plays an integral part in every Christian conversion. The intellectual element provides the conceptual framework in which conversion takes place; and repentance enables conversion to be truly a "turning," a change of direction; but it is through the affective element that conversion can run deep, coming from and taking over the heart. The affective dimension brings integration—whole-person integrity and unity.

The affective element is not merely an emotional experience associated with conversion (though it may well include this). Much evangelical preach-

---

[22]Leo Tolstoy, *My Confession, My Religion: The Gospel in Brief* (New York: 1899), quoted in *Famous Conversions*, ed. Hugh T. Kerr and John M. Mulder (Grand Rapids, Mich.: Eerdmans, 1983), p. 134.

ing and worship seek to create and sustain "the emotional landscape of conversion," as Bruce Hindmarsh has put it.[23] It is one of revivalism's proclivities: using emotion to foster conversion rather than recognizing that the affective is an essential element of conversion. The consequence, in my observation, has been that revivalism has not fostered emotional transformation.

The affect is a necessary element in a Christian conversion, not merely the catalyst or context in which conversion happens—indeed for many it is a critical component in the process of coming to faith in Christ. John Calvin stressed that true faith is not merely a matter of intellect: "faith cannot possibly be disjoined from pious affection."[24] He particularly stresses the importance of inner assurance, which he links to true faith and calls "security of the heart"[25] (something we often associate with Wesley and not with the Reformed tradition). The ministry of the Spirit includes both illuminating the mind and providing "the confirmation of the heart," he says, because "there is more distrust in the heart than blindness in the mind; and it is more difficult to inspire the soul with security than to imbue it with knowledge."[26]

Taking affect seriously. Many evangelical Christians were raised with an assumption that emotions are not only secondary or incidental but positively dangerous. They are *at best* an icing on the cake, to be taken only in moderate quantities. Young people have been taught that feelings are the "caboose" of a train on which facts and faith are the lead cars. Emotions, we were taught, are not to be trusted; they are not a pivotal point of reference. This kind of teaching became particularly insidious in the common assumption that "emotional" people are not to be trusted—and women were generally thought to be more emotional. It was constantly implied that we can trust only reason and rationality, and that we must depend on those who are cerebral and intellectual.

But emotions, far from being incidental, are central to what it means to be human. The mistrust of emotions that many of us learned is ironic because the critical place of affect is deeply embedded in the evangelical heritage. The further irony is that that mistrust was reinforced by a pro-

---

[23]D. Bruce Hindmarsh, *John Newton and the English Evangelical Tradition: Between the Conversion of Wesley and Wilberforce* (New York: Oxford University Press, 1996), p. 321.
[24]Calvin *Institutes* 3.2.8.
[25]Ibid., 3.2.33.
[26]Ibid., 3.2.36.

pensity within revivalism. Revivalism appeals to emotions in order to incite conversion, yet many churches in the revivalistic tradition subsequently teach people to discount emotions in their spiritual lives. But this is not consistent with the evangelical heritage. Both Jonathan Edwards and John Wesley recognized the primary place of emotion and affect, affirming that redemption that does not bring joy is not true redemption, for Christ has come that our joy would be complete. Jesus himself went to the cross for the joy set before him, and he did so with the anticipation that our sorrows would be addressed and that our mourning would be turned to joy.

The emphasis on affect is based on the implicit assumption that we are created to be emotional people and that we live Christianly and with integrity only when we live "from the heart," from the core of our being. So we are learning that the people we can *really* trust are not those who are purely cerebral but those in whom there is an integration of heart and mind, those who know how to live with integrity from the heart and respond emotionally to God, others and their world—and whose lives are lived out of a center of joy, even in a broken world.

The joy of our salvation. The affective element of conversion has diverse expressions. For some it is comparable to the experience of falling in love. June O'Conner notes that Dorothy Day's relationship with Forster Batterham prepared her for what would ultimately be a relationship with God. Although not in isolation from previous experiences of love and affection, "Day's falling in love with Forster [was] profoundly influential . . . in her recognition of and receptivity to God."[27]

O'Conner builds on the thought of Bernard Lonergan and Walter Conn, who speak of the affective as the ability to reach out beyond oneself for the good of others. The affective dimension of conversion involves a radical reorientation of passionate desire. It is the awakening and reorientation of our deepest feelings, without which there can be no ultimate transformation. Unless a conversion, at some point and in some way, captures us this deeply, it will never be all-encompassing. Until we abandon ourselves emotionally to God, our conversion will always be one-sided or one-dimensional.

For C. S. Lewis, an Oxford intellectual, conversion required a deep and unequivocal certainty that he would be placing his faith and his life in

---

[27]June O'Conner, "Dorothy Day's Christian Conversion," *Journal of Religious Ethics* 18, no. 1 (1990): 163.

something that had rational or intellectual integrity. Christian faith had to make sense; it had to hold together conceptually. Nevertheless, though a search for intellectual certainty played a major part in his experience, his conversion was the fruit of a search for something more mysterious and profound.

In *Surprised by Joy* Lewis demonstrates that his journey was, in the words of David Leigh, "less an intellectual homecoming than an imaginative rediscovery of the ultimate meaning of his early emotional experiences."[28] Lewis and G. K. Chesterton have helped me to see that within each person there is a profound desire or longing, a passion for joy. It takes on different forms for different people, but at rock bottom our hunger is for joy.

As noted, for some discovering and experiencing joy is comparable to falling in love. For others the longing for joy is expressed in a search for "father." In the late 1990s I viewed two films within days of each other: *Smoke Signals,* a Native American production, and *Central Station,* an award-winning film produced in Brazil. In each story the young male protagonist is traveling by bus over a barren landscape with a single prevailing and almost desperate aim: to find and to know his father. Poignantly, in the end he finds only traces of memories of one who is there no longer. The gospel is good news to many because it leads them to a Father who grants them identity, security, meaning, purpose, intimacy—and ultimately joy.

Others seek joy less as "falling in love" or "finding father" and more as an adventure—the romance of exploration and ultimate discovery. For others the pursuit of joy is a longing for intimacy. For still others it is a longing for innocence: the joy of play or childhood delight in a toy.

Joy is found in pleasure, in the satisfaction of one's deepest longings. Almost inevitably, if we fail to find our joy as satisfaction in God we will seek it elsewhere: in material or sensual pleasure, in the exercise of power and control, or in the pursuit of honor and recognition. This is what makes joy, as the reorientation of our deepest desires toward God, so crucial to an authentic conversion. What is significant is not the particular vehicle or dominant motif or image that facilitates the experience of joy. The main point is that the discovery of joy is neither incidental nor

---

[28]David Leigh, "The Psychology of Conversion in Chesterton's and Lewis's Autobiographies," in *G. K. Chesterton and C. S. Lewis: The Riddle of Joy,* ed. Michael H. MacDonald and Andrew A. Tadie (Grand Rapids, Mich.: Eerdmans, 1989), p. 294.

optional; it is essential to the experience of a Christian conversion.

I must stress that the conversion of the intellect does not automatically lead to the conversion of the affect. As David Leigh points out, while both C. S. Lewis and G. K. Chesterton came to an intellectual conviction about the truth of the gospel, their conversions were not purely intellectual.[29] They did not include particularly ecstatic experiences but rather a profound sense, intellectual and emotional, that they had found Joy (uppercase, Lewis style).

Assurance of forgiveness (knowing that we are loved). Central to the affective element in conversion is an assurance of forgiveness. There is no transformation, no true conversion, no ultimate freedom, emotional or otherwise, unless we know at the core of our being that we are forgiven—that our sins are no longer held before us or over us, that we are freed from the burden of guilt and that in Christ we are accepted and loved.

While this element has been essential within all Christian traditions, perhaps none has captured it quite as powerfully as Wesleyan Methodism. The tradition has been deeply shaped, of course, by the experience of Wesley himself, who through the mysterious working of God's grace felt his "heart strangely warmed"; he went on to say, "I felt I did trust in Christ, Christ alone, for salvation: an assurance was given me that He had taken away my sins, even mine, and saved me from the law of sin and death."[30]

The central expression of this emphasis on affect is the extraordinary hymnology for which the movement is justly famous, particularly the hymns of John's brother Charles Wesley. These lyrics capture the stunning freedom and joy of knowing that one is forgiven, accepted and loved by the Creator of the universe:

> And can it be that I should gain
> An interest in the Savior's blood?
> Died He for me, who caused His pain,
> For me, who Him to death pursued?
> Amazing love! How can it be
> That Thou, my God, shouldst die for me?

And in another hymn:

> Oh, for a thousand tongues to sing
> My great Redeemer's praise,

---

[29]Ibid., pp. 302-4.
[30]John Wesley, *The Journal of the Rev. John Wesley, A.M.,* ed. Nehemiah Curnock (London: Epworth, 1909), 1:476-77.

The glories of my God and King,
The triumphs of His grace!

Jesus! the Name that charms our fears,
That bids our sorrows cease;
'Tis music in the sinner's ears,
'Tis life and health and peace.

And yet again:

Arise, my soul, arise!
Shake off thy guilty fears;
The bleeding Sacrifice
On my behalf appears.
Before the throne my Surety stands,
Before the throne my Surety stands:
My name is written on His hands.

My God is reconciled,
His pardoning voice I hear;
He owns me for His child,
I can no longer fear.
With confidence I now draw nigh,
With confidence I now draw nigh,
And Father, Abba, Father, cry.

Faith: the posture of radical dependence. But though this assurance—the deep confidence and joy in one's forgiveness—is critical, the affective element of conversion involves more. I find it most helpful to explore the full range of the affective through a consideration of faith as the posture of radical dependence. Emotional abandonment of one's self to the mercy and forgiveness of God is the essential point of departure, but the affective element of conversion goes beyond this.

Faith is both belief and trust. Faith is the first act of Christian discipleship; it is by faith that we begin, when we accept God's gift of life through Jesus Christ. But we are God's people not only when we believe in Jesus but also when we walk by faith. Indeed, the premier mark of Christian identity is that we are people of faith. We call the church the community of faith for the simple reason that God's primary requirement of us is that we would trust him and show this trust in obedience. Nothing pleases God more. There is nothing that he longs for more than that we be people of radical faith. So it is fair to say that the central means by which we mature in our Christian walk is the strengthening of our faith.

We often speak as though to mature as a Christian is to grow in holiness—less sin, more righteousness, a maturity in thought, word and deed. But perhaps it would be more appropriate to consider holiness to be derivative of faith. This means that the focus of our nurture, pastoral care and discipleship should be the strengthening of faith.

According to this understanding, a lack of faith is a lack of trust. When we do not trust in God, we essentially place our trust and confidence elsewhere. Our greatest need is to trust in the One who has made us, to place our faith in the only One who merits it.

Faith building is rarely the focus of contemporary programs of Christian discipleship and nurture. But it *was* the focus of older approaches to spiritual direction and guidance, such as that of the Spanish mystics and the medieval spiritual writers. This emphasis also appears in the reflective writings of the Danish thinker and writer Søren Kierkegaard. His commentary on the life of Abraham presents the patriarch as the preeminent example of faith. Kierkegaard helps us see that in the end the only thing that will ultimately bless God is our faith—not our morality, not our accomplishments, not our faithful service, not the quality of our relationships, not the depth of our wisdom or knowledge of truth, but our faith. And it is the faith of radical dependence.

So we see that joy does not flow only from knowing that our sins are forgiven; it ultimately comes from resting the whole of who we are in the arms—the wisdom, goodness and power—of the Creator of the universe.

Assurance begins with knowing we are loved and forgiven; and to this we return daily and weekly in our daily prayers and our public worship. We never graduate beyond this fundamental principle; it is the foundation for our growth in faith. But conversion must include the faith of radical dependence, for then and only then do we find complete rest for our souls.

Assurance is vital to the Christian experience. But true assurance does not foster complacency; it nurtures vital spiritual growth. Thus the "once saved always saved" motto is true in a sense; yet it is often misguided, leading people to put focus on a false sense of security rather than on a dynamic growth or transformation, as called for in 1 Peter 1. And such a transformation is fueled by growth in faith.

I Have Decided to Follow Jesus

It is the clear witness of the New Testament that a Christian conversion includes a transfer of allegiance, evidenced in a resolution to live in obedience to the Lord Jesus Christ. In the words of Lesslie Newbigin, "There cannot be a separation between conversion and obedience. To be converted in any sense which is true to the Bible is something which involves the whole person. It is a total change of direction which includes both the inner reorientation of the heart and mind and the outward reorientation of conduct in all areas of life."[31]

I have chosen to speak of this as the *volitional* element of conversion on the assumption that there is no true and lasting conversion that does not incorporate the will. An authentic encounter with Christ Jesus, whether it be a mystical vision or a sobering discovery of truth, will always lead one to action in the world, to a desire to live in truth and serve the truth.

Two expressions of the volitional. The volitional element of conversion has two particular expressions; both represent the desire and will to obey. And it is imperative that we note that obedience in Christian conversion is the obedience of freedom and joy. Such obedience is welcomed and actually sought.

First, the volitional element of conversion includes moral reform: we take responsibility for our behavior in intentional response to the character and will of God. Its expression is a longing for righteousness evident in obedience to God's moral will.

Second, the volitional also includes the orientation of one's life energies toward the service of the One who has granted us salvation. The fundamental expression of this orientation is an obedience of sacrificial service. In coming to Christ we become participants in the reign of Christ and means by which the reign of Christ comes into our world. We become witnesses in word and deed to the reign of Christ. God's saving grace is extended to our lives not ultimately for our sake but for the sake of others.

In an authentic conversion this moral realignment never stands alone. A one-dimensional conversion leads to legalism on the one hand and "crusadism" on the other. But in a genuine conversion, when a transfer of allegiance is accompanied by truth, repentance and trust, this realignment becomes an expression of a commitment to faith, hope and love. That is, the transfer of allegiance is an expression of the love of God and the love of neighbor. We come to love righteousness not as an end in itself but as the reflection of God's character. We love holiness because we love God. And our devotion to service for Christ in the world is not the devotion of a

---

[31]Lesslie Newbigin, *Open Secret* (Grand Rapids, Mich.: Eerdmans, 1978), pp. 150-51.

zealot; it is the loving service of one who gives his or her life for another in the name of Christ.

The freedom of obedience. The volitional element in a Christian conversion assumes that freedom comes with obedience rather than autonomy. The human heart longs for freedom. We were created to be free; we are alive when we are free. Deep within each of us is a longing for the joy, vigor and vitality of essential freedom. We know that oppression is death, that imprisonment robs us of life; at the core of genuine humanness is freedom.

But obedience to Christ is central to freedom. To be a Christian is to make a radical choice, a fundamental act of allegiance (Rom 6:17): to be obedient from the heart, from the depth of our being. Once sin exercised dominion over our lives; we were in bondage. Now we are to consider ourselves as dead to sin and alive to God. We are called to think this way and act this way. Romans 6:4-19 speaks of this as fundamental to the Christian life: if we are to live in freedom—the freedom of holiness and life—we must make a choice.

Without an act of surrender, we will live frustrated lives, torn between a desire for God and a desire for what God has created. We will be bewildered and confused, caught between our longing for what is good and for what we know is wrong. We either are surrendered to Christ or we are not.

Paul acknowledges in Romans 6:19 that the metaphor of slavery has its limitations; it can be pressed too far. Even for his original hearers, the image of slavery would have been revolting in many respects; they would have had immediate difficulty relating the horrors of slavery to the freedom that they experienced in Christ. But the apostle still uses the metaphor to make a simple point. To be a Christian is to make a fundamental choice, a critical transfer of allegiance from sin to Christ. Freedom is found in allegiance to Christ. And our freedom is a freedom to embrace and live in righteousness. It is freedom not to do as we please but to live in truth. We are set free from darkness to become slaves of the light.

There is no freedom in moralism, in being subject to nothing but rules and regulations. Freedom is found when we die to the law and embrace Christ. Freedom is found in Christ, in union with him. We belong, as Paul says in Romans 6:4, to another.

There is a certain irony here but also an important distinction. We are called to holiness, and its full expression will be obedience to Christ, reflected in love of and fulfillment of the law of God. But the law itself cannot be our taskmaster. Our allegiance is not to the law but to Christ.

Our freedom arises from union with Christ and obedience to Christ, not from some external code or law.

It is much the same in marriage, actually. Marriage is sustained by a covenant of commitment and faithfulness. But as husbands and wives we are devoted to persons. A man is in love with his wife, not with the rules and regulations that make for a good marriage. A woman loves her husband, not techniques for good communication. The rules, guides and techniques are means to an end, but following them is not the same as authentic devotion.

Conversion and vocation. Paul's conversion and call constituted one event. While this may or may not be the case for others, in conversion we all acknowledge that we no longer live for ourselves but for another. Our transfer of allegiance means a fundamental reorientation of our life and work: we choose to work for Christ and his reign.

Jesus proclaimed that the first disciples would no longer be fishers but rather fishers of people. And while not all were called to leave their previous occupations in this way, all were called to see their lives and their work as "for the Lord" (Col 3:23). So the call to Christ is also a call to offer the whole of our lives and particularly our work in the world to Christ in response to his saving grace.

To become a Christian, then, includes the realization that our life is now lived in the service of another, as an expression of love for God and for our neighbor. To become a Christian is to accept the call of God on our lives, a call over which we do not have control. All we can do is humbly accept this call with grace, as Mary received the word of the angel that she would be the mother of the Messiah.

I suspect that the seeds of our vocation—who we are and who we are called to be—are always somehow found within the experience of our conversion, as was the case for the apostle Paul. If this is so, it reinforces the importance of knowing our own conversion well, of articulating our conversion narrative as a basis for self-knowledge and for the focus of our energies in response to God's gracious work and call.

A Christian conversion has ethical implications. But the transfer of allegiance goes beyond a resolve and willingness to become moral; it encompasses a radical and complete realignment of one's deepest passions. Through conversion an individual comes to live with a growing appreciation of the reign of God in the world. This leads to a new pattern of behavior and work within a community that in word and deed witnesses to the truth and glory of Jesus Christ. In coming to faith, we see the world through a new set of lenses. We no longer think only in terms of our own needs and personal aspirations; through the gospel we are transformed into men and women who turn from a self-centered focus to see the bigger picture, including the social and economic implications of our actions. The gospel is a call to identify with those on the margins, especially those who are different from ourselves.

The heart of the matter, though, always remains the question of one's response to and loyalty to Jesus Christ. Conversion has an ethical dimension; conversion and obedience cannot be separated. However, we cannot equate conversion with the abandonment of a particular moral evil or with a profound resolution of the will. Rather, conversion is always rooted in one's loyalty to and love for Jesus Christ. A conversion leads to commitment. But it is commitment to a Person, the Lord Jesus Christ. This must be distinguished from other legitimate commitments, even religious commitments—whether it is a commitment to the ethics of Jesus (moral behavior) or to the church and its activities and ministries, or to justice and social action, or to mission and evangelism. These are good, but none of them lies at the center of an authentic conversion, which is commitment to Jesus. Anything else is nothing but commitment to a cause. It may be a good and legitimate cause, but it is not the same as a commitment to Jesus himself.

So we cannot stress the need for or call for a radical commitment to Christ without insisting that this devotion in service arises out of an encounter with Christ. No one will give themselves in generous obedience to Christ until they meet, know and are overwhelmed by the beauty, wonder, intelligence, strength and love of Jesus. In the end, if we devote ourselves not to a cause or a principle but a person, it is because we have met this Person. Jonathan Edwards, who insists that the evidence of true conversion is the practice of faith, phrases it wonderfully well:

> By the sight of the transcendent glory of Christ, true Christians see him worthy to be followed; and so are powerfully drawn after him: they see him worthy that they should forsake all for him: by the sight of that superlative amiableness, they are thoroughly disposed to be subject to him, and engaged to labor with earnestness and activity in his service, and made willing to go through all difficulties for his sake.[32]

Conclusion

In the end, the defining center and focus of conversion remains the same:

---

[32]Edwards, *Religious Affections*, p. 395.

Jesus Christ. In coming to Christian faith, we are choosing to love Jesus in response to his love for us. Our understanding, our deepest passions and joys, our resolve to repent of sin, our submission to the truth are all but expressions of the simple reality: a Christian is one who has chosen to know, love and serve Jesus.

8

Three Elements That Support & Enable

The Sacramental, the Charismatic & the Communal

We now come to a consideration of three elements of conversion of a different sort than those considered thus far. These three are not so much the fruit of grace as the means by which we know and experience divine grace.

Baptized into Christ

The longer ending of the Gospel of Mark includes the declaration "The one who believes and is baptized will be saved" (Mk 16:16). This is one of several scriptural statements about conversion impressive for their stunning simplicity. In this case belief and baptism are highlighted as necessary elements in a Christian conversion; the first speaks of the internal disposition of the heart and mind, the second of an external sacramental action.

Just a symbol? When Corazon Aquino led the people's revolution in the Philippines in 1986, overthrowing Ferdinand Marcos and his cronies, there was a color that symbolized the aspirations of the people. It had first come into prominence a couple of years earlier when Aquino's husband,

Ninoy Aquino, returned from self-imposed exile. He had been in the United States but had decided that he must return to the Philippines. He did not necessarily intend to carry out anything dramatic; all he knew was that he had to return home. A popular song about yellow ribbons "on an old oak tree" inspired hundreds of people who went to meet his flight and welcome him home, and they decked the airport in yellow.

Ninoy Aquino was assassinated right there at the airport, moments after he disembarked from his airplane. But the color worn that day to celebrate his return was not forgotten; it became the symbol of his aspirations, the longings of his people and eventually the revolution. After Cory Aquino became president no one was surprised that at her inauguration she wore yellow, as she did at every major event for quite some time.

No one planned it. It was not scripted. It just happened: yellow became the symbol of the revolution. That is why I find it very strange when anyone speaks of a symbol as "just a symbol."

I wear a wedding ring, and it is certainly not "just a symbol." It represents the most important relationship I have on this earth. It is quite small, a minor part of my wardrobe, of what I wear every day, but it says more about me than anything else I have. It says that I am a one-woman man, devoted and dedicated to and in love with one person, my wife.

If I were to come home someday without the ring on the fourth finger of my left hand, my wife, Joella, would surely notice its absence. And if in reply to her inquiries I replied, "Well, it's just a symbol," she would find this very strange. In actual fact it is a powerful symbol of something fundamental and basic to our lives, and it speaks of that commitment day in and day out in a way that words can only begin to tell.

To be human is to use symbols. We use them in our play. We use symbols to capture our national identity, our important relationships and even our deepest spiritual commitments. So it is not surprising that Jesus used and instituted symbolic actions as part of his ministry, or that symbol and symbolic action are important to the church.

Symbolic actions play a critical role in the whole of human life, but they take on particular significance in a study of religious experience. Louis Dupré gives particular attention to the role of symbol and symbolization in religious experience; he actually insists that a religious act cannot exist *except* by symbolization.[1] Study of religious experience requires

---

[1]Louis Dupré, *Religious Mystery and Rational Reflection: Excursions in the Phenomenology and Philosophy of Religion* (Grand Rapids, Mich.: Eerdmans, 1998), p. 7.

awareness of the two essential components of the religious act: the symbolization (which constitutes the objective) and the subjective religious experience. If we isolate the experience, we are lost in the romantic; if we only analyze the religious symbols, we are left with what Dupré calls the "scaffolding of the living act."[2] The two are intrinsically united: "the inner intention [is] indissolubly linked to the outward expression."[3] Because a religious experience focuses on the transcendent, it necessarily requires symbolic representation to have concrete existence in the world. Dupré insists that without symbolic action, that which "re-presents" the past event, "religion evaporates into a purely interior attitude, in which salvation is remembered but not renewed."[4]

Dupré fully recognizes that symbolization is always inadequate; it is finite. Thus, he contends, religious symbols need the word that links "religious intention to expression."[5] But having acknowledged this limitation, he stresses that "without symbolic meanings, historical facts could never become objects of religious faith."[6]

This has extraordinary significance for our understanding of conversion. It is a powerful reminder that symbolic actions are neither trivial nor incidental; they are essential means by which religious change is experienced and expressed. Indeed, a formal religious rite or symbolic action allows sacred reality to be present and immediate. This sacred reality is no longer merely a past event, but a past event that is present to us. The rite enables the present to be sanctified by the past. "Through its rites," Dupré says, "faith reactivates the sources of salvation."[7]

Still addressing the matter of symbolization, Dupré further notes that through ritual the individual and the society interpenetrate one another.[8] Symbols are never purely individual; they are always the actions of a community. So symbolic activity in ritual enables the individual experience to be penetrated by the communal identity, and vice versa. For example, in baptism the community endorses, affirms and participates in the conversion of an individual—and actually *mediates* that experience. The experience of the individual is profiled and enabled through a symbolic action.

---

[2]Ibid., p. viii.
[3]Ibid., p. 7.
[4]Ibid., p. 82.
[5]Ibid., p. 8.
[6]Ibid., p. 13.
[7]Ibid., p. 82.
[8]Ibid., p. 81.

In much the same way, the act for the individual has the equally positive effect of fostering and renewing the experience of the whole community.

Holy Communion as symbolic action. Jesus ordained that the church practice two symbolic actions. Some contend that he even commanded more. But there are at least two, and these two symbolic actions lie at the center of the life and witness of the church: baptism and the Lord's Supper, or Holy Communion. For thinking about baptism it is helpful to first consider the meaning of Communion. Christ mandated that the church, as a regular part of its worship, remember his work on the cross and the resurrection by sharing the bread and the cup. We are called to eat and drink together, as a Christian community, for the bread represents one body— when broken, the body of Christ broken for us. The cup represents the blood of Jesus shed for our forgiveness. Jesus spoke of this supper as the celebration of the new covenant in his blood.

Jesus' staggering words have occasioned much discussion: "This is my body, broken for you." Roman Catholics understand the Lord's words literally. The body and blood are not just represented in the bread and cup; the elements, through consecration, actually become the body and blood of the Lord Jesus.

The Protestant Reformation, though, brought a backlash against this literalism, and many evangelicals insist that the bread and the cup are but *tokens*—something to hold in your hand, something to eat and drink, but certainly not anything that could be called the body and blood of Christ Jesus.

Both groups have missed something fundamental: Jesus was using symbolic language when he said, "This is my body." If I hold up a picture of Joella and say, "This is my wife," no one wonders with amazement that she is so small and paper-thin! Not for a moment. When I say, "This is my wife," anyone who hears knows that these words are meant to *represent* something (or better, someone).

The "evangelical" response would be to treat that picture as just a token, having no meaning in and of itself. But symbols communicate deeply—more deeply than words. The photograph of Joella is far more meaningful to me than merely the word *wife*. When I enjoy this photograph, I am enjoying Joella. It is not literally my wife. But neither is it "just a photograph."

A photograph and a symbol are not the same; but in the same way, the bread and the cup are not *just* symbols. They *are* symbols. Which means that when we partake of the bread and the cup we partake of the Lord himself—of his grace and strength and blessing (1 Cor 10:16).

This is not something magical; we are not manipulating grace. But neither is it mechanical, with our participation being incidental or irrelevant. A symbol communicates a deeper reality. But just as a Canadian flag means nothing or little to a non-Canadian, and just as a wedding ring means nothing if we do not honor the meaning of marriage, the elements of the Lord Supper, the bread and the cup, mean nothing if there is no faith in Jesus Christ. A symbol has meaning only if we take seriously that which is symbolized.

A. B. Simpson, a spiritual author in my own tradition, understood and taught the power of Christ's real presence in the life and witness of the church in the Lord's Supper:

> In speaking of the Lord's Supper (1 Cor. 11:29) the apostle blamed them for "not discerning the Lord's body." Roman Catholics teach that in the Lord's Supper the bread and wine are converted into the actual flesh of Christ. But this is the shadow of truth; namely, that in the Lord's Supper the physical life of Jesus Christ is imparted to us as well as his spiritual blessing. It would do us no good if we could actually eat the flesh of Christ; it would be profane cannibalism. But if we can receive that which lies back of His flesh, His vital strength into our being, that is all we need. And that is the real substance of the resurrection body. He is the embodiment of life and power, and by the Holy Ghost He imparts to us that life and power as we worthily receive the sacrament and discern Him in it.[9]

Precisely *because* the Lord's Supper is symbol, we "discern" Christ in the symbol and we know the grace of his resurrection body when we eat and drink of the bread and the cup.

Baptism not optional. The same is true with the second symbolic action that was ordained by Christ: water baptism. It is the symbolic action by which we mark that we are *in* Christ. In conversion we celebrate the inner transformation that comes by faith and repentance; but this inner reality needs to be sacramentalized, and this sacramental action testifies to the inner reality of the Spirit's work.

A convert is a person who has been baptized. Baptism is a necessary sacramental dimension of a Christian conversion, the external expression of an inward reality. It is a vital *part* of conversion, not merely a sign of conversion. The New Testament does not speak of converted people who

---

[9]A. B. Simpson, *Lord for the Body, Tracts for the Times,* Divine Healing series (New York: Christian Alliance Publishing, c. 1900).

are not baptized. In Matthew 28 those who make disciples are commanded to baptize them. And in the accounts of conversion in Acts (the Ethiopian, Saul, Cornelius, Lydia, the Philippian jailer), though in each case different elements are emphasized, there is one common element: water baptism. It should not surprise us that all the conversions described in Acts include water baptism. This is to be expected for two reasons: (1) Jesus commanded his followers to make disciples by baptizing them— baptism is essential to the act of becoming and making a disciple and thus we are not disciples unless we are baptized; and (2) in the landmark proclamation of Peter, following his sermon on the day of Pentecost, when those who heard him asked what they should do, he declared that they should repent and be baptized for the forgiveness of their sins.

Is it necessary to be baptized? Yes, if we take symbol seriously. Is it necessary for me to wear my wedding ring? Ask my wife! Of course it is. It is not an incidental mark of my identity. If I am married and do not wear my ring, am I still married? Of course I am. But that is not the point. Why would I *not* wear the ring? And why would a person who has transferred allegiance to Christ not accept the symbolic action mandated by Christ?[10]

Conversion, biblically conceived, has both an outward and an inward dimension; it includes baptism as the external sign of the inward expression of faith and belief. The external and the internal are distinct but inseparable. Baptism without faith and repentance is nothing more than water on the body. But faith and repentance without baptism are also inadequate, for we are embodied souls.

Historically, Roman Catholic missionaries such as Francis Xavier emphasized baptism and downplayed faith and repentance. Their urgency was to get converts baptized; they assumed that faith and repentance would eventually follow. Protestant missionaries often take the

---

[10]Often Christians appeal to the thief who was crucified with Christ, noting he was assured he would meet Jesus in paradise that very day. They conclude that surely this means a person does not need to be baptized. A possible response to this kind of thinking is to note that in actual fact everyone has a choice: you can be baptized or you can be crucified. It's up to you, I suggest, tongue in cheek. Thomas Aquinas had a more pastorally sensitive response to the question. He argued that it is sufficient to desire baptism—this from someone who could hardly be accused of suggesting that baptism is not necessary. He contended that it is sufficient if someone dies while desiring baptism. He further would have stressed the need for an adult convert to be fully instructed before coming for baptism. See Thomas Aquinas, *Summa Theologiae: A Concise Translation,* ed. Timothy McDermott (Westminster, Md.: Christian Classics, 1989), p. 564.

opposite tactic: seek faith and repentance and assume that baptism will eventually follow. However, the biblical ideal runs counter to both of these approaches. The New Testament, taken as a whole, calls for both the internal expression of belief, repentance and trust and the outward sign of baptism; it is not one or the other but both/and, for "the one who believes and is baptized will be saved" (Mk 16:16).

Without faith and repentance baptism means nothing; it is, in the words of 1 Peter 3:21, simply "a removal of dirt from the body." But with faith and repentance, baptism is absolutely essential. Again, 1 Peter 3:20-21 says that "baptism . . . now saves you . . . as an appeal of God for a good conscience, through the resurrection of Jesus Christ."

Baptism is not a *means* of salvation. The priority of faith and repentance in the Scriptures is hardly debatable. But this does not mean that baptism is optional. The apostolic writers make a very close connection between conversion and baptism, and we can hardly do otherwise. To do so would be to rationalize baptism away rather than to humbly accept the clear biblical evidence and mandate.

In Romans 6 Paul takes it for granted that those who are believers are baptized people. It simply is not optional. In Galatians 3:27-29 the basis of unity in the Christian community is baptism into Christ. The remarkable language of Titus 3:4-7 makes a close connection between baptism and regeneration:

> But when the goodness and loving kindness of God our Savior appeared, he saved us, not because of any works of righteousness that we had done, but according to his mercy, through the water of rebirth and renewal by the Holy Spirit. This Spirit he poured out on us richly through Jesus Christ our Savior, so that, having been justified by his grace, we might become heirs according to the hope of eternal life. (Tit 3:4-7)

Many evangelicals insist that "water" (or "washing") here cannot be a reference to baptism. But this is due largely to the assumption that there is no close link between baptism and conversion.[11] In contrast, R. T. France

---

[11]Gordon D. Fee explores the options of interpretation of this text and concludes that though potentially the "washing" of verse 5 could allude to baptism, it is in fact a metaphor for spiritual cleansing. Having said this, Fee acknowledges that the more literal interpretation would be more consistent with the normal understanding of how "regeneration and renewal" are used. But, he says, this puts "more emphasis on baptism than the full context warrants." Yet the context is clearly speaking of regeneration, and one wonders why a reference like this could not be taken quite literally (Gor-

concludes that our tendency to see baptism as a symbolic, optional extra, or to be embarrassed by the inclusion of a physical act as part of the spiritual process of conversion, contrasts with the strongly "realist" language of the New Testament about the saving significance of baptism (e.g., Jn 3:5; Rom 6:3-4; Gal 3:27; Col 2:12; Tit 3:5; 1 Pet 3:20-21). While there are no New Testament grounds for believing that baptism *by itself* makes a person a Christian, the idea of an unbaptized Christian is equally foreign to its thought.[12]

Without baptism a believer was not considered part of the New Testament community of faith. Several church historians and theologians have noted that when baptism is neglected or intentionally ignored, substitutes are invented or borrowed to take the place of this mandated rite of initiation. The most obvious example is the altar call, which for many years was an indispensable feature of evangelism, so much so that there are yet some who cannot think of evangelism except in the context of mass crusades that conclude with "invitations." Charles Finney actually viewed the altar call and the "anxious seat" as replacements for baptism, thus essentially acknowledging the need for some kind of rite or ritual.

The very nature of the human person requires a tangible, concrete, enfleshed action that is congruent with what is happening internally. It is both logical and compelling therefore to acknowledge and embrace the divinely given action of water baptism.

The meaning of baptism. Baptism is a symbolic action given by Christ to the church as an external act that speaks of an internal reality. First, it symbolizes the experience of forgiveness. In 1 Peter 3:20-21 we read that "baptism . . . now saves you," but with the stress that this is not a cleansing of the body but a symbolic cleansing of the conscience. Second, baptism speaks of the presence of the Spirit in our lives. In Acts 2:38 Peter urges his hearers to repent and be baptized for the forgiveness of sins, with the assurance that they would receive the gift of the Spirit. Third, baptism symbolizes our union with Christ in his death and resurrection (Rom 6:1-4).

Baptism, then, represents our identity with Christ—we have died with him to sin, and with him we have risen to new life, as we see so clearly in Romans 6:4. Indeed, as Douglas Moo points out, *baptism* is a shorthand

---

don D. Fee, *1 and 2 Timothy, Titus,* New International Biblical Commentary [Peabody, Mass.: Hendrickson, 1984], p. 205). As R. T. France suggests, would not the original hearers have taken these words as a reference to baptism?

[12]R. T. France, "Conversion in the Bible," *The Evangelical Quarterly* 65, no. 4 (1993): 306.

way of referring to conversion—the whole experience of being with and in Christ. Through baptism we are present with Christ in his death and resurrection; through baptism we are united with Christ.[13]

In the past I was prone to see Romans 6 as making obvious reference to baptism by immersion: the submersion of the believer as a kind of death—as we die with Christ—and coming out of the water to show our rising with Christ. But I see now that this presses the imagery too far. There is still plenty of reason to support immersion baptism, but this text and its imagery do not serve as justification for full immersion. A photograph looks like that which it represents. But not so a symbol. Baptism is not necessarily meant to *look like* what happens when we are united with Christ; it is meant to *symbolize* that reality.

Through baptism we have been marked, we have been identified with another; we have become one with Christ in his death and resurrection. In becoming Christians, and through baptism, we are united with Christ. In this union Christ has freed us not only from our guilt but also from bondage to sin, from the power that sin might hold over us. In all of this baptism is a mark—a benchmark, a symbolic identification with Christ, much as a wedding ring marks me as a married person. And just as a wedding ring symbolizes a change of identification—from single to married— and thus a change of behavior, baptism symbolizes a change of both identification and behavior.

And just as a married person cannot be nonchalant about behavior, even so a Christian cannot be complacent about sin. Conversion to Christ involves a rejection of sin. Toleration of sin would be fundamentally incompatible with our union with Christ. Or, to reverse this and state it positively, if we are in Christ then we are called to live for Christ. And the capacity to live for Christ is granted to us through the union we have with Christ through baptism. Paul stresses this: the new life we have is made possible through the union with Christ we experience in our baptism (actually *through* our baptism, as it would be appropriate to read the Greek preposition *dia* in Romans 6:4).

It is not that a Christian never sins after baptism. Rather, there is a resolve to live in the light of Christ rather than in a pattern of habitual sin. Moreover, the Christian has assurance that the power of sin has been broken, for our primary identification is now with Jesus Christ. Our baptism,

---

[13]Douglas Moo, *Romans 1-8*, Wycliffe Exegetical Commentary (Chicago: Moody Press, 1991), p. 371.

then, speaks of our hope—our confidence in the work that God is doing in our lives. We are marked through baptism with an assurance that God has begun a work in us that he will bring to completion. Baptism is a sign that the work of Christ in the cross and the resurrection was not in vain but has been applied to us, to you and me.

As baptized people, we know that we have started down a new road. On the outside we may not look much different from non-Christians. Actually, in many cases a non-Christian may look more moral or more civil and have more graces. But we know, and the act of baptism is our constant mark and assurance, that a new work has begun in us. We may not feel like new people, and some days we may not act like new people, but we know that we are baptized, and this fact is a constant assurance that God is at work in us because we are one with Christ Jesus.

All of this makes sense only if we take seriously our identification with Christ through baptism. It is my impression that most Christians have little awareness of the significance of their baptism. It is viewed as a past event, not as a dynamic reality in the present. Romans 6 calls us to live more intentionally in the light of who we are in Christ, an identification that is marked, symbolized and mediated through our baptism.

Though I do not walk around holding my left hand in front of my face so I can always see my wedding ring, I am always conscious that I am married, that I have a wife and that she is my true love. If I woke up one morning and the ring was not on my hand, I would feel that something was missing. There is a sense in which I am always conscious of my wedding ring.

Similarly, Paul calls us to live with a continuous consciousness that we are baptized, so that we feel the awkwardness of behavior that is inconsistent with our baptism and so that we embrace behavior that is consistent with who we are in Christ. We would do well to begin each day with an awareness of our baptized identity—who we are in Christ.

The Lord's Supper is a wonderful opportunity to renew our baptismal vows and confirm again before God and one another that we are united with Christ in his death and resurrection. For this Table calls us back to first principles—to establish afresh who we are, to resolve once more to live consistent with that identity, to appropriate Christ's grace to walk in union with him.

Baptism, then, is an ideal way to sacramentalize the inner reality of faith and repentance. It speaks of repentance and the forgiveness of sins; it calls forth our faith and our resolve to live in loyal identification with

Christ. It is personal but also communal, indicating our personal commitments but also our common commitments as the community of faith.

Restoring the interconnection between baptism and conversion. Baptism is commanded in Scripture as integral to conversion. Symbolic actions are essential elements of any religious experience, for external actions affirm and complement internal faith and repentance. The symbolic significance of baptism makes it a rich rite of passage for the new believer. It follows then that the Christian community must find a way to reintegrate conversion and baptism. Only then will our understanding and practice of Christian initiation have integrity; only then, I would contend, will it truly foster spiritual transformation. William J. Abraham says that "separating conversion from baptism, a practice that is such a marked feature of modern evangelism, is a theological scandal. . . . It is imperative, then, that the church find a way to reunite conversion and baptism in a coherent, unified process of initiation."[14]

We must resist any inclination to speak of baptism as *subsequent* to conversion; our language must be in agreement with that or the New Testament, which consistently integrates the two. Some, perhaps out of a fear of implying baptismal regeneration, insist on always keeping the two separate. But surely we should come as close as the New Testament itself comes to linking baptism and God's regenerating grace. Surely we should make such a close link that we could *potentially* be accused of "baptismal regeneration." Why? Because the Scriptures themselves make this link.

Having made this close connection, we can affirm, of course, that baptism itself does not regenerate; we are made new as we respond in faith to the saving grace of Christ. But this faith is necessarily accompanied by the external act of baptism. In other words, though we affirm the necessary link between baptism and the other elements of conversion and affirm that baptism is integral to conversion, we acknowledge that while inseparable they are distinct.

This is not only the case when it comes to the relationship between faith and baptism; similar care must be taken regarding the connection between baptism and the gift of the Spirit. Though Gordon D. Fee affirms the high place of baptism, he insists that a careful reading of the New Testament reveals that one does not receive the Spirit *through* water baptism. While Paul often links the two, he does not so link them that you cannot have one without the other. As Fee puts it, "In no text does Paul associate

---

[14]William J. Abraham, *The Logic of Evangelism* (Grand Rapids, Mich.: Eerdmans, 1984), p. 133.

the gift of the Spirit with water baptism, either as cause and effect or as occurring experientially at the same time."[15] We see this particularly in the case of Cornelius. Peter himself had implied if not actually declared that those who repent and are baptized would receive the gift of the Spirit. But then he discovers that for Cornelius the gift of the Spirit came prior to baptism. And in recognizing this, he resolves immediately that Cornelius should be baptized.

In other words, we must act obediently, both as new believers and as leaders in our Christian communities; baptism should happen as early in the process as appropriate, with a bias toward earlier rather than later. There is little if any reason for delay, especially for an adult.

It follows then that references to our baptism should be a regular part of our worship and conversation. Just as Paul makes comfortable reference to baptism as an important benchmark in the Christian life in Romans 6, in our worship, preaching, teaching and conversation about our Christian experience, we should foster awareness that we are a baptized people. Baptism should be highlighted as the symbolic action capturing the reality that we are new people in Christ.

Finally, a word about infant baptism. This is an ancient practice, and many traditions within the church affirm this approach to baptism and conversion. A child is baptized on the basis of the faith of the parents and is thereby incorporated into the covenant community of faith. My own preference is to acknowledge that a newborn child is a part of the church family, dedicated by the parents and the church community to God. But the act of dedication is an act of the parents: they dedicate themselves to teach and guide their child to know God. Then the young person can choose to be baptized when he or she is ready to take adult responsibility. Though this is my preference, the same result comes when a person who was baptized as an infant comes into adulthood having been confirmed, having chosen to appropriate the faith of the parents. Thus baptism is no less integral to conversion for those who practice infant baptism.

Have You Received the Gift of the Spirit?

At conversion Christians receive the gift of the Spirit. This is the gift of God himself, indwelling them in grace, power and love. But evangelical Christians differ on whether this gift is appropriated consciously and also

---

[15]Gordon D. Fee, *God's Empowering Presence: The Holy Spirit in the Letters of Paul* (Peabody, Mass.: Hendrickson, 1994), p. 862.

whether it is necessarily received at conversion.

Two dominant views among evangelicals. There tend to be two dominant views or theological positions. After summarizing them briefly, I will suggest that perhaps the resolution of this debate is found in a "third way."

Some insist that the Spirit is received by all believers *automatically*. They are of the opinion that the Bible teaches that if a person believes and repents then, whether consciously or not, she has received the Spirit. The gift does not need to be prayed for or requested; it just happens. Those of Baptist and Reformed traditions generally hold to this view, linking the gift of the Holy Spirit directly with conversion and insisting that it happens automatically when one believes, while resisting the idea that it is a conscious experience or a gift to be actively sought.

Others believe the reception of the gift of the Spirit happens subsequent to conversion. This view most frequently occurs within Pentecostal or charismatic circles, but it is also found in different forms within other traditions that trace their roots to the late-nineteenth-century Holiness movement. Often language of "baptism" or "filling" is used to speak of a distinctive experience of divine grace. Some use language of sanctification to speak of this event, but the most common older term is "baptism in the Spirit." Within my own tradition, for example, the Christian and Missionary Alliance, sanctification is spoken of as a "crisis subsequent to conversion."

This position involves the conviction that vital to an authentic Christian experience is a conscious reception of the Spirit. Those who hold to this view may ask a person if they have been filled with the Spirit. The Pentecostal camp has traditionally viewed "speaking in tongues" as the definitive evidence—the evidential sign—that baptism in the Spirit has taken place.

These two views represent two very different streams within the evangelical Protestant tradition. One gets the impression that there are "Calvary" people who speak of the cross and Jesus, and there are "Pentecost" people who speak of Pentecost and the Spirit. It is all too possible that this divide between evangelical Christians will continue to grow, to the detriment of the church and its mission.

Perhaps there is another alternative, a way forward that comes by rethinking the nature of conversion. Thinking of conversion as a protracted experience gives us a new way to think about the experience of the Spirit. That is, it may well be that both groups are right, and that we can draw on the strengths of both positions by rethinking our understanding of conversion—especially if New Testament models of conversion bear out such a perspective.

Unfortunately, the Spirit is a relative nonentity in the conscious experience of most Christians. They do not have a dynamic theology of the Spirit that shapes and informs their experience of God's grace and Christian faith. Yet even a cursory reading of Paul's letters would highlight that the Spirit is absolutely critical in the Christian life, and that the apostle was deeply conscious of the presence and ministry of the Spirit. Paul's life was lived in intentional response to the Spirit.

It is a basic premise of the New Testament that receiving the gift of the Spirit is essential to conversion. What follows is an attempt to affirm this reality and to incorporate the wisdom of the Pentecostal, Holiness and charismatic traditions that call us to an intentional reception of this gift—within a framework that is distinctly Reformed.

The gift of the Spirit and the language of the New Testament. The promise of the Spirit is essential to the meaning of conversion. It is not an extra, above and beyond conversion. Rather, the gift of the Spirit lies at the heart of prophetic promises regarding the redeeming ministry of the Messiah. He would baptize his people with his Spirit. How then can we speak of the salvation won by the Messiah if it does not include this dimension? It is inherent to what it means to be a follower of Jesus, one who has been graced by his salvation. The promise of the Spirit was an essential component of the new covenant. The promise given to Abraham for the Gentiles included the promise of the Spirit (Ezek 36; Gal 3:14). John the Baptist spoke of Jesus as the One who would baptize in the Holy Spirit. Thus the experience of the Spirit is a vital part of entering the kingdom of God; it is not supplemental or incidental to the New Testament idea of what it means to be initiated into Christian faith. Indeed, it would be fair to insist that the defining mark of the first Christians, described for us in the book of Acts, was that they were people of the Spirit.

Clark Pinnock makes the interesting observation that Christians commonly speak of conversion as a time when people "receive Christ," yet the New Testament emphasizes confessing Christ as Lord and receiving the gift of his Spirit. It is not wrong, as Pinnock notes, to speak of "receiving Christ." But this is not the emphasis of Scripture. The pressing question in the New Testament is not whether you have been "born again" but whether you have received the Spirit.[16] Somehow we need to restore to the

---

[16]Clark H. Pinnock. *Flame of Love: A Theology of the Holy Spirit* (Downers Grove, Ill.: InterVarsity Press, 1996), pp. 164-65.

life and witness of the church the close connection between the gift of the Spirit and conversion.

It is helpful to clarify something about New Testament language with respect to the gift of the Spirit. Of the four models of conversion already described, those that are intentionally post-Pentecost in their description of the Christian experience (Acts, Paul and John) all make explicit reference to the Spirit. They use different language and different metaphors, but they speak of the same reality. John speaks of "rebirth by the Spirit" and records in John 20:22 that Jesus exhorted his disciples to "receive the Holy Spirit." Luke, in his Gospel and in Acts, refers to "Spirit baptism." In Paul's letters the most common expression is "filling of the Spirit." Most likely all these terms refer to the same reality: reception of the gift of the Spirit.

On one and only one occasion Paul speaks of the baptism of the Spirit (1 Cor 12:13); his usual terms are "filling" and "walking in the Spirit." The Spirit, for Paul, is someone to whom we are subject (rather than to the flesh) and someone who infills us as the Spirit of Christ. Thus submission and infilling go together. Indeed, submission to the will of God is the prerequisite for the infilling of the Spirit.

Luke does not use "baptism in the Spirit" language exclusively. A comparison of Acts 1:5 and 2:4 shows that "baptism" and "filling" are both used and used synonymously. The expression "filling of the Spirit" can refer to an initial experience of the Spirit and also to a process, the ongoing experience of the Christian, as in Ephesians 5:18.

All of this points to the profound reality that receiving the gift of the Spirit is integral to the experience of conversion. James Dunn has effectively shown that the book of Acts, the only section of the New Testament that could conceivably support a distinction between conversion and Spirit baptism, actually affirms that the gift of the Spirit is an essential dimension of conversion. He demonstrates that Acts 2:38 ("Peter said to them, 'Repent and be baptized every one of you in the name of Jesus Christ so that your sins may be forgiven; and you will receive the gift of the Holy Spirit' ") serves as a kind of paradigm of the nature and meaning of conversion: "Luke probably intends Acts 2:38 to establish a pattern and norm for Christian conversion-initiation in his presentation of Christianity's beginnings."[17]

---

[17]James D. G. Dunn, *Baptism in the Holy Spirit* (Philadelphia: Westminster Press, 1970), p. 90.

The rest of Acts is a history of the proclamation of the gospel and its reception in various communities. It includes the preaching of the apostles as well as accounts of how the early Christians discovered and appropriated their new faith. And though the ideal may be Acts 2:38, the actual experience was not necessarily so tidy. Cornelius was baptized *after* he received the gift of the Spirit. His experience of the Spirit did not come automatically with belief, repentance and water baptism, as is implied in Acts 2:38. But this does not mean that the gift of the Spirit is not an essential component of Christian conversion. At most, it implies that reception of the Spirit may be distinct from the acts of belief and repentance (distinct but ultimately inseparable). So Scripture does not support the Wesleyan-Holiness or Pentecostal two-step paradigm of conversion and sanctification.

The experiential reality. Yet beyond the exegetical question, we must also consider the church's experience, and here the Wesleyan-Holiness and Pentecostal heritage offers wisdom that all Christians would do well to hear. My comments above might seem to support the position that the gift is received automatically when one believes and repents. However, exegesis alone cannot be the basis for distinguishing the relationship between the gift of the Spirit and conversion. Invariably our theological formulation and our experience are informed by a spiritual tradition and a theological heritage.

The experience of the church shapes and informs the theology of the church. Though Scripture always must remain the primary source of our theological formulations, experience (along with tradition and reason) also has a formative influence in the beliefs, doctrines and teachings of the church. Biography informs our theology. Paul's conversion experience, as part of the canon, has shaped the life and doctrine of the church. And the experience of the founders of theological movements has shaped the character and convictions of those participating in those movements. Rather than deploring this fact, we can celebrate it and learn from it.

The purpose of theology is to edify the church. But more, theology has the task of interpreting the experience of the church in light of divine revelation. So the theological task includes helping the Christian community make sense of experience—recognizing that our experience of the Spirit invariably influences the perspective we bring to divine revelation and that Scripture must remain primary in the development of our theology.

This approach to theological method has led me to reappraise my own tradition, the Christian and Missionary Alliance. Let me now speak directly out of this tradition, as a means of enabling others, within their traditions, to come to terms with the meaning of the gift of the Spirit.

For the Christian and Missionary Alliance (C&MA), A. B. Simpson's experience was a primary factor in the formulation of doctrine and in the development of the theology of the denomination he founded. This can be said without apology. Critical aspects of Simpson's theology were determined not by exegesis but through his own experience. As I have wrestled with theological questions, I have concluded that only in recognizing this can we eventually resolve the tension that many C&MA members feel between Simpson's weaknesses in theological and exegetical method, his experience, and the influence of both in the doctrine of the C&MA.

Simpson's experience. A. B. Simpson was raised a Presbyterian, and though his mature theology cannot be termed "Reformed," he did maintain Reformed doctrines of sin and justification by faith, and he upheld the priority and sovereignty of grace in the lives of Christian believers. He acknowledged his faith in Christ as a young man (age fifteen) and eventually entered public ministry as a Presbyterian pastor.

Yet Simpson felt a growing discontent with the depth of his spiritual experience; his dissatisfaction grew more acute when he read William E. Boardman's *The Higher Christian Life* (1858 edition). This book impressed Simpson in two ways: (1) Christian believers could enjoy spiritual vitality and inner strength far beyond what he was currently experiencing, and (2) this more profound experience was to be found in Jesus Christ himself. Simpson decided that he would be content with nothing but an experience of Christ comparable to what Boardman described.

At this time throughout North America, and to some degree in Britain as well, there were a variety of movements that were emphasizing a similar message. Broadly speaking, these could be termed "holiness movements": despite some critical differences all affirmed the possibility of an experience of grace and divine holiness that was deeper or higher than normal Christian experience.

The conviction was that this more profound level of experience could be justified from Holy Scripture. Many believed the phenomenon of Pentecost pointed to two phases of salvation: first an experience of Christ and Calvary, then an experience of the Spirit and Pentecost. Some spoke of the second as a baptism in the Spirit that would enable the Christian to move into greater spiritual vitality. Others, especially those from a Wesleyan tradition, spoke of this deeper experience of grace as "perfection" and emphasized the possibility of being freed from sin for a perfect love.

Boardman's book was the primary influence in Simpson's life at this point. The Holiness movement (particularly D. L. Moody) challenged and encouraged him as well. Sometime between 1872 and 1875 Simpson had a dramatic and life-changing experience of divine grace, a turning point in his experience with Christ. He was empowered for ministry, and his desire to turn from sin and live in righteousness was markedly strengthened. This came about fifteen years after his first experience of Christ as a young man.

A third critical experience came in 1881, when Simpson experienced a complete emotional and physical breakdown. He heard teaching that led him to believe that he could be healed, and he received a unique, miraculous healing that he recognized as the gift of the Holy Spirit. And he saw that the grace of God called him to a complete, moment-by-moment emotional dependence on Christ. This was the culmination of Simpson's spiritual journey: a critical and deliberate transfer of trust in himself to trust in Christ, with recognition of the all-sufficiency of Christ. He describes this realization in his famous sermon "Himself." The experience seems to have been the most significant for the formulation of his theological convictions. Yet it was also a culmination of the motivations and insights he had received through reading Boardman's book.

Simpson's doctrine. Simpson adopted a basic Wesleyan-Holiness paradigm to explain the nature and goal of Christian experience. Though his own pilgrimage was marked by three distinct moments, he was deeply immersed in the Holiness movement of his day, and he adopted and taught the notion of conversion followed by a crisis of the Spirit.

Simpson's thought differed in some notable ways from the teachings of his contemporaries: he rejected the perfectionism of the Wesleyan Methodists, and he did not accept the suppressionism of the Keswick movement. It would probably be an overstatement to call him a pre-Pentecostal. But he was definitely part of the broader movement that accepted, adopted and encouraged a two-step model of Christian sanctification, with a postconversion event referred to as either the "second blessing" or the "baptism of the Spirit," seen as enabling the believer to experience the "deeper life."

Simpson's doctrine includes the following notable features. First, sanctification is not optional but essential; election is for sanctification. Simpson would even say that the experience of sanctification is inherent in salvation. He spoke of salvation as conversion plus the baptism of the Spirit, and on more than one occasion he raised doubts about the genuineness of the spiritual experience of those whose initial experiences of belief and repentance were not complemented by transformation through a conscious reception of the Spirit.

A third way. Gordon D. Fee makes a sobering observation:

> The general loss of the dynamic and experienced life of the Spirit *at the beginning of the Christian life* also accounts for the frequent malaise and unfortunately all too frequent anemia of the individual believer throughout much of the church's later history. This is obviously not true of everyone, of course. But it does in part account for the rise both of the monastic movement and of various Spirit movements throughout its history.[18]

On the one hand, we can respond by affirming that the gift of the Spirit is an integral part of becoming a Christian. Fee himself makes reference to 1 Corinthians 12:13 ("For in the one Spirit we were all baptized into one body—Jews or Greeks, slaves or free—and we were all made to drink of one Spirit") as a reference to "their common experience of conversion, . . . in terms of its most crucial element, the receiving of the Spirit."[19] This conversion gift is symbolized by water baptism, which Acts 2:38 links directly with the gift of the Spirit. As a theological premise, we must affirm a close identification between baptism and the Spirit. The one represents the other. However, baptism does not actually mediate the gift of the Spirit; and for many a full actualization of the Spirit may in reality come quite some time after water baptism. The problem is that many, especially those of a Wesleyan or Pentecostal persuasion, have concluded that this delay has biblical warrant.

Simpson is typical of other writers of the late nineteenth century in building a case for a second crisis of sanctification on texts such as Acts 19—an example of Christians who were baptized with water but had not experienced the baptism of the Spirit. He reasons on this basis that the one does not automatically lead to the other, that it is possible to have one without the other. Simpson concludes that the two baptisms are distinct and must be appropriated as separate acts of faith.

Pentecostals are also inclined to focus on the experience of the Samaritans in Acts 8, where it seems clear that those who had come to Christ had a subsequent experience:

> Now when the apostles at Jerusalem heard that Samaria had accepted the

---

[18]Fee, *God's Empowering Presence*, p. 900.
[19]Ibid., p. 181.

word of God, they sent Peter and John to them. The two went down and prayed for them that they might receive the Holy Spirit (for as yet the Spirit had not come upon any of them; they had only been baptized in the name of the Lord Jesus). Then Peter and John laid their hands on them, and they received the Holy Spirit. (Acts 8:14-17)

This is a more appropriate text to work with than Acts 19, for a good case could be made that Acts 19 is an example of individuals who were sincere seekers but not actually Christians, precisely because they had not received the Spirit. Whichever way this text is read, the Acts 19 account exemplifies conscious awareness of the Spirit as the defining evidence of whether or not persons were believers.

The promise of Acts 2:38 was that if Peter's hearers were baptized they would receive the gift of the Holy Spirit. Yet the Samaritans had believed and been baptized, but they had yet to receive the gift of the Holy Spirit. So Peter and John laid hands on them and prayed that they would receive this gift. As John Stott notes, Luke does not tell us here how Peter and John knew these people had not received the gift but merely that they "discovered" this to be the case.

How do we make sense of this disparity between Acts 2:38 and the experience of the Samaritans? Some, of course, argue that this is the biblical pattern (conversion followed by a later filling by the Spirit or Spirit baptism). Stott responds that there is no way the Samaritan experience can be viewed as "normative," for the whole New Testament clearly assumes that the gift of the Spirit is integral to conversion.

Going to the other extreme, then, others argue that this was not a two-stage experience, that actually these Samaritans were brought to Christ through Peter and John and their experience with Philip was not a genuine conversion.[20] And finally, many non-Pentecostal evangelicals conclude that this was a unique situation: the church in Samaria was first being evangelized, so this was a first step outside of the apostolic community in Jerusalem.

But this seems highly speculative, at best. Better to agree that indeed the Samaritan experience is not normative, but also to affirm that no experience is normative. And further, for belief and baptism to be separated from an experience of the Spirit may not be all that unusual. Yet this does not mean that an experience of the Spirit is not inherent in conversion.

---

[20]John Stott, *The Spirit, the Church and the World* (Downers Grove, Ill.: InterVarsity Press, 1990); see Stott's overview of the two views, pp. 150-55.

We must take seriously the concern that Simpson and others in the Wesleyan-Holiness and Pentecostal traditions raise. These traditions appropriately highlight the presence of the Spirit and rightly call all Christians to receive this gift and live with a conscious awareness of the Spirit. These traditions see great value in knowing for certain that one *has* received the gift of the Spirit. However, the New Testament witness links this reception of the Spirit directly with the initial experience of conversion rather than being "subsequent to conversion." The resolution, it would seem, is to affirm that the gift of the Spirit is inherent in conversion but also to recognize that a Christian conversion is a complex event—and in many cases a conscious appropriation of the Spirit may actually be experienced distinct from (and likely separated in time from) the other elements of conversion.

Traditional Holiness and Pentecostal theology tended to distinguish conversion from the gift of the Holy Spirit. Some even went further and made a distinction between baptism of the Spirit and sanctification. This was an unfortunate set of distinctions, yet in hindsight we can see that in their social and ecclesial context this distinction made sense. While it may have fit their situation in the nineteenth and early twentieth centuries, this theological paradigm is not congruent with either the text of the New Testament or current realities in the church.

However, this does not mean that the Holiness-Pentecostal theological conviction was devoid of truth. To the contrary, these traditions have effectively called the whole Christian community to greater appreciation of the place of the Spirit in the life of the believer. And while I argue that there is no scriptural warrant for a separation of conversion and the gift of the Spirit, these traditions call us to consider that the gift of the Spirit should be received in a conscious, intentional act that is integral to our conversion experience.

Not all need to have a definite or conscious experience of receiving the gift of the Spirit. However, it is clearly the witness of Scripture that a Christian should not live with a perpetual uncertainty regarding whether the Spirit dwells within them. Those in the Wesleyan-Holiness-Pentecostal traditions insist that such an uncertainty is abnormal. Hence they call us to receive the gift.

What really matters is whether we are currently conscious of the presence of the Spirit. If a person says that she does have such an awareness, whether she had a distinct moment of receiving the gift of the Spirit is not a matter for concern. But if someone is in doubt, those from the Holiness-

Pentecostal traditions would urge us to pray with her to receive the Spirit. I am convinced, however, that we need to see such an experience as not subsequent to conversion but inherent in coming to Christ—and thus part of a complex, extended process of conversion.[21]

If this proposal is valid, the implications are twofold. First, we would teach and preach that in coming to Christ we can and must receive the gift

---

[21]I am confident that Simpson himself, if he were still teaching and preaching, would be formulating his theology differently now from the way he did a century ago. My sense is that he would have moved on from the Wesleyan-Holiness paradigm, which was appropriate in the late nineteenth century given the urgent need to bring renewal and revitalization to a dormant church. There are two seeds in the thought of Simpson that lead me to this conclusion.

1. He had definite reservations about the status of those who had been regenerated but not sanctified. He called them half saved. He recognized that justification and sanctification, though distinct, are inseparable.

2. Simpson agreed that if new believers were properly taught, there would be no significant length of time between their conversion and their reception of the gift of the Spirit. Ideally, he believed, these would be part of a single event in the life of the believer. His only insistence was that the gift of the Spirit was received in a separate and distinct act of faith. Of interest is his comment that it was quite acceptable if the two were received in the same prayer, so long as there were two distinct acts of faith, receiving both regeneration and sanctification.

Commenting on the place of water baptism in the initiation into Christian faith, Simpson wrote, "In the divine plan, sanctification is closely connected with justification, and assumed as immediately following it. The fact is, that in the Christian life of many persons, it comes at a later period. But this is not God's intention, and this assumes that sanctification is to accompany, or immediately follow, the first action of faith. . . . In [Romans 6, sanctification] is spoken of as something immediately connected with their baptism, and to which that act committed them" (A. B. Simpson, *The Epistle to the Romans* [Harrisburg, Penn.: Christian Publications, c. 1930], pp. 137-38).

And elsewhere: "We are willing, however, to concede that the baptism of the Holy Ghost may be received at the very same time a soul is converted. We have known a sinner to be converted, sanctified and saved all within a single hour, and yet each experience was different in its nature and was received in proper order by a definite faith for that particular blessing" (A. B. Simpson, "The Baptism of the Spirit: A Crisis of an Evolution [sic]," *Living Truths* 5 [1905]).

This then led George Pardington, a disciple of Simpson, to conclude the following: "Indeed, where there is right Scriptural teaching no interval of time need occur after conversion before the Holy Ghost is received. Unfortunately, however, this is seldom the case. Generally an interval of time—and often it is a long period—does occur. . . . We cannot refrain from saying that we believe God never intended that there should be a barren waste of Christian experience between regeneration and sanctification, but that conversion should be immediately followed by a life of victory over sin and self in union with the indwelling Christ and through receiving the gift of the Holy Ghost" of the Spirit, a gift that is known by faith as we submit our lives to the lord-ship of Christ. We would reject as unbiblical a sharp distinction between initial faith and repentance and a later reception of the Spirit. Rather, we would teach about the gift of the Spirit as an essential element in our evangelism.

Second, we would lead those who are coming to Christ through a simple act of consciously receiving the gift of the Holy Spirit. This could include placing hands on a new believer and asking the Father that they receive the gift of the Spirit. But it is imperative that this be done at the time when the person coming to faith is ready to receive this gift. Ideally, all new believers, perhaps on the occasion of their baptism, should have a prayer offered that they would know and receive the Spirit. But if not then, at some point it needs to happen as an indicator on their journey of faith. Such a prayer need not be marked by an outward sign or evidence, emotional or otherwise. It would simply serve as a benchmark for the believer. They would be charged to walk in the Spirit, for by faith we believe that they have been granted the gift of the Spirit.

If a Christian doubts that he has been forgiven, we lead him to an assurance that his sins have been forgiven. Similarly, if a believer doubts that he is filled with the Spirit, we lead him to a conscious appropriation of the gift of the Spirit. With new believers, we take the window of opportunity to introduce them early, consciously and intentionally to the presence that is prepared to dwell within them.

This moment, perhaps when a person is prayed with for this gift, is not in itself a transforming moment. Rather, it is an event or experience that will *enable* transformation. It is a benchmark from which that person will live as he or she chooses to walk in the Spirit.

Many have particular expectations regarding what they will experience or feel when they invite the Spirit's filling. I wonder if it is better that they have no striking experience at that moment, lest they continue to associate the Spirit with that particular emotion or experience. This is, I suggest,

---

(George Pardington, *Outline Studies in Christian Doctrine* [New York: Christian Alliance Publication, 1916], p. 163).

So Simpson himself did not insist on the two-step paradigm, a crisis "subsequent to conversion." We have hints that he would have been quite prepared to see the reception of the Spirit inherent in the act of coming to Christ, receiving Christ and consecration for the service of Christ. The Wesleyan-Holiness paradigm, then, is not in itself an essential component of the Alliance doctrine of sanctification. What is essential to the Alliance heritage is that the gift of the Spirit is received as an act of faith distinct from belief and repentance.

an unfortunate byproduct of the charismatic movement. In some cases it has so associated the gift of the Spirit with a particular sign, such as speaking in tongues, that many are left wondering whether their experience is legitimate. And leaders unfortunately assume that particular sign or manifestation must be present to validate the Spirit's work. But the work of the Spirit is manifested in many diverse ways; and we must not limit the Spirit to one defining expression.

While some have wanted to limit the expression of the Spirit's gift, others resist the idea that we can ask for this gift, believing that it is inconsistent with their theological traditions. Understandably so. But I have been teaching on the nature of conversion for several years, in five different theological schools. As part of the course I usually ask students to articulate their conversion narrative, to help their critical reflection on religious experience. It amazes me how frequently students, regardless of their denominational backgrounds, will make reference to a conscious reception of the gift of the Spirit. It makes no difference if they come from Baptist, Lutheran, Wesleyan or Pentecostal backgrounds. Interestingly, those from traditions that do not teach a conscious reception of this gift have experienced it while visiting a Pentecostal or charismatic church. If they eventually return to the denomination of their upbringing, this conscious reception of the Spirit remains a vital part of their experience. Unfortunately, though, it is not integrated in the theology and practice of their longtime community of faith. And thus, tragically, it seems like an anomaly in their experience.

Some have linked the gift of the Spirit with conversion but have insisted that the gift need not be asked for; it is received automatically. I would argue that it is unquestionably part of conversion; however, conversion is often a protracted experience. Further, there is value in intentionally praying for and receiving the Spirit. This act is not subsequent to conversion but an integral part of what it means to come to Christ. And it is equally imperative to affirm that this experience comes in the gracious timing of God.

So it is legitimate to ask someone, When you believed in Christ, and when you were baptized, did you receive the gift of the Spirit? If they did, then we can celebrate the life of God and encourage one another to walk in the Spirit. If they say that they have not received the Spirit or have doubts about it, we can urge them to pray for and appropriate this gift of life. And the church has always affirmed the value of a formal, intentional act, symbolized through the laying on of hands.

Again, ideally the request for the gift of the Spirit would happen in connection with water baptism. It seems entirely appropriate that after a person is baptized we pray that they be filled with and empowered by the Spirit of the Living God. In such a case, then, baptism is not so much a witness to others as an event in which we are united with Christ and filled by his Spirit.

And the end result should be a stronger affirmation of the place of the Spirit in a Christian conversion.

Becoming Part of the Family of God

A genuinely Christian theology of conversion will explicate this foundational religious experience with particular reference to the community of faith. This critical aspect of conversion needs to be addressed from two sides. On the one hand the Christian community *mediates* conversion, particularly through its language of conversion. This will be the topic of a subsequent chapter.

God's redemptive purposes. On the other hand, conversion includes incorporation into Christian community, and this will be the focus here. Normally evangelicals emphasize that a new convert needs to become part of the church. Though this comes from a valid conviction, it overlooks an accomplished fact: for the early church in the days of Acts, incorporation into Christian community was *part of* coming to faith, and further, Paul assumes that all believers are part of the church. As he stresses in Ephesians 2, once we were not part of the covenant people of God, but now through Christ we are no longer foreigners and aliens; we are members of God's household. To put it simply: to be Christian is to be a participant in the community of faith. St. Augustine had a point when he suggested that if you do not have the church as your mother, you cannot claim that God is your Father. Our union with Christ is unavoidably linked to our union with the body of Christ.

Thus the corporate significance of Christian faith is not sufficiently faithful to the New Testament when left to a mere suggestion that once a new believer comes to faith it is advisable that they join a church. Becoming part of a community of faith is so critical to becoming a Christian believer that the New Testament cannot conceive of the Christian in isolation from the community. In coming to faith in Christ we become members of the new humanity of which Christ is head. And this new humanity is linked not only with Christ but also with each other in human solidarity. We are one people.

This is rooted in the very mission of God: through Abraham God intended to form a *people*. The redemptive purposes of God are not fulfilled in the salvation of individuals here and there. Rather, God is forming a people who will bear God's name, worship God and witness to God's reign. He has formed this people through sending his Son, and this people is now conceived as the body of Christ, the fellowship of the Spirit. However, we also anticipate that day when at the consummation of the reign of God the community of faith, as a single, dynamic entity, will appear as a glorious bride before the Lord Jesus Christ. And God will choose to dwell among the people, the one people of God.

Paul explicitly states that this communal identity is essential to the spiritual well-being and growth of the individual Christian. Ephesians 4:11-15 reminds us that we grow into Christ Jesus as each member of the community of faith does its part. We do not grow up in Christ in isolation from one another. We cannot. Our only hope for spiritual maturity, radical transformation, is to be united in love with fellow believers and learning to mature in mutual dependence.

Consequently, we cannot conceive of conversion in purely individual terms. The community of faith mediates our conversion, and conversion must include incorporation into that community. We are not disembodied souls; our faith must find expression in concrete, tangible relationships that reflect God's mission to form one people who represent a new humanity. Conversion then must include a commitment to Jesus Christ within the fellowship of the people of God.

We may resist this on account of the failures of the church, the obvious flaws in the life of Christian communities with which we are familiar. But the Christian faith necessarily finds expression in the lives of flawed people who together embody the reality that we are still fallen and in sin but also our hope of ultimate transformation in Christ. By becoming participants in a community of faith, we identify with who we are together, in all our weaknesses and flaws, and also with who we hope to become in Christ through the work of his Spirit.

This incorporation into community is symbolized by baptism. It represents the forgiveness of sins, union with Christ and the gift of the Spirit. But baptism, which is mediated by the community, also represents incorporation into the covenant people of God.

For many, this incorporation into the family of God will also be represented by a formal process of becoming a member of a local church. While this might be a vital means by which we live out this dimension of our conversion, formal membership does not in and of itself constitute an element of conversion. Rather, in coming to Christ we become participants in a community of faith, a community where we have the opportunity of corporate worship, of teaching and learning, of receiving grace, encouragement and discipline, of being means of grace to others through service, a community where we learn to love and be loved in Christian fellowship. To be a Christian is to be a member of a community of faith. To become a Christian means to enter into this common life. It is that straightforward.

A necessary qualifier. While it is imperative that we stress the corporate element of conversion, the affirmation needs to be qualified. We must always distinguish between the church and Christ; they are not one and the same. Union with the church is not synonymous with union with Christ; submission to the church is not the same as submission to Christ. Coming to faith in Christ will necessarily at some point mean incorporation into a community of faith. But the only way that some will eventually come to a mature understanding and encounter with Christ is to deliberately leave the church, or at least the church of which they have been a part. I am thinking in particular of second-generation Christians and perhaps of Christians in countries where a state Christian religion sees faith and citizenship as virtually synonymous.

We affirm that incorporation into congregational life is an essential element of a Christian conversion. But this element can never be the only element of an authentic conversion; it can never stand alone. Further, even as one of several elements, it still needs qualification.

The primary Christian identity or loyalty is never to the church. A truly converted person *always remains differentiated,* neither consumed by the community nor subsumed by the community. That is, the individual remains an individual whose primary loyalty and identity are found in Christ and not in the community.

Thus it is appropriate that in a listing of the elements of conversion, loyalty to Christ and a transfer of allegiance come prior to incorporation into community. Such an intentional logical ordering makes sense (even if, as we shall see, it is not always the experiential order).

Some Christians such as Simone Weil never come to terms with the church, even though their conversions are surely authentic. But we must see them as exceptions rather than the norm; perhaps we need to pay attention to such exceptions as reminders that our commitment is ultimately to Christ and not to any human organization.

The conversion of some may well include a break—deliberate or unintentional—from community. Such a break frees the person from what has become an oppressive influence that would otherwise actually discourage an authentic conversion. Ideally, of course, a reintegration happens at a later date.

Some implications. All of this has tremendous implications for how we think about conversion and the life of the church. In a subsequent chapter I will stress that evangelism is most authentic when it arises from communities of faith that can effectively incorporate new believers. It means that we necessarily raise cautions regarding crusade evangelism and televangelism, which are disembodied and disconnected from community. It means, of course, that we encourage and enable new believers to become members of communities of faith where they will experience the joy of giving and receiving authentic love (Rom 12:9-21), and that we view this responsibility as an essential part of authentic evangelism, rather than merely an outcome or ideal byproduct of enabling people to come to faith.

Our thinking about conversion, then, leads us to affirm the value of formal links with Christian communities. The formal act by which we make public our church membership can be a critical and meaningful sign of commitment to Christ and response to his call into Christian discipleship. We come to see commitment to Christ as necessarily expressed in a responsible commitment to a community of Christian believers.

As will be stressed in the closing chapter, for many if not most, conversion to Christ actually begins with "conversion" to the church. Like any of the other elements of conversion, the communal can come first in a person's experience. Indeed we will increasingly find that this element of a Christian conversion comes early in people's experience: a person first becomes a participant in the life of a community of faith and only then, as a loved member of the community, comes to Christian faith.

9

Growing Up Christian

Conversion &
Second-Generation
Christians

Few things engross the hearts and concerns of Christian parents more than the spiritual lives of their children. Parents long for their children to choose to be followers of Jesus. But within the Christian community this longing comes up against what for many is a confusing predicament: a deep uncertainty about what it means for a child of Christian believers to become a Christian. While we are far from a consensus within evangelicalism, I hope that what follows can contribute to the conversation and perhaps encourage some—both parents and the children of Christian believers—to make sense of the religious experience of second-generation Christians.

The Unique Status of the Children of Believers
First we must acknowledge that conversion for first- and second-generation Christians is *not* the same; it *is* possible to "grow up in the faith." The dynamics of coming to adult faith are perceptibly different for those whose parents have sought to raise their children in the Lord.

The children of believers are, in the language of Paul, "holy" or "sanctified" (1 Cor 7:14). But though these children have a special identity before God,

every Christian tradition affirms the need for a conscious adult appropriation of the faith of one's parents. Even the traditions that practice infant
baptism call for an adult appropriation of Christian faith. And even in the
covenantal community of Israel, the promises of God were passed on to
the next generation only if it was a "believing" generation. Thus Deuter-
onomy 1:37-40 speaks of the judgment of God that excluded rebellious off-
spring from entering the land that had been promised to Israel. It is
therefore critical that we discern what it means for persons to adopt the
faith of their believing parents. Their parents' faith must become their
own faith.

However, having stressed the need for each individual to make a conscious decision, I would plead just as urgently that we recognize that the
conversion of second-generation Christians has a different character.

The way we treat children and respond to them within the Christian
community is highly significant. Our attitude toward children is an important indicator of the level of our faith and the quality of our life together.
Jesus welcomed children and urged all of us to remember what it means
to be in the kingdom by seeing it through the eyes of a child. Therefore a
Christian community must be a child-affirming place.

However, while this sets the tone for our response to children and
their faith experiences, it does not do away with the need for critical
reflection and even hard choices as we nurture adult faith in those who
are raised within our communities. We must not sentimentalize the words
of Jesus. To take children seriously we need to take seriously the process,
structures and means by which they come to adult faith.

The Bible itself gives very little indication of how the children of
believers make the transition into full, mature involvement in the Christian community. There is no explicit teaching on how second-generation
Christians embrace a full adult faith in Christ. Timothy was clearly
brought up in the faith; Paul speaks of the sincere faith that lived first in
his grandmother Lois and his mother Eunice (2 Tim 1:5), and later the
apostle urges him to continue in what he has learned and believed from
childhood (2 Tim 3:14-15). But while Timothy may be an example of a second-generation Christian, Scripture does not give an explicit outline of
how this transition happens.

Timothy's experience is hardly instructive, beyond the crucial reference to instruction. Neither should we draw too much from such texts as
Proverbs 22:6, which some read as promising an assured outcome: "Train
children in the right way, and when old, they will not stray." This is a prov-

erb, not a guarantee; it articulates a general truth. It does provide prover-
bial wisdom, but it does not grant pastoral guidance for a Christian
community seeking to enable its young people to come to adult faith.

The Age of Accountability

This means that we must draw heavily on the wisdom of our Christian
heritage, learning from various streams of the church. Many traditions
speak of "the age of accountability." Christian churches have historically
recognized that there is a particular period or transition when a young
person becomes personally responsible for his life and actions. In many
ancient cultures this was assumed to happen at age twelve or thirteen;
within ancient Jewish communities this was the age when a young man
could properly take his place as an adult member of the religious community.

In the traditions that practice infant baptism, the "age of accountability" has historically been the time when a young person was expected to
move toward confirmation and first communion. Among the Puritans, a
young person was not permitted to take Communion until at least age
fourteen, assumed to be the minimum age at which a person could be said
to be "accountable." Other traditions have been more flexible but have
normally placed this age somewhere between seven and fourteen (the
Council of Trent set it between seven and twelve).[1]

Those traditions that follow adult or believers' baptism have historically viewed the "age of accountability" as that point at which an individual is viewed as capable of making a personal and genuine profession of
faith—to know the truth, make a genuine repentance and understand
what it means to be a disciple of Christ. Again, this would normally mean

---

[1]The Puritans overemphasized a particular kind of conversion narrative, which meant
they never were really able to resolve the matter of second-generation conversions.
Those from covenantal traditions assumed that their children were part of the covenant if they were baptized and that with good instruction they would eventually have
an authentic conversion and become active members of the church. But this did not
necessarily happen, and the result was great debate about whether their children in
turn should be baptized, and if so, how many generations removed from converts
could children and grandchildren be baptized. The resolution the Puritans came to
was that the children and grandchildren of believers would be baptized, but if they did
not have a definitive conversion experience they would have only partial membership
in the church (a provision termed the "halfway covenant") and could not receive the
Lord's Supper. See Jerald C. Brauer, "Conversion: From Puritanism to Revivalism,"
Journal of Religion 58 (1978): 237.

that baptism would happen at the very earliest in one's early teens.

While historically accountability was expected to occur during the teen years, recently in many Baptist circles, and denominations influenced by the Baptists, there has been a growing tendency to baptize younger children, without any sure biblical or theological rationale. Some have called this practice "toddler baptism," a descriptor that is not far off the mark.[2] It cannot be called believer or adult baptism; this is not a decision by a person capable of taking adult responsibility. The problem with this practice is that it takes no account of genuine *adult* responsibility for moral choices and life decisions.

Generally it has been assumed that the "age of accountability" is a critical point of transition in a person's life from childhood to adulthood. But the matter has been complicated considerably by the development of a distinctive period of "adolescence," a concept foreign to most traditional societies, a kind of no person's land between childhood and adulthood. And the phenomenon of adolescence is, if anything, expanding; it has no clear boundaries. In fact some sociologists have begun speaking of "post-adolescence" to refer to individuals in their mid to late twenties who may have the appearance of adulthood but have not really begun taking personal responsibility for their lives. Many would suggest that there are gender and cultural differences that further complicate the setting of a particular age of accountability. In some cultures young women move toward maturity and personal responsibility much earlier than men.

Complexity and Mystery

Richard Lovelace makes the following observation: "Calvin comments that John the Baptist was filled with the Holy Spirit even in his mother's womb and that the timing of regeneration in the lives of believers is therefore mysterious, *especially in the children of believers.*"[3] This is an appropriate reminder that the conversion of the children of believers cannot be managed or controlled. And this is complicated by the fact that adolescence is a vague, indeterminate period of time. God works in different ways in different lives. We cannot force the hand of God or the work of the Spirit with anyone, and this principle has immediate application to the children

---

[2]Timothy George, "You Must Be Born Again—But at What Age?" *Christianity Today*, March 1, 1999, p. 62.

[3]Richard Lovelace, *Dynamics of Spiritual Life* (Downers Grove, Ill.: InterVarsity Press, 1978), pp. 107-8 (emphasis mine).

of believers. For both theological and developmental reasons we should avoid pressing young people to make a decision, or be baptized, or acknowledge adult faith before they are intellectually, emotionally and socially ready to do so.

We must let young people respond in their own time; and there is no ideal time to come to faith. Earlier is not necessarily better. What makes the transition a good one and enables an authentic conversion is the following: first, that it is unequivocally *their own* faith, and second, that their experience becomes a basis for personal transformation. God does God's work in God's time. Pastoral care of young people enables them to be sensitive to what God is doing in *their* lives and to respond appropriately. We must avoid the understandable inclination to advise them what they *should* be experiencing and what they should do; instead we should be in conversation with them about what is actually happening in their lives.

Peer pressure, parental expectations and the intentional guidance of pastors and other religious leaders are often less than helpful in this process. We must avoid prematurely calling for or encouraging a decision or a statement of personal belief. *Letters to a Niece* by Friedrich Von Huegel suggests that it is a law of our earthly lives that young people are unequipped, up to the age of thirty at the earliest, "for any final negative decision as to religion"—that is, "definite, institutional religion." This means that parents and seniors must do all that they can to not provoke "the young to any indiscriminate revolt against such definite institutional religion."[4]

> Such seniors may have the deepest experience of what such definite, institutional religion means in and for *their own* lives, but they ought simultaneously to make clear to themselves that their own formed conviction has been an affair of time, and that they must not presuppose it as extant in the young, as simply transferable to the young by command or even by careful teaching.[5]

Von Huegel does not mean that religious instruction should be abandoned. His intent is that we should accept with grace and patience the limitations inherent in the transfer of religious faith from one generation to another. "We will have gained a great point," he says, "if they leave your hands with only a little definite religion, but with a sense that there may well be more in it than they can, so far, see for themselves."[6]

---

[4]Friedrich Von Huegel, *Letters from Baron Friedrich Von Huegel to a Niece* (London: J. M. Dent, 1928), pp. 51-52.
[5]Ibid., p. 52.
[6]Ibid.

Adult Identity

A second-generation conversion may well be linked to adult identity; frequently conversion is the act by which a person becomes an adult. This is a critical life transition: from submission to parents' authority to submission to God's authority, from a faith mediated through parents to a faith expressed directly to God, from following parents' sense of right and wrong to assuming moral responsibility for one's life, from loyalty to parents to fundamental loyalty to God.

I suggest that parents should not baptize their own children, because it confuses the role of parents with the vital mediatorial role of the Christian community. Baptism is not a family rite; it is a church rite. The power of baptism for second-generation Christians lies in part in its symbolization of an adult faith that one has separate from one's parents. Christian parents' goal for their children is that they come into their own adult faith. So everything should be done to reinforce and symbolize that what is being expressed is not the faith of the parent but the faith of the child, embraced within the Christian community. Even if a parent is a pastor of the church, I think it is wiser that someone who is not a parent officiate at the baptism.

The next chapter deals at length with religious autobiography and conversion narratives. However, it is worth noting here that second-generation Christians often find it particularly challenging to discern the contours of their conversion experience. Their story tends to lack a clear beginning and end. Often I have heard young people say things like "I have always believed in God" or "I have always loved Jesus." They may be expressing frustration, wondering whether they have had a genuine conversion.

However, even second-generation Christians can identity key influences—the character of their religious upbringing, persons who played significant roles in their spiritual awareness, key events—and the theological significance of the influences and events. The most critical question for a second-generation Christian is really quite straightforward: When did I begin to assume adult responsibility for my life? There are three vital marks of adult responsibility: identity, security and loyalty. A child finds identity, security and loyalty in his parents; when we assume adult responsibility as Christians, we find our identity in Christ, we find our security in Christ, and we ultimately give our loyalty to Christ. We have never really *become* Christian until we recognize that loyalty to our parents is not synonymous with loyalty to Christ.

In some form or another, all seven of the elements we have studied are essential and will find expression in second-generation believers' transition to full adult faith. God works differently in different lives, but there are some fundamental commonalities. The seven common elements will be present in a second-generation conversion as much as in any other. These elements may not be *as* evident, and second-generation conversion will likely not be as dramatic. The experience may be "flatter" emotionally, but it is still a *Christian* conversion, a distinctive appropriation of personal faith in Christ. It may be harder to discern definitive turning points in such a life journey. However, if the child of believers is becoming a Christian, then the elements of a Christian conversion must still be experienced if he or she is to begin well. And a key aspect will be the process of becoming an adult.

The Need for Patience

For many children of believers, the religious community in which they have grown up has been omnipresent and virtually synonymous with God, so that their only hope of coming to adult faith is to actually leave the church. Often parents despair when their children leave the church in their late teens or early twenties. Ironically, though, this may be a critical and necessary act for their children, an essential part of coming to their own adult faith. We long for the estrangement to pass quickly; we fear that they may never embrace a mature Christian faith. Yet we have no choice but to patiently allow them to respond to God in their own time. Nothing can be rushed or forced, and parents gain nothing by pressing their children or even asking them where they are in their Christian lives. They will come to adult faith in their own time. As often as not they will come back into the church through another door.

I left the church in my late teens and came back to the church through the ministry of Francis Schaeffer and his associates. They gave me a fresh language of conversion and of faith; and they were the catalyst I needed to come to terms with the faith that had been nurtured in me as a child. I realized that if I were to embrace the faith of my parents, it would likely mean that I would affirm many elements of my childhood faith but also challenge it.

We parents are all too prone to compare our children to the children of our peers. And we do not have a language of conversion and faith that really enables us to talk about the spiritual lives of our children. The language of religious experience inherited from revivalism is black and white: one is either in or not, "following the Lord" or not. Our young people are in a phase of life that is as crucial as any other, but we have no way to speak of it positively and hopefully.

When second-generation Christians later delineate their conversion narratives, they may well speak of that adolescent phase as a time "when I was not following the Lord." But to say this is to fail to appreciate that God was *as present* to us in our time of "wandering" as in the times when we felt very connected to the church.

If conversion is an adult experience, what is the religious potential of children? Many second-generation Christians (as well as those whose parents were not believers) had significant spiritual experiences when they were very young. We must celebrate these moments; these are wonderful gifts from God. But as we look back on these childhood experiences and the early prayers we prayed to "receive Jesus into my heart," we should not attribute more meaning to them than they actually had. In many cases these prayers and spiritual acts expressed a heartfelt desire to please our parents. This is not to discount these experiences; it is merely to put them in their context.[7]

They are significant moments that we can in later years see as markers of God's love and presence in our lives and of our own desire to love God and follow Jesus. But I believe these experiences should not be called conversions. The New Testament notion of conversion is far more complex; further, it calls us to assume adult responsibility for our lives.

Implications for Ministry to Youth
The church's experience with second-generation Christians is a constant reminder that the transition to adult faith is a complex matter that does not lend itself to easy solutions. For people of faith, this is a continuing concern. We cannot abandon children to their own devices; yet neither can we manipulate their lives so that they imitate us. We are forced to think critically and courageously, and perhaps to accept that in the end this is something we cannot manage or control.

There are some things we *can* do. First, we make it a priority in our churches to establish a context of community and learning for our young

---

[7]See Sofia Cavalletti, *The Religious Potential of the Child*, trans. Patricia M. Coulter and Julie M. Coulter (New York: Paulist, 1979), particularly the preface by Jerome W. Berryman. My read of Cavalletti's work suggests that in a consideration of childhood spiritual experiences more weight should be given to spontaneous experiences than to those that came in response to the prompting of an adult.

people where they are affirmed and encouraged. A Christian congregation should provide opportunity for exploration, discovery and learning,
but always without the pressure of "decision." The emphasis of such youth
ministry is conversation about the nature of Christian faith and the character of their religious experience. We must provide settings where teens
and young adults can describe and discuss what *is* happening to them
rather than what adults think *should be* happening to them. It makes good
sense to foster conversations in which young people have as much opportunity to speak and be heard as they have to listen to their elders. The role
of a youth minister, then, should be like that of a spiritual director, helping the young interpret and give meaning to what they *are* experiencing
rather than telling them what *should* be happening in their lives. Most of
all, the youth minister, on behalf of the whole church, communicates an
unqualified acceptance.

Randall Balmer observes that many congregations have hired youth
pastors whose primary responsibility is to keep young people within the
evangelical camp, and they are often judged for the degree to which they
facilitate commitments. This is motivated by what Balmer aptly calls the
"greatest fear that haunts evangelical parents . . . that their children will
not follow in their footsteps."[8] The problem is that many churches assume
that the youth worker will both "carry the mail and deliver it." The youth
minister who is ostensibly responsible for this critical task often is relatively young in the faith and hardly in a position to bear the spiritual, emotional and relational weight of enabling second-generation Christians to
make a transition to adult faith.

Mike Yaconelli suggests that three models reflect the unspoken expectations of most congregations: an entertainment model (program centered), a charismatic youth leader model (the youth pastor bears sole
responsibility for pastoral care of the youth) and an information-centered
model that focuses on religious instruction. He argues that all three models are deficient largely because each fails to build on the fundamental
strength of a Christian community—it is a community participating
together in spiritual practices that form women and men in the Christian
faith.[9]

Often the weight of responsibility for the conversion of young people

---

[8]Randall Balmer, "Adirondack Fundamentalism," *Reformed Journal,* June 1989, p. 15.
[9]Mike Yaconelli, "Youth Ministry: A Contemplative Approach," *Christian Century,* April
    21-28, 1999, pp. 450-53.

rests entirely on the shoulders of parents and youth ministers. It would be far better to recognize that the transformation of our young people will take place within the normal routines and practices of congregational life, that the whole congregation shares the weight of responsibility for the spiritual well-being of the young, and that a youth minister should be rather like a docent, a person who walks alongside another, as in an art gallery, describing and helping to interpret what is happening without having to make sure that anything would actually happen. The responsibility to bring about change, reformation and transformation lies in the hands of God; God will do in God's time what only God can do. Again, the context for religious change and transformation, the setting in which God works, is the whole of congregational life, not merely the youth program. We must assure parents and encourage them that the weight of responsibility for the formation of their children is not theirs alone; we hold it together as a community.

Actually I would question whether a parent can be *the* critical player in enabling his or her children to come to faith. Obviously parents are tremendously formative and influential; parents set the stage, so to speak, for the conversion. But when it comes to the actual resolve to appropriate adult faith, it may be necessary for parents to be in the background. The presence of a parent may complicate the most fundamental issue at hand, the need to move out from under one's parents' faith and to appropriate faith for oneself.

In most of the conversion narratives I have read in my teaching ministry, the most effective catalysts for the definitive moments in a conversion process are not parents or peers but the peers of parents—a pastor, a teacher or coach, a Sunday school teacher or a neighbor. The blessing, encouragement and challenge of these other adults often enable a young person to assume an adult faith. In many cases youth ministers are too young to play this role; they have barely moved through adolescence themselves.

Thus it is imperative that adults in Christian community recognize the importance of being present to the children of our peers. For them, at all ages but particularly in their teens and early twenties, there is no substitute for our blessing and encouragement.

In conclusion, two comments about the sacramental actions of the church. First, the posture I am proposing suggests that we would provide regular opportunities for baptism or confirmation, without pressure or expectation that the children of believers be baptized any sooner than they are personally ready. We should enable our youth to understand the meaning of baptism; what it means and what it does not mean. Further, regular and easy references to baptism in our sermons and conversations should show it to be a vital and life-giving benchmark of Christian experience, always with the implication that it is available to those who are ready to make such a commitment. For example, when a child under fourteen asks about baptism, we can explain that baptism is for those who are older and that when they are at least fourteen they will be welcome to receive it. Nothing is gained by rushing baptism; and a great deal is gained by waiting until they are at least this age. Many would benefit by waiting even longer. In my judgment, fourteen should be the *minimum* age.

However, I propose that we move away from a specific age by which a person is expected to or becomes free to participate in Holy Communion. It seems increasingly that the wisest approach is openness and full participation. Our young ones *are* members of the community of faith through the commitments of their parents. In the traditions that baptize adult believers, an open approach to the Table would acknowledge that children are members of the covenant community even though they cannot yet assume adult responsibility for their lives, evidenced in baptism. For now they come to the Table under the spiritual authority and identity of their parents. And they are welcome.

This approach will certainly not alleviate all the concern and stress that parents feel for the spiritual well-being of their children. But surely we will live with greater grace and freedom if we can be confident that God will do God's work in God's time in the lives of our children—and that our children's spiritual well-being is the responsibility of the whole community of faith, not merely of the parents or the youth minister.

10

The Rhythms of Grace

This extended reflection on conversion has a twofold objective: (1) to enable us to make sense of our own experience and (2) to empower Christians to enable others to come to faith in Christ. The first speaks of religious autobiography; the second speaks of evangelism in the life of the church. In both cases we are impressed by God's grace, particularly as it is captured in a classic Presbyterian phrase, "the rhythms of grace." Our stories are about the goodness and mercy of God. Our own experience and that of others is all superintended by the mercy, grace and providential care of God. We can all sing "Amazing Grace."

A conversion is really nothing other than an encounter with the risen Lord Jesus Christ. Christ comes to us as the personal embodiment of the mercy of God, and Christians know that in Christ Jesus they have been "found." They were lost, and now through the amazing grace of God they have been restored to their Creator. All this is gift.

Christians know that this grace is neither earned nor discovered on their own. Every conversion narrative highlights the wonder of a God who seeks and finds us and then in mercy invites and draws us into fellowship. Christ is our demonstration of the love of God, a love that is personal and sacrificial.

Christians also speak of the *mystery* of divine grace. This book is an intentional analysis of Christian conversion. But the analysis is not meant to explain mystery. Astronomers, those who analyze the heavens, are most aware of the wonder and mystery of the cosmos. In a similar way, this study should lead us to a greater appreciation of the wonder and mystery of God's work in the lives of his children.

God's mercy and goodness, God's amazing grace, are the fountainhead from which the Christian life springs. Paul speaks of the Thessalonian believers' conversion as being more than the fruit of his own preaching; through the work of the Holy Spirit his words were received with joy (1 Thess 1:5-6). And the consequence was simple: these women and men were transformed by grace. They received strength in the midst of trial and persecution and were an example to believers in other parts of the world, witnessing in word and deed to the power of the gospel. This is what we mean by conversion: through the Spirit, women and men are transformed by the Word; experience pervasive joy and peace in the midst of a broken world; courageously walk in the way of the cross; and live by faith, hope and love, signs of the triumph of God's grace.

Yet we will not appreciate the wonder of God's grace unless we are prepared to accept two things that evangelicals are prone to deny. The first is that God works slowly; the second is that God works through social and cultural contexts. Evangelicals have been inclined to see a conversion as a powerful sign of God's grace when it is dramatic and punctiliar. For some reason, a conversion is viewed as less miraculous when it extends across many months or years. When asked to testify, such a person often responds, "I don't have much of a testimony," meaning that he does not have a dramatic story of his coming to faith.

As this study has shown, the wonder of God's grace is precisely that God works slowly; this calls us to marvel at God's grace and mercy. God is not necessarily impressed with speed; God's inclination is to work slowly and incrementally in our lives, moving at the speed of our hearts. In John 16:12 the Gospel writer quotes Jesus: "I still have many things to say to you, but you cannot bear them now." This is really the character of all of God's work in our lives. God is attentive to us and draws us nearer at a pace that we can *bear*. If God overwhelms us, it is because we are ready to be overwhelmed! But the primary pace of God's working is incremental attention to the progress of our souls.

We may wonder about some of the early chapters of our lives—where God was when we were far from the church—or where God is in others' lives. In either case we fail to wonder at God's grace, which works slowly.

An extended, complex conversion is no less miraculous than a punctiliar, dramatic one. If we knew God better we would see that God works slowly. The wonder of grace is *precisely* that it is subtle, slow and incremental.

Second, God works through the ordinary social and cultural contexts in which we live and work. Evangelicals are prone to assume that identifying important social influences somehow minimizes the work of God. Unfortunately, religious experience is viewed as more authentic and meaningful, that is, "miraculous," when no mediating cause or influence is detected—God just broke into a person's life.

The wonder of the incarnation is the extraordinary reality that God took on human flesh. We know God only because God became one of us. The reality of Christ's humanity is not an obstacle to our knowledge of God; it is the very means by which we are able to know God.

In the same way, without reservation we can affirm that God works in a historical, social and cultural context. Always. The wonder of God's grace is that it takes shape in the ordinary forces and influences that make up who we are. We cannot understand our own lives until we see how God has been at work within the influences that shape us. Even further: just as we do not know Jesus the Christ except as we know Jesus in his humanity, we do not understand the Spirit's work in our lives until we understand our social and cultural context. The more attentive we are to our context, the more we appreciate the particular ways the Spirit of God is present with us.

Religious experience is socially conditioned; religious traditions shape and inform religious experience. I am not saying the individual is socially *determined,* but we must acknowledge the influence of social institutions in our religious experience. This relationship is not dictatorial; we are never prisoners of our culture, social conditioning or religious institutions.

Consequently, the church will be a place where women and men discover Christ as Lord when it is attentive to the social dynamics in which people live and work. A theological reflection on conversion must always be complemented by studies of the social, cultural and psychological factors that influence religious experience. A study of the psychology of conversion, or the sociology of religious experience, does not diminish the wonder of God's gracious work; it puts the work of the Spirit in its context. God does not work in a vacuum. Gaining understanding of this human context enables us to appreciate the wonder of God's working.

Religious Autobiography: Telling Our Stories
In reading Paul's letters one is struck by the ease with which the apostle

speaks of his own conversion and also the way he makes reference to—
appeals to—the conversions of his readers. He assumes that his readers
have enough awareness of their conversion that it can serve as a benchmark for their spiritual growth and development. One way we can foster
this awareness for ourselves is to do intentional reflection on our own
experience through a spiritual exercise—the writing of our conversion
narrative.

Religious autobiography is a vehicle for self-understanding and thus
potentially a vital aspect of a person's education—self-knowledge through
a personal, reflective and critical review of one's religious experience.
This exercise can foster critical thinking in two ways: we look back to
make sense of the past, and we look forward to build on this understanding.

Making Sense of the Past

First, religious autobiography is a means by which we can begin to make
sense of our past: highlighting religious influences, illuminating personal
motives and life patterns. It is a vehicle for critical analysis through the
classic spiritual exercise of reminiscence: review experience but then go
further, interpreting it and the influences that enabled it.

In recounting religious autobiography, we identity key events or markers in our lives and then formulate a theological interpretation of them. It
is an adult reflection that recognizes that no one develops in a spiritual
and religious vacuum. Many experiences and influences have made us
who we are today. But then, having identified important events and influences, we *interpret* them. We consider them in the light of the words of
Scripture and the church's understanding of conversion. I came to growing clarity about my own experience through a careful reading of John
Wesley's journal. His experience helped make sense of mine.

As we strive to give theological meaning to the events and influences of
our lives, both Scripture and our spiritual heritage are vital resources.
They help us reflect on influences and events with critical appreciation—
to get some distance from them but also gain ownership of them.

This exercise also is a means by which we can identify the religious
language that has shaped our experience. Many assume that their religious language is a given; they fail to see how its clichés and jargon have
little if any actual meaning in their experience. Intentional reflection on
our religious influences can help us get some distance from this language
and begin to find a more authentic language to speak of our experience.

In the end no one can interpret religious experience for another; we each must necessarily do this for ourselves. This does not mean that a pastor or spiritual director or friend cannot play a vital role in helping make sense of your past, but there is only one authoritative interpreter of your experience: you. And through this exercise we can respond to the call to think of ourselves with "sober judgment" (Rom 12:3).

The value of religious autobiography lies in part in the fact that we all see the world through the lens of the particular, the lens of our own experience. So each person really has only one vantage point from which to appreciate God's redemptive work—his or her own experience.

Yet wonderfully, in coming to terms with our own religious experience we appreciate our uniqueness but also see more clearly how we are all cut from the same cloth. This is the value of the study of religious biography and of including conversion narratives in the life of the church: the conversion narrative of another sheds light on my own experience, and I see that my experience is but another version of the classic Christian story. Writing one's conversion narrative is an act of testimony—of witness to one's identity as a person graced by God.

Looking to the Future

Second, religious autobiography has the capacity not only to make sense of the past but also to help us be all that we are called to be. Self-knowledge is a key building block for personal development, learning and vocational discernment. And religious autobiography can be a significant benchmark in our spiritual lives. When the apostle Paul appeals to his readers' conversions, he calls them to faithfulness and maturity. Similarly, a review of the past should foster our sense of common identity in Christ and facilitate our understanding and courage to embrace the future.

It is not an act of sentimentalism or nostalgia. In reviewing our past we can take greater responsibility for our spiritual growth and well-being. We have greater clarity about who we are and how God works in our life, how the Spirit is attending to us and thus how we should attend to the Spirit. We can more fully see how our spiritual beginnings foster our spiritual formation.

Knowing where we have come from, we can more fully take responsibility for our lives. We are less inclined to see ourselves as victims of past influences, and we can build on the positive influences that have formed us. Many find that the rendering of their conversion narrative leads them to a particular course of action. They may come to see their need for a more intentional program of spiritual formation. Others may conclude that they need clinical counseling. They may gain greater clarity about career, work and vocation. All gain a clearer self-identity, a mature and well-informed context for taking responsibility for their lives.

The act of religious autobiography is a search for meaning, *personal* meaning. If it is done well, it enables us to accept that we have been given gifts—those positive influences along the way. But we also see that we have liabilities and limitations. When we clearly see these and name them, they are less likely to control the next chapter of our lives. Rather than blaming these influences (viewing ourselves as victims), we can make the best of them, learn from them and move on.

A conversion narrative reveals what is at the heart of our personal identity: what drives us, the emotional, intellectual or spiritual longing that makes us who we are. When we name our deep longings we will not be blind-sided and driven by them; instead we can tame our longings so that they are a constructive source of energy and direction.

A clear sense of one's own religious experience, made accessible through a conversion narrative, is potentially a very significant source of strength, especially in a cultural context that does not nurture Christian faith. We cannot look to cultural and religious traditions to sustain our faith; we must look to our own experience to make sense of our past and embrace the future with courage. Effective religious autobiography requires avoidance of simplistic deductions and one-to-one correlations with the experience of others. While Wesley's experience helped me make sense of my own, my experience was certainly not a parallel to his.

Guidelines for a Conversion Narrative
In a conversion narrative, as much as possible we need to avoid religious jargon, clichés and catch phrases. When someone tells me, "I received Jesus into my heart at age seven," I urge them to recount the event in the light of what influenced their behavior and what the context was. I want them to tell me what actually happened. It may indeed include an experience of the risen Christ, but they need to find language that captures more fully what happened and what it means.

Authentic conversion narratives avoid the pressure to smooth over times of ambiguity and uncertainty. We are at our best when we turn from any pressure to tie up loose ends. We are not writing an ideal conversion narrative; we are telling our story *as it is*. This means that we do not overstate the experience or the significance of events and influences along the way. Poor journalism is marked by sensationalism, histrionics and over-dramatizing events. A good journalist tells it as it is without whipping up more emotion or tension than the situation warrants. In the same way, good religious autobiography trusts the quality of the experience itself to carry the narrative. We can tell our story without having to explain everything; we can recount events even when we are not sure of their full significance. In the end we will find that we have a greater appreciation of the actual meaning of the events and influences that make up our past.

Writing spiritual autobiography shows that different people experience conversion in dramatically different forms and by different means. The order in which the elements are experienced proves to be very different. And the degree to which different elements are important varies according to each unique set of circumstances and previous experiences.

We must remember, of course, that though every conversion experience is unique and particular, not all religious experience is *Christian*. While a complete narrative will identify non-Christian influences and may speak of them as positive, a conversion is not Christian unless it has certain essential elements or components. Again, no two football games are alike, but not just anything is a football game. In the same way, not all religious experience is authentic; not all Christian experience is so thoroughly Christian that it makes for a good beginning.

So we must not sentimentalize or approach our experience nostalgically. To make religious autobiography formative we must approach the task *critically* and *theologically*. We put together an account of our conversion, and then we subject it to a critical analysis informed by the historic church's understanding of the nature of conversion.

Not all the elements identified in this study will be equally significant to each person. Some readers will not agree that there are seven elements in a Christian conversion. However, the evidence suggests that each element I have identified will find *some* expression in a Christian conversion. And together they are offered as a vehicle for critical reflection on personal experience and the experience of the church.

Lewis Rambo makes a distinction that can help as we seek to identify the psychological, social and cultural factors that formed the context for our conversion experience.[1] We can consider (1) the macro context, the

---

[1]Lewis Rambo, "The Psychology of Conversion," in *Handbook of Religious Conversion*, ed. H. Newton Malony and Samuel Southard (Birmingham, Ala.: REPress, 1992), pp. 163-65.

cultural and linguistic milieu in which we were formed, (2) the micro context, the world of family, religious community, work and neighborhood, and (3) the individual context. While conversion never happens in a historical vacuum, the primary focus of our narrative should be the third. The events of our *individual* experience actually carry the narrative. We must be attentive to the social, cultural, religious and historical influences on our experience, but what we highlight is not the context but what *happened:* what *we* experienced, what turning points made us who we are.

A conversion narrative is a snapshot that captures how we see our own religious experience at one particular moment. It is important that we recognize that *one* writing of our story is not the *last* writing. We tell our story, but we do so knowing that over time we may see things differently. We can rethink our narrative, realizing the significance of still other influences. This often is the case for those who rejected the religious context of their youth. Years later they may come to a new appreciation of their spiritual roots. They see more clearly how certain people played a crucial role in their spiritual formation.

A well-formed conversion narrative creates intellectual and emotional distance from childhood and early Christian influences. We see them in a new light; they are no longer taken for granted or taken to be more than they were. We become aware that when severed from our religious roots our connection to ourself is lost. A critical appreciation of our past keeps us from both an uncritical appropriation of those influences and an overreaction against them.

Religious autobiography helps some begin to appreciate the multiple influences in their lives. They see how they came under diverse religious influences and are able to put them in context and note the ways (both positively and negatively) their identity was shaped. Marie Theresa Coombs and Francis Kelley Nemeck say we need to recognize that the primary, central experience of conversion may happen early, but the full effect is not realized until a much later point in our experience.[2]

Further, we are wise to attend to threshold events, occasions on which the whole experience hangs (and around which the narrative may well take shape). A pivot may be an experience that at the time seemed insignificant, but later we realize it was the turning point of our whole experience.

---

[2]Marie Theresa Coombs and Francis Kelley Nemeck, *The Spiritual Journey: Critical Thresholds and Stages of Adult Spiritual Genesis* (Collegeville, Minn.: Liturgical Press, 1987), p. 135.

It may be that key events seem to encompass the whole experience, but later we see them in a broader context. Writing soon after his Aldersgate experience, John Wesley spoke of this event almost as if it were the totality of his conversion. But in later years he came to see it as part of a whole, something that made sense only in the light of his previous commitments. Thus over time we come to a holistic interpretation of our experience that enables us to read later events in the light of earlier turning points; each giving meaning and significance to the other.

Psychologists suggest that conversion turning points often occur when there is inner stress or turmoil. Some people experience disorientation: they are overwhelmed by a sense of guilt, dislocation or abandonment, and they seek resolution. Others do not experience tension but longing. Changes, crises or events open them up to new possibilities; they see themselves and their potential in a new light. Their conversion is not so much a resolution of the past as an embracing of new possibilities for the future. For many, conversion is an expression of self-identity and personal responsibility. It is helpful to be attentive to the emotional energy that sustains the whole conversion experience when we write our narrative.

Finally, a conversion narrative necessarily includes reference to the individuals who played a formative role in enabling us to come to faith. Rarely is there a single decisive influence—one person who "led us to Christ"; usually a whole host of individuals played a part. We need to acknowledge parents, grandparents, religious leaders or pastors, peers, friends and even those who played a role without consciously doing so.

Religious autobiography on first glance may seem very personal. And in a sense it is. It celebrates the grace of God extended to a particular person. But the hero of the story is God, not the person recounting the narrative. A conversion narrative is not constructed; we do not craft our lives or ourselves. Rather, we live in response to the grace of God; who we are is a testimony to God's initiative. The conversion narrative is evidence that we ground our lives neither in this world nor in a world of our making, but in God. The narrative is, then, an act of thanksgiving and humility.

The Church as a Midwife of Conversion

Critical reflection on the nature of conversion should enable us to make better sense of our own experience, but it is also an opportunity to rethink the life of the church and its approach to evangelism. Communities of faith are called to foster genuine conversions to Christ, conversions that are good beginnings, effective foundations for the Christian life. We are called not for our own sake but to be means through which others come to Christ. But we assume this responsibility *together*. And together we seek to be communities that enable women and men to come to Christ and mature in their faith. This is not the responsibility of religious leaders or specialists in evangelism but of the whole community acting in concert.

However, we will not be able to act effectively unless our evangelism reflects a sound theology and experience of conversion. All too frequently our approach to evangelism is not congruent with how women and men *actually* come to faith. Evangelism is first and foremost the act of a community of faith, not of specialists who seek to "win" people to Christ in isolation. It means that we see the church as a midwife and nurturer of a process.

Many who become Christians come to faith while already a part of a Christian community. Many congregations are developing models of Christian initiation in careful response to seekers who are already participating in congregational life. These models of initiation provide adults with opportunities to learn about Christian faith, observe Christians as they live in community, discern the work of the Spirit in their own lives and count the cost of following Jesus.

But it is important that all of this happens without overt pressure to become Christians. We gladly acknowledge that there are some (perhaps many) in the midst of congregational life who are coming to faith, but in their own time. The church thus offers true friendship and hospitality. Individuals are encouraged to participate in worship, learning and service, so that seekers work side by side with Christians as volunteers in acts of charity and generosity.

The implications of this are enormous. What makes a congregation evangelistic is not that it has special evangelistic programs and practices. Rather, all the church's activities are structured and conceived of as means by which people are acclimated into Christian faith, understanding and commitment. It is not that *everything* is evangelism (this would undercut the distinctive character of worship, for example; worship is worship). It is rather than everything serves an evangelistic end, teaching people the language of faith and encouraging their faith, understanding and commitment.

In this model there are no predetermined agendas. People are free to respond or to reject the gospel as they choose. The community seeks to foster honest searching, honest questions, honest responses. Both our young people and adult seekers need this kind of patient friendship and care.

Again, this model involves the whole community, not merely those who are designated as evangelists, pastors or leaders. As Karen Ward insists, *ordinary* congregational life forms the foundation and context in which initiation of adults takes place; ministers and laypersons, are equally involved in the give and take of enabling individuals to respond honestly to the gospel.[3] Several elements make up this approach to evangelism.

Our Witness Is to Christ

Our primary call is to witness to Christ Jesus himself. For the apostle Paul this meant a passion to preach Christ. True preaching is essentially the proclamation of Jesus Christ. But authentic preaching always happens within the context of a community that embodies in its worship, life and ministry what it means to be followers of Jesus. Preaching is embodied in the context of worship, the worship of the crucified and risen Christ, and of a living community that bears witness in word and deed to Christ.

This does not mean that preaching itself is necessarily the particular occasion for our conversion, but preaching forms one of the essential contexts in which we come to faith in Christ. The *means* of conversion is the Word of God; we are born again by truth (Jas 1:18), particularly the *preaching* of truth (1 Pet 1:25). The mind and heart and will engaged with truth ultimately encounter the witness and enabling of the Spirit that makes conversion possible. But it must be stressed again: this truth is proclaimed within the context of a worshiping community that seeks to live the preached Word.

Our Confidence Is in the Spirit

Our confidence is not in our methods or actions or words (or preaching) but in the Spirit. Lesslie Newbigin makes a sobering observation: "There is no direct proportion between the organized efforts of [the church in its evangelistic or mission endeavors] and the actual event of conversion."[4] The church is the *venue* in which conversions take place and are fostered,

---

[3]Karen Ward, "Making Adult Disciples: Rite for Our Times," *Christian Century,* March 24-31, 1999, pp. 348-50.

[4]Lesslie Newbigin, quoted by George R. Hunsberger, *Bearing the Witness of the Spirit: Lesslie Newbigin's Theology of Cultural Plurality* (Grand Rapids, Mich.: Eerdmans, 1998), p. 169.

but the church is never the *cause* of conversion, which remains always the irreplaceable work of the Spirit. We must abandon all language of "winning" souls (or people) to Christ. That is simply not the task of the church; it is the work of the Spirit and the Spirit alone.

Even the apostle Paul refused to see himself as the pivotal player in the lives of his readers. "What then is Apollos? What is Paul? Servants through whom you came to believe, as the Lord assigned to each. I planted, Apollos watered, but God gave the growth. So neither the one who plants nor the one who waters is anything, but only God who gives the growth" (1 Cor 3:5-7).

We are not "soul winners"; we are not manipulators of what only God can do; we are not fishers of "men" in the sense that we need to reel them in. God does God's work in God's time. We therefore err when we seek to legitimize ourselves or our congregational life by the number of converts we have "won." Some plant, some water, some harvest. But no one person ever "wins" another to Christ. No conversion is ever the fruit of merely one person's words or actions. This is not to minimize the part we play in the religious experience of another. But when we appreciate the diverse and amazing ways in which people actually come to faith, we realize that this can happen only through a process that is orchestrated by God's Spirit.[5]

Helping People Respond to God's Work

Evangelism is essentially encouraging others to respond to the work of the Spirit in their lives. The primary responsibility of the community of faith is to encourage conversation about how God is already at work in our lives. We seek to foster a posture of response to the initiative of the Spirit. We work together to recognize the subtle but distinct ways the Spirit of God is at work in our lives, individually and corporately. Evangelism then includes spiritual direction, helping others discern and be attentive to the prompting and direction of God, the rhythms of grace in their lives.[6] Rather than telling them what they *should* do and experience, we walk beside them, asking them what they *are* experiencing and helping them make sense of what is happening.

Newbigin issues an insightful call for radical trust in the work of the Spirit and in people's capacity to hear and respond as *they* interpret the

[5]Hunsberger, *Bearing the Witness*, p. 170.
[6]Ben Campbell Johnson, *Speaking of God: Evangelism as Initial Spiritual Guidance* (Louisville, Ky.: Westminster John Knox, 1991).

witness and call of the Spirit. And this has particular implications when we speak of crosscultural evangelism/missions. George Hunsberger ably observes, "Newbigin claims for every 'fresh work of the Holy Spirit' in conversion, especially as that occurs for one who hears the gospel communicated across cultural lines, a necessary and 'radical discontinuity' with all former expressions of Christian discipleship."[7]

We can then rightly insist that the evangelist is never lord over the convert; rather, they are followers together of one Lord. Both become servants of the tradition that bears witness to Jesus Christ in community; both are called to live in the world in a way that by the Spirit they understand to be consistent with the reign of Christ.

Community of Grace, Community of Discipline

Sustaining a balance between being a *community of grace* on the one hand and a *community of discipline* on the other is essential. The church is unequivocal in extolling the claims of the gospel, but simultaneously the church ought to refuse to judge others.

We can be a community of grace that accepts people just as they are, fully believing that they will accept their Christian identity and responsibility in their time (that is, in the timing of the Spirit's work in their lives). We must be patient with one another. At the same time, we are free to proclaim that we live under the claims of the gospel. We do not proclaim a cheap grace; rather, without reservation we call one another to be full disciples of Jesus Christ.

While all people are accepted when it comes to joining the community, it is another matter to be in leadership within the community. All are welcome, but leadership in preaching and teaching, in worship and service, necessarily requires meeting a clear set of criteria. There is a community within the community, and while the inner community cannot be elitist or segregated, without apology we hold leaders to a level of commitment that may not be required of others in the community.

Worship and the Sacramental Life of the Church

The sacramental actions of the community of faith do not belong to the church; they are God's work *through* the church. But they are entrusted to the church as vital means by which faith is sustained, hope renewed and love made more perfect.

---

[7]Hunsberger, *Bearing the Witness*, p. 171.

These sacramental actions lie at the heart of what it means to be a worshiping community. We long for an approach to evangelism that not only brings people to Christ (or restores them to Christ) but also helps them enter into a mature, full and dynamic Christian life as participants in the community of faith. Robert Webber suggests that for this to happen, we need to be awakened to the formative power of the liturgy, and thus to practice an evangelism that is both evangelical and catholic: *evangelical* in being rooted in the historic gospel, *catholic* because its practice is rooted in precedents set by the universal church. Webber's conviction is that women and men are called "into Christ and his church through a conversion regulated and ordered by worship."[8] Our worship, insofar as it reflects the ancient worship practices of the church, is itself a proclamation, in word and deed, of the gospel.

Worship is the central act of the community, yet it is but one of the acts that empower people to know, love and serve Christ. And it all takes time. It has always taken time, but this is particularly the case in our current sociocultural context.[9]

Intellectual discovery and exploration will be ordered around the preaching and teaching of the ancient text, and affective and volitional development is fostered by the mutual service and joint love of the community of faith. Both will be framed by common worship. But this emotional and intellectual formation will take time, potentially a great deal of time. Our evangelism must allow people to come at their own time and at their own pace.

Conclusion

"Do not be afraid of the laborious pace of conversion," Søren Kierkegaard aptly exhorts.[10] It does take time, and reviewing our own experience or

---

[8]Robert E. Webber, *Celebrating Our Faith: Evangelism Through Worship* (San Francisco: Harper & Row, 1986), p. 1.

[9]Douglas Coupland is a Vancouver-based Canadian writer who first introduced the phrase "Generation X" to common speech. In his novel *Life After God* the characters have a common characteristic: none has a religious upbringing: "You are the first generation raised without God." If women and men of our day are going to come to knowledge of Jesus, many of them begin with no spiritual infrastructure within which to place their newfound faith. Their coming will take time, and they need a community of faith that is marked by patience and grace.

[10]Søren Kierkegaard, *Practice in Christianity,* ed. and trans. Howard V. Hong and Edna H. Hong (Princeton, N.J.: Princeton University Press, 1991).

hearing that of others is a good reminder. A good beginning takes time; it cannot and does not need to be rushed.

In Glenn Tinder's conversion narrative he describes his Christian Science upbringing, the horrors of war and his own seemingly unforgivable acts in that war, and then his long and capable career as an academic. Through it all he notes the subtle ways he gradually became conscious of the presence of God—a God of grace and forgiveness and the God of all truth. He concludes, "I still have not described the actual event of my becoming a Christian. There is good reason for this: no such event occurred. I can only say that I was not a Christian during my time as a graduate student and a young instructor, whereas well before reaching the age of fifty I was."[11]

Tinder uses a wonderful image to capture a critical dimension of his experience of God's grace. A friend would often hike in the Sierra Mountains, in foothills inhabited by mountain lions. When Tinder asked if he had ever seen one of the big cats, the friend responded that he had never actually seen one, but that often on a return trip he had come across "the tracks of a mountain lion near his own tracks made earlier in the day." Thus he knew that the mountain lion had been out of sight, paying close attention to him. Tinder says, "My friend's experience might serve as a parable of my own life with God. I can't claim ever to have had even a glimpse of God. When I look back on my life, however, I see his tracks all around the places where I have been."[12]

All is gift. Christians know that the grace of God is nothing they have earned or manipulated; neither have they discovered it on their own. Every conversion narrative highlights the wonder of a God who seeks us, finds us, and in mercy invites us and draws us into fellowship with God. We can all look back and see traces of the gracious work of God.

---

[11]Glenn Tinder, "Birth of a Troubled Conscience," *Christianity Today*, April 26, 1999, p. 37.
[12]Ibid., p. 38.

Names Index

Scripture Index